Images and Stories of

TCU's First 100 Years

Other Books by Gene Allen Smith

ed. *Coloring Texas History: A Texas History Coloring Book*, with LeAnna Schooley

In Harm's Way: A History of the American Military Experience, with David Coffey and Kyle Longley

ed. *From Colonies to Countries in the North Caribbean: Military Engineers in the Development of Cities and Territories*, with Pedro Luengo-Gutiérrez

The Slave's Gamble: Choosing Sides in the War of 1812

ed. *Nexus of Empire: Negotiating Loyalty and Identity in the Revolutionary Borderlands, 1760s–1820s*, with Sylvia L. Hilton

ed. *A British Eyewitness at the Battle of New Orleans: The Memoir of Royal Navy Admiral Robert Aitchison, 1808–1827*

Thomas ap Catesby Jones: Commodore of Manifest Destiny

ed. *Historical Memoir of the War in West Florida and Louisiana in 1814–15: With an Atlas*, by Arsène Lacarrière Latour (1816)

Filibusters and Expansionists: Jeffersonian Manifest Destiny, 1800–1821, with Frank Lawrence Owsley, Jr.

Iron and Heavy Guns: Duel Between the Monitor and Merrimac

"For the Purposes of Defense": The Politics of the Jeffersonian Gunboat Program

Images and Stories of

TCU's First 100 Years

Gene Allen Smith
and Jackson W. Pearson

A Joint Project of the
Center for Texas Studies at TCU
and TCU Press

TCU Press
Fort Worth, Texas

TCU | 150 1873 2023

Library of Congress Cataloging-in-Publication Data

Names: Smith, Gene A., 1963- author. | Pearson, Jackson W., 1991- author.
Title: Images and stories of TCU's first 100 years / Gene Allen Smith and Jackson W. Pearson.
Description: Fort Worth, Texas : TCU Press, [2023] | Includes bibliographical references. | Summary: "Authors Gene Allen Smith and Jackson W. Pearson discuss the history of the first 100 years of Texas Christian University through photographs. This reflection commemorates the sesquicentennial of the founding of the university"-- Provided by publisher.
Identifiers: LCCN 2022047065 | ISBN 9780875658407 (hardback)
Subjects: LCSH: Texas Christian University--History. | Texas Christian University--History--Pictorial works.
Classification: LCC LD5311.T382 S65 2023 | DDC 378.764/5315--dc23/eng/20220930
LC record available at https://lccn.loc.gov/2022047065

TCU Press

TCU Box 298300
Fort Worth, Texas 76129

Design by Bill Brammer

FOREWORD

The history of Texas Christian University is fascinating, complete with some twists and turns, triumphs and challenges, that make for a good read. What is even more fascinating are the photographs of that time period that represent this rich history. The story of TCU—its founding and its evolution over one hundred years—inspires me and countless other history nerds. I enjoy looking at the past, because by evaluating the past we can think forward for the future. These incredible photographs brilliantly capture TCU's journey, one of determination and fortitude as a young private university in Texas growing to bright, shining university star-status on the national stage. We have grown through the years, and these photos depict our growing pains, our coming into our own, and our confidence as a nationally acclaimed and multifaceted university.

As we recount the past, we must also address "the rest of the story" about our heritage. TCU has reflected the culture of the times, and there are things in the past that we regret. That said, we must acknowledge and embrace our past in order to move forward—together.

In 2020, the Board of Trustees and the Chancellor's Office commissioned an academically based, historically focused initiative designed to investigate TCU's relationship with slavery, racism, and the Confederacy. This Race & Reconciliation Initiative (RRI) resulted in a Reconciliation Day held in April 2021, whereby TCU publicly made a statement of acknowledgment. We believe that through this research and through further study, we can help the university embrace an active role in reconciliation and the healing of our community. The journey continues . . . as we look back and look forward toward a more inclusive campus setting where all feel welcome.

CHANCELLOR VICTOR J. BOSCHINI JR.

CONTENTS

Introduction

The year 2023 will mark an important milestone for TCU. It will mark the sesquicentennial of the founding of the university. TCU is one of the oldest continuously coeducational institutions west of the Mississippi River. Addison and Randolph Clark started the school in Fort Worth during the fall of 1869 as the Disciple-based Male and Female Seminary of Fort Worth, reportedly with thirty-three female students and twenty-two male students, all ranging in age from early grade-school level to late adolescence. It was founded in downtown Fort Worth at a time when Hell's Half Acre—populated with saloons, brothels, and gambling dens—was a raucous red-light district that emerged because of the cattle drives beginning in the 1870s. But soon the need for more classroom space and the desire to remove the youngsters from the "human wreckage and debris" of Hell's Half Acre prompted the brothers to relocate their school from Fort Worth to the sleepy community of Thorp Spring. Within three years the institution had received a charter from the state of Texas, establishing the 1873 founding of the school, and student enrollment had increased.

During the time in Thorp Spring, 1870–1896, the university adopted the new name AddRan Christian College, incorporated student codes for dress and behavior, and established fields of study. The time in Thorp Spring also denoted major changes for the school and its foundation of faith. In 1889 the Clark brothers agreed to turn control of the school, including all of its assets and debts, over to the Brotherhood of the Christian Churches of Texas, the church governing body in the state, hoping it would bring financial stability. This decision created the link between the institution and the Disciples of Christ faith that has subsequently guided the school for more than 130 years. The connection with the Disciples while at Thorp Spring had other consequences, however—including the 1894 "organ incident" that marked a split between the Disciples of Christ and the emergent Church of Christ. The doctrinal split almost immediately resulted in greatly reduced enrollment, increased financial problems, and ultimately resulted in an agreement by the Board of Trustees to move the school to Waco, where the Waco Christian Church and the Waco Commercial Club promised to provide the financial support needed for the school's survival.

The move to Waco in 1896 saw the school grow and develop academically and athletically, with the creation of the new name Texas Christian University, an official university Horned Frog mascot, a football team, and adoption of purple as the official color for the school. The emergence of the *Skiff* newspaper in 1902 permitted students to share their perceptions of the school and the surrounding community as well as of the state of Texas. Year round educational terms and a broadening of the fields of study brought increased enrollment, permitting the school to challenge crosstown rival Baylor University for students and stature. TCU seemed to be growing, advancing, and prospering in Waco until the faithful night of March 22, 1910, when the campus Main Building—the largest educational building in the southwestern United States—went up in flames. The catastrophe forced the board of trustees to decide whether to remain in Waco or to relocate somewhere else.

The fateful decision to leave Waco and return to Fort Worth in the fall of 1910 for the 1910–1911 school year marked TCU's return to the city where it all began. TCU temporarily held classes downtown while the new campus was under construction on "the hill" southwest of the city. By the fall of 1911, the new campus—four buildings: Main, Clark Hall, Jarvis Hall, and Goode Hall—was ready for students, marking the last major move TCU would make. Since 1911, the campus has evolved, developed, and merged with the city of Fort Worth, and enrollment has steadily grown. In 1923 the university celebrated its golden jubilee, while in 1973 TCU celebrated its centennial. During 2011 the university marked the centennial of its return to Fort Worth and its new campus. In 2023, TCU will celebrate its 150th anniversary—its sesquicentennial.

TCU and our hometown of Fort Worth have enjoyed a partnership of growth, mutual enrichment, and community throughout the twentieth century, but the recent new millennium has brought unprecedented cultural and physical progress to the university. Through strategic planning, vision, and generosity, today TCU is a campus that honors our history as we look to the future. The current Horned Frog family includes approximately eleven thousand students from across the country and throughout the world, and a global network of more than ninety thousand living alumni who flash the Horned Frog sign. The original 1873 charter stated that AddRan Christian University would fulfill its mission to "promote literary and scientific education." Today we promote the same message for men and women of character to acquire a liberal arts education and strive to serve the greater good.

Chancellor Victor Boschini and TCU Press Director Dan Williams approached me in early 2020 about a photographic history of the first hundred years of the university's existence. I agreed to undertake this responsibility with the assistance of Jackson W. Pearson, a student nearing the end of the PhD program in history here. Because of the 2020 Covid pandemic, we could not conduct research in libraries and archives until the late fall of 2020. Since that time, we have organized the format, written scores of vignettes, and scoured thousands of photos about TCU history, selecting many that illustrate the stories we want to tell. What you have here is images and stories of TCU's first one hundred years.

The images reproduced in this book are not all that are available or even a complete photographic history of TCU. We have chosen to highlight common and uncommon stories about the university and provide images, because a picture is worth a thousand words. Many readers will know of some of these stories, while they will know nothing at all of other included stories. For example, how many people knew that there was a March 1917 airplane crash on campus, damaging modern-day Reed Hall? Fortunately, no one died, but this represents an important event in the history of the school. So rather than trying to offer a full or complete pictorial story of the institution 1873–1973, we have incorporated images of buildings, chancellors, board of trustee members, faculty, staff, male and female students, major events, sporting teams, and even physical reminders of what the TCU campus has become—including a vignette and images of the oldest tree on the current TCU campus. The organization and layout of this book is based on providing short vignettes (generally 250-400 words) on a variety of topics through the first hundred years of the school's existence. These short stories can whet your appetite for more information about TCU. They are designed to be short enough that the book can easily be read in stages, leaving it on the coffee table in your living room, on your bedside stand, or even in your bathroom. Material on the TCU experience in Fort Worth, in Thorp Spring, in Waco, and the return to Fort Worth constitute the first three chapters and take the story through the first fifty years, or half of the book. The second half, chapters four through six, highlight the academic expansion, financial growth, physical development, increase in enrollment, and social, racial, and academic evolution of this institution of higher learning during the years 1923 through 1973.

The images we have chosen come from a variety of repositories. There are many, many more images of TCU, including more of some of the events we have documented. What we have tried to do is find little-known images to combine with well-known images to offer new views of the topics we have highlighted. The TCU Special Collections includes invaluable images and scrapbooks from throughout the institution's history; these scrapbooks frequently suggested topics for the vignettes. *TCU Magazine* has graciously permitted several images to be reproduced for this volume. Photos of the city and many of special events in the school's past have generously come from the Fort Worth Public Library. The Baylor Special Collections include photos that illustrate the time that TCU was in Waco, 1896–1910, while the Tarrant County Archives has photos that detail the period of World War I (1914–1918). The *Star-Telegram* Collection of newspaper photos, housed in the Special Collections at the University of Texas-Arlington, have provided many images of people, sporting and academic as well as political events, and pictures of the evolving and developing campus. The Granbury Old County Jail Museum has permitted us to use two photos from TCU's time in Thorp Spring. Finally, we have also included a few images from the estates of Sue Monk Kidd, Bob Lilly, and Ben Procter, and images from a book by Stella Brooks, *Unbelievable: The Unmasking of Harrison Miller Moseley*.

Most of the book's vignettes for this project have been written by Gene Allen Smith (thirty-four) and Jackson W. Pearson (twenty-two). Stories about the Thorp Spring period were contributed by Robert D. Burriss (four), while athletic stories and development of the Worth Hills campus were provided by Mark Z. Mourer (four). Caroline Collier (four) wrote some vignettes about the 1960s and 1970s, while Sylviane Ngandu-Kalenga Greensword (two) drafted a couple of stories about African Americans and racial events in TCU's past. Throughout all of the stories and images, we have tried to provide a snapshot that represents a much larger story of the school's development—from a small rural academy beginning to provide higher education to eager students, to a university in Waco educating Texans, to a major Fort Worth comprehensive university providing education to students from across the nation and from throughout the world. While a century has greatly modified and changed much of what was once AddRan Christian College and is now TCU, that progress continues even today and, we trust, into tomorrow!

CHAPTER 1

The Beginnings: From Fort Worth to Thorp Spring, 1873–1896

ABOVE
"Downtown Fort Worth," 1885. Street Scenes, A-0002.jpg. Historic Photograph Collection, Fort Worth Public Library Archives. Courtesy of the Genealogy, History and Archives Unit, Fort Worth Public Library.

The Clarks and Slavery

It was a slip of paper about the size of a small index card. Discovered in the archives of the Clark Family Records, it outlined a contract to lease the labor of an enslaved boy and how he should be treated. The contract also called for the boy to receive proper clothing and food. The signature at the bottom of the agreement was that of the boy's owner, Joseph Clark, father to Addison and Randolph Clark, founders of Texas Christian University. That small slip of paper represents the sum total of the Clark family's direct participation in slavery or the slave trade. It is unknown when or under what circumstances Joseph acquired the boy. There is also no record that Addison or Randolph ever owned slaves. Most likely, the slaveholding venture of the Clark patriarch was brief, though the Clark family lived their entire lives in a region where chattel slavery was an accepted part of life.

BELOW
Contract between Joseph A. Clark and John Harris in which Harris agrees to pay Clark $150.00 for the use of his enslaved boy, George, for one year. Dated, February 1, 1856. Clark Family Papers, Series II: 1751; 1773-1781; 1841-1969; and undated. Box 36. Joseph Lynn Clark Papers, MS 156. Courtesy of TCU Archives and Special Collections, Mary Couts Burnett Library. Texas Christian University.

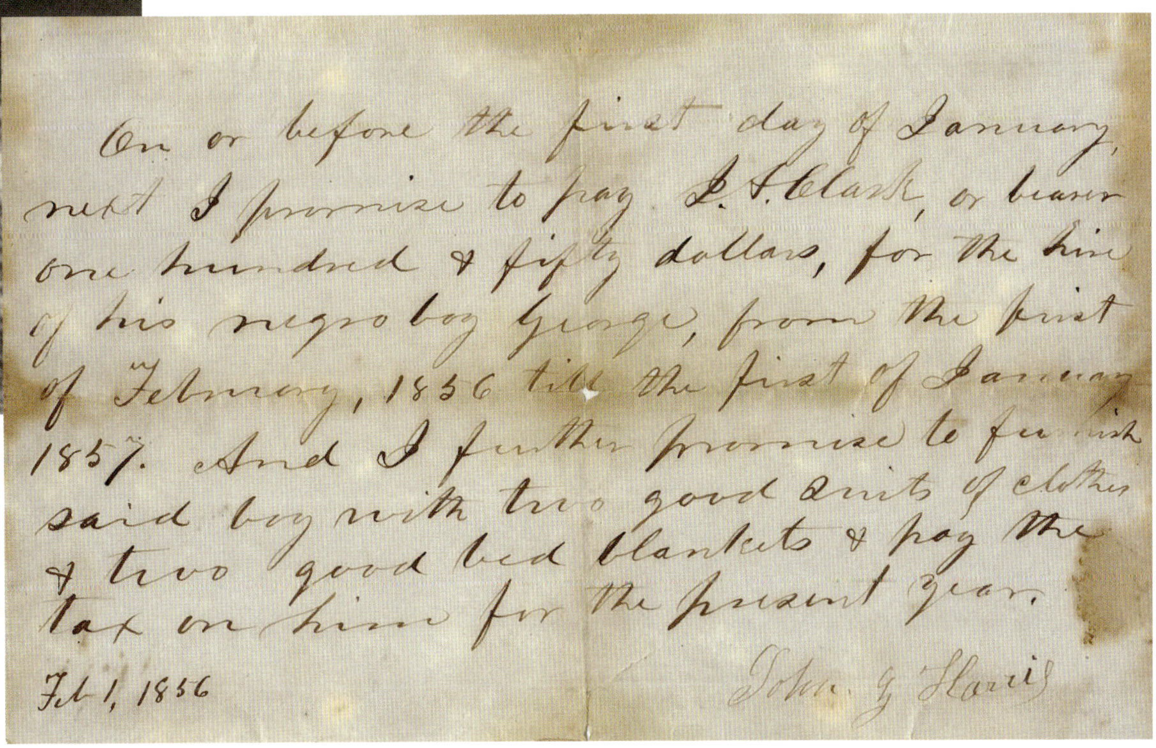

On or before the first day of January next I promise to pay J. A. Clark, or bearer one hundred & fifty dollars, for the hire of his negro boy George, from the first of February, 1856 till the first of January 1857. And I further promise to furnish said boy with two good suits of clothes & two good bed blankets & pay the tax on him for the present year.

Feb 1, 1856

John G. Harris

CITY NATIONAL
BANK BUILDING
HARDWARE
DAGGETT & HATCHER
DRUGS
DRY GOODS

The Clarks and the Civil War

As the South raced into war to protect its institution of chattel slavery, Addison Clark, like his father, urged caution. Randolph referred to talk of secession's consequences as "the noise of war." The Clark brothers' reticence toward war flowed from both their strong Christian beliefs and their pragmatism. As scholars of the Restoration Movement, the Clarks were greatly influenced by the writings of Alexander Campbell, the prominent theologian considered one of the fathers of the Disciples of Christ. Campbell opposed war in general, and he often denounced the Civil War specifically. Addison and his father Joseph understood the precarious situation in which the South placed itself in waging a war to save slavery. The North possessed strong advantages in terms of population and industrial capacity. War for the fledgling Confederacy would not be easy, an opinion shared not just by the Clarks, but also by Texas Governor Sam Houston, a unionist. Nevertheless, Texas forged ahead with secession, a decision that Randolph viewed with foreboding, characterizing the final days of peace as "the silence before the storm," after which "the peal of thunder came."

Addison and Randolph were nineteen and seventeen, respectively, when Texas seceded from the Union and joined the Confederacy in 1861. Formal hostilities began with the Battle of Fort Sumter in April of 1861, but Addison and Randolph remained at home in Texas, refusing to join what they felt was a losing proposition. Addison held out hope that a national leader would emerge to save the country from what he termed "political fools." Despite being old enough to enlist, Randolph stayed behind and spent the first two years of the war helping Joseph run the family grain-milling business. It was not until the next year that Addison made the agonizing decision to enlist, quite likely understanding that if he did not, he would probably soon face the prospect of being drafted into the Confederate service. He joined a unit heavily composed of other members of his Disciples congregation who had joined the war effort earlier.

LEFT
"Cotton Sale in Downtown Fort Worth," 1878. Street Scenes, A-0033.jpg. Historic Photographs Collection, Fort Worth Public Library Archives. Courtesy of the Genealogy, History and Archives Unit, Fort Worth Public Library.

TCU's Origins

Looking at the TCU seal, it proudly denotes 1873 as the year when the institution was chartered. Yet its origins recall an earlier time when Addison and Randolph Clark and Fort Worth were struggling with post-Civil War Reconstruction. Facing political and religious divisions in the city, during the fall of 1869 the brothers opened their private Disciple-based Male and Female Seminary of Fort Worth—the first continuously coeducational institution west of the Mississippi River. The exact location of the school remains in doubt, ranging from a claim that it was on the block between Fourth and Fifth Streets facing Main, to another that it was on the south end of Jones and Calhoun, between Ninth and Fourteenth Streets. Regardless, the school began with ample students, reportedly thirty-three female students and twenty-two male students, all ranging in age from early grade level to late adolescence. With the institution's emergence, it enrolled more women than men!

RIGHT (ABOVE)
Photograph of "Joseph and Hettie Clark," 1869. TCU Photograph Collection, RU 53. Photo Number: 1137. https://repository.tcu.edu:443/handle/116099117/3389. Courtesy of TCU Special Collections. Mary Couts Burnett Library. Texas Christian University.

RIGHT
Sanborn Map Company, Sanborn Fire Insurance Maps. "Fort Worth, Texas, 1885, Sheet 1." Sanborn Fire Insurance Maps Collection. https://collections.lib.utexas.edu/catalog/utlmaps:022b254b-7b6e-4316-8c61b79d0d8d05c7. Courtesy of the Perry-Castañeda Library Maps. University of Texas Libraries, University of Texas at Austin.

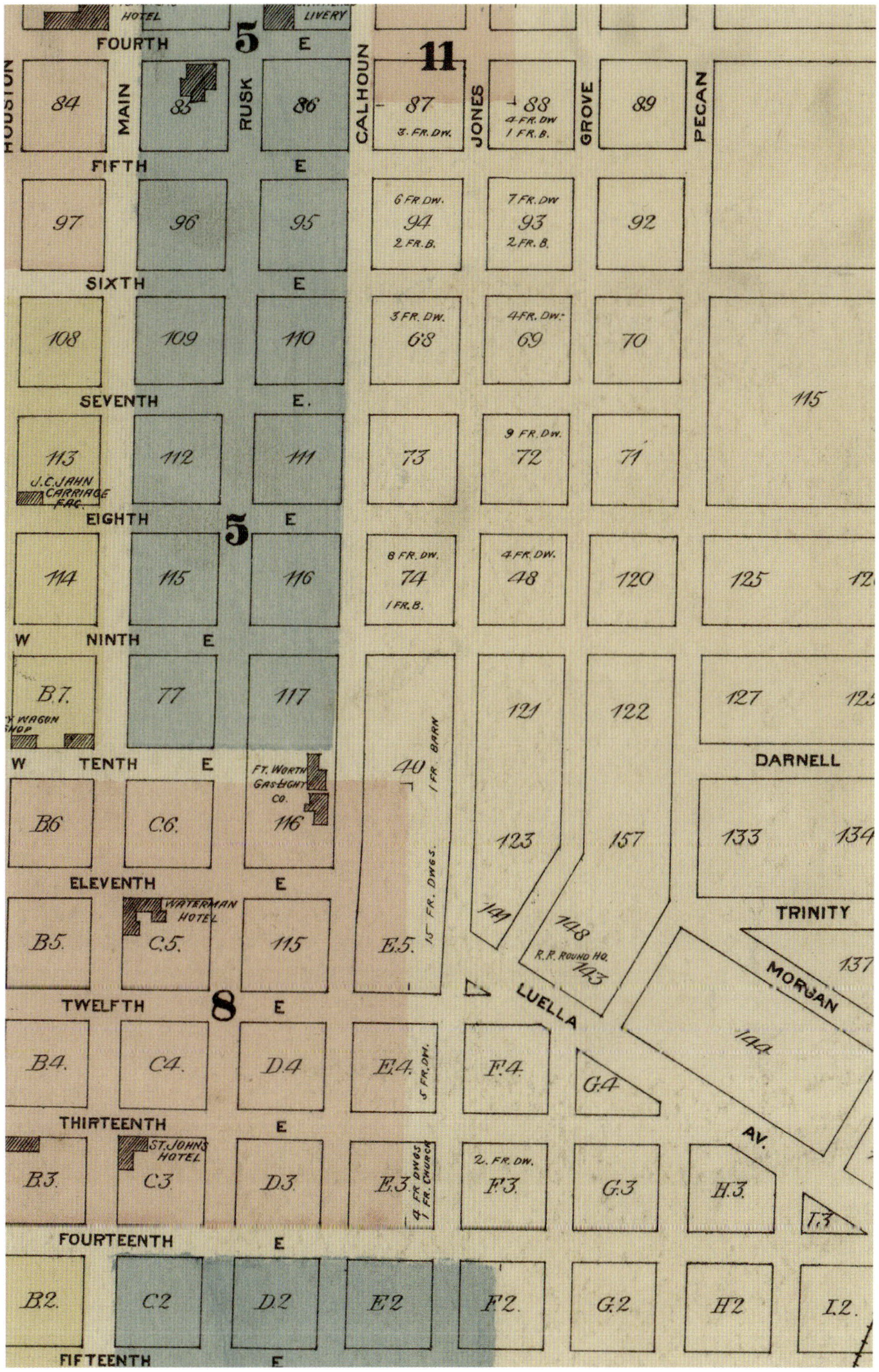

ABOVE

Clipping of Sanborn map showing Jones and Calhoun from Ninth to Fourteenth Streets. Sanborn Map Company, Sanborn Fire Insurance Maps. "Fort Worth, Texas, 1885, Sheet 1." Sanborn Fire Insurance Maps Collection. https://collections.lib.utexas.edu/catalog/utlmaps:022b254b-7b6e-4316-8c61-b79d0d8d05c7. Courtesy of the Perry-Castañeda Library Maps. University of Texas Libraries, University of Texas at Austin.

Leaving Fort Worth

Hell's Half Acre—populated with saloons, brothels, and gambling dens—was Fort Worth's raucous red-light district that had emerged because of the cattle drives beginning in the 1870s. But by the 1870 fall school term, the Clark brothers needed space. They moved their school to a series of buildings located on the south end of Jones and Calhoun, between Ninth and Fourteenth Streets—"soon surrounded by human wreckage and debris." According to Randolph, "The town boys, the boys from the farms and ranches, rough, but clean, were dazzled by this glitter of vice and caught like insects around a streetlamp. It might have been the better part of valor to have remained and fought the flames in an effort to prevent the fire from spreading, but we thought more of saving those who could be kept out of the burning. . . ." The brothers relocated their school to sleepy Thorp Spring.

ABOVE
"Add-Ran College Dormitory," n.d. TCU Photograph Collection, RU 53. Photo Number: 231. https://repository.tcu.edu:443/handle/116099117/3034. Courtesy of TCU Special Collections. Mary Couts Burnett Library. Texas Christian University.

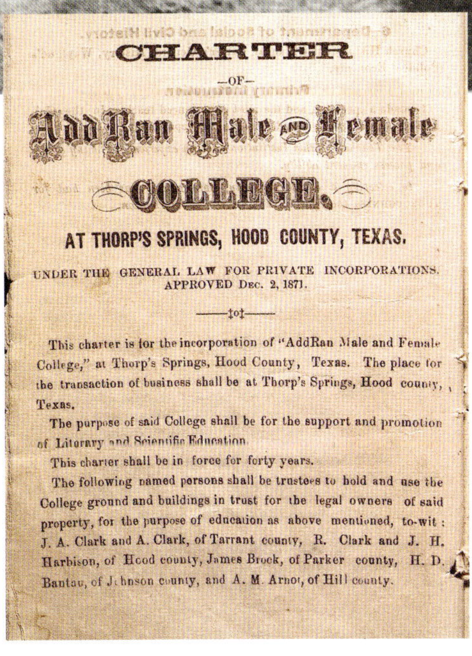

CHARTER
—OF—
AddRan Male and Female
COLLEGE,
AT THORP'S SPRINGS, HOOD COUNTY, TEXAS.

UNDER THE GENERAL LAW FOR PRIVATE INCORPORATIONS.
APPROVED DEC. 2, 1871.

This charter is for the incorporation of "AddRan Male and Female College," at Thorp's Springs, Hood County, Texas. The place for the transaction of business shall be at Thorp's Springs, Hood county, Texas.

The purpose of said College shall be for the support and promotion of Literary and Scientific Education.

This charter shall be in force for forty years.

The following named persons shall be trustees to hold and use the College ground and buildings in trust for the legal owners of said property, for the purpose of education as above mentioned, to-wit: J. A. Clark and A. Clark, of Tarrant county, R. Clark and J. H. Harbison, of Hood county, James Brock, of Parker county, H. D. Bantau, of Johnson county, and A. M. Arnot, of Hill county.

Charley Thorp

Charley Thorp played an instrumental role in the early development of AddRan College. He was born around 1853 to an enslaved Black mother while his father—listed as "unknown"—was White. Colonel Pleasant Earl Thorp, founder of Thorp Spring, purchased Charley's mother between 1850 and 1854. After emancipation in 1865, Charley stayed in Thorp Spring and remained close to Col. Thorp. The 1880 census listed him as a member of Thorp's household. According to oral history, Col. Thorp's slaves (including Charley) helped build Thorp Spring's infrastructure, including the building used by AddRan College.

Charley had a complicated personal life. He fathered at least seven children between 1883 and 1896. He finally settled down with Kate Lee, his third wife, and purchased 137 acres of land from Col. Thorp in 1894. Charley and Kate had a volatile relationship, and they officially separated by 1910. Despite his personal struggles and complicated family life, Charley remained highly regarded in the local community of Thorp Spring and at AddRan College.

LEFT
Charter of Add-Ran Male and Female College at Thorp Spring, Hood County, Texas, 1873. "Add-Ran College, Thorp Spring, Hood County, Texas, 1873-1874 Catalogue." (Fort Worth: Printed by T. B. Marshall, 1873), 12. Charter is on page 12. TCU Catalogs Collection. https://repository.tcu.edu/handle/116099117/41565. Courtesy of TCU Special Collections. Mary Couts Burnett Library. Texas Christian University.

Charley did not allow his inability to read or write determine his life. After his emancipation, he oversaw Col. Thorp's personal affairs. Thus, when Col. Thorp recruited TCU founders Addison and Randolph Clark to Thorp Spring, Charley began employment for AddRan College. He worked at the college for more than twenty years until its move to Waco in 1895. Charley oversaw many of the nonacademic duties and responsibilities at AddRan, including security, discipline, janitorial, scheduling, landscaping, and repairs. Also known as the "fire chief" of Thorp Spring, Charley received praise for his altruism while Kate performed laundry and nursing services for the school.

Despite working for an educational institution, Charley's family did not receive educational lessons from the school that they helped build. Their children attended the nearest Black school in Granbury, but its program ended at the eighth grade. Charley Thorp died in 1927 in New Mexico. Upon learning of his death, Randolph Clark lamented that Charley's lack of formal education was an intellectual injustice for all.

ABOVE
Sallie Chism Clark with Charley Thorp and Family, 1913. Series II: Box 66. Joseph Lynn Clark Papers, MS 156. Courtesy of TCU Archives and Special Collections, Mary Couts Burnett Library. Texas Christian University.

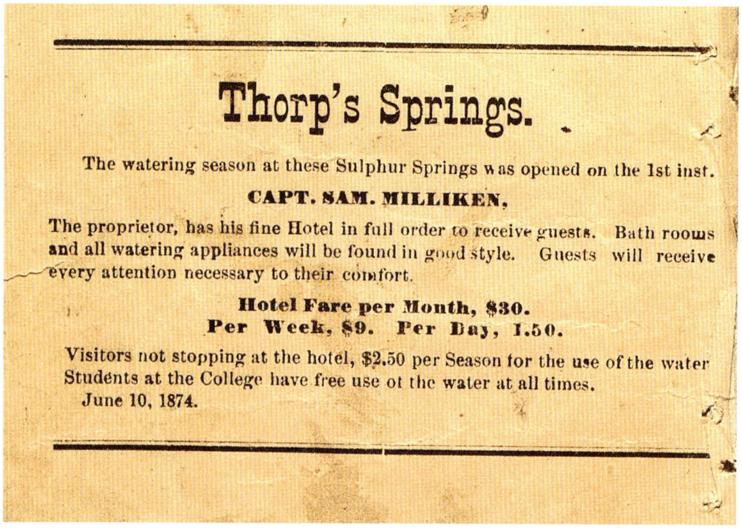

Thorp's Springs.

The watering season at these Sulphur Springs was opened on the 1st inst.

CAPT. SAM. MILLIKEN,

The proprietor, has his fine Hotel in full order to receive guests. Bath rooms and all watering appliances will be found in good style. Guests will receive every attention necessary to their comfort.

Hotel Fare per Month, $30.
Per Week, $9. Per Day, 1.50.

Visitors not stopping at the hotel, $2.50 per Season for the use of the water. Students at the College have free use of the water at all times.
June 10, 1874.

ABOVE
Description of Thorp's Springs in "Catalogue of the Officers and Students of AddRan College for the session ending June 19, 1874." Pdf page 19. (Fort Worth: Printed by T. B. Marshall, 1873), 19. TCU Catalogs. https://repository.tcu.edu/handle/116099117/41565. Courtesy of TCU Special Collections. Mary Couts Burnett Library. Texas Christian University.

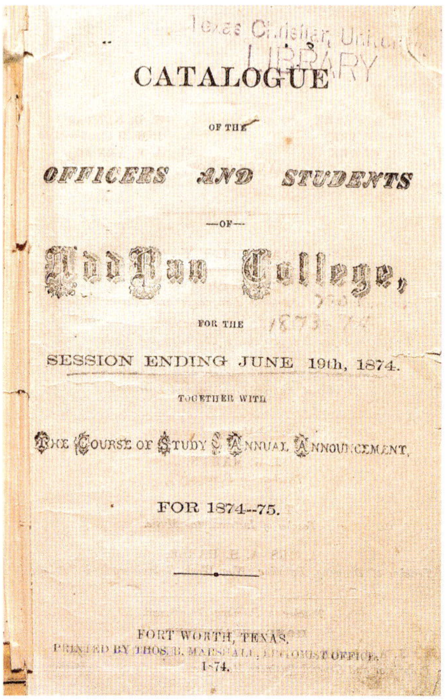

CATALOGUE
OF THE
OFFICERS AND STUDENTS
—OF—
AddRan College,
FOR THE
SESSION ENDING JUNE 19th, 1874.
TOGETHER WITH
The Course of Study & Annual Announcement,
FOR 1874–75.

FORT WORTH, TEXAS.
PRINTED BY THOS. B. MARSHALL, [illegible] OFFICE.
1874.

LEFT
Title Page of "Catalogue of the Officers and Students of AddRan College for the session ending June 19, 1874." Title page is on pdf page 2. (Fort Worth: Printed by T. B. Marshall, 1873), 2. TCU Catalogs Collection. https://repository.tcu.edu/handle/116099117/41565. Courtesy of TCU Special Collections. Mary Couts Burnett Library. Texas Christian University.

ABOVE (TOP)
Image of main building at Thorp Spring campus. "Thorp Spring, TX," 1892. TCU Photograph Collection, RU 53. Photo Number: 1418. https://repository.tcu.edu:443/handle/116099117/3344. Courtesy of TCU Special Collections. Mary Couts Burnett Library. Texas Christian University.

ABOVE
Students outside main building at Thorp Spring Campus. "Add-Ran Christian University Students," 1890–1892. TCU Photograph Collection, RU 53. Photo Number: 2341. https://repository.tcu.edu:443/handle/116099117/2839. Courtesy of TCU Special Collections. Mary Couts Burnett Library. Texas Christian University.

Student Codes at Thorp Spring

At TCU today, students meander around campus in yoga pants, baggy sweatshirts, and loungewear. But in 1892, this attire would have violated AddRan Christian College's Victorian Era dress code, which stipulated that students dress "uniformly plain and neat . . . without vain or extravagant adornment." For classroom settings, faculty expected girls to wear "grey woolen goods . . . with checked gingham apron and a bonnet." For public outings, it specified that they should wear "a black cashmere dress and black hat—with black and white trimmings." The catalogue assuaged parental budgetary concerns, assuring them that since the "judgement of girls cannot be relied upon in making judicious purchase, all of their shopping will be done by supervision of the matron." For the boys, the codes stipulated that they should wear gray "Janes or Cassimere" with a black hat. It also stated that "the first suits were to be purchased from merchants at AddRan . . . 'at as low a price as can be obtained anywhere in the State.'"

In line with Victorian and Progressive notions of morality, the codes also dictated student behavior, expressly prohibiting students from "consuming alcohol anywhere" or attending any "exhibition of an immoral tendency; no race course, billiard saloon, bar, or tippling house." They urged students to abstain from tobacco use on campus and prohibited smoking in public. The codes also banned students from possessing "fire-arms, a dirk, a bowie-knife, nor any other deadly weapon." Perhaps most surprisingly, it even required students to "abstain . . . from card playing, even for amusement." Times have certainly changed!

ABOVE (TOP)
Dormitory for boys at Thorp Spring Campus. "Dormitory for Boys, Built in 1887," 1890. TCU Photograph Collection, RU 53. Photo Number: 1371. https://repository.tcu.edu:443/handle/116099117/2385. Courtesy of TCU Special Collections. Mary Couts Burnett Library. Texas Christian University.

ABOVE
Dormitory for girls at Thorp Spring Campus. "Dormitory for Girls," 1880. TCU Photograph Collection, RU 53. Photo Number: 225, PN Number: 556. https://repository.tcu.edu:443/handle/116099117/3855. Courtesy of TCU Special Collections. Mary Couts Burnett Library. Texas Christian University.

RIGHT
Image of Add-Ran Christian University Faculty on pamphlet. "Add-Ran Christian University Faculty," 1892. TCU Photograph Collection, RU 53. Photo Number: 2100. https://repository.tcu.edu:443/handle/116099117/2789. Courtesy of TCU Special Collections. Mary Couts Burnett Library. Texas Christian University.

Decision to Turn Over to Disciples of Christ

The 1880s was a time of great economic growth in the United States, but not everyone profited from the expansion, especially not small private Christian colleges located in rural America. AddRan had struggled financially since its inception, but the Clark family always found a way for the institution to endure. As time progressed, it became obvious the school needed an endowment to survive.

Part of the financial issues facing AddRan lay in Addison and Randolph's insistence on keeping school affordable. The college had no matriculation fee, did not charge for incidentals, nor make a profit from student housing. Addison and Randolph strongly believed that access to an education was for anyone willing to study hard and abide by the school's rules. This approach, while altruistic, differed markedly from most institutions of higher learning.

Addison and Randolph founded AddRan on the principles of the Disciples of Christ, but the Disciples did not financially endow the institution. AddRan, as constituted at the time, simply was not financially sustainable. While the college had many supporters, none possessed the means to sufficiently endow the school, personally or collectively. In 1889 the Clarks reached a painful conclusion. The only remaining option for Addison and Randolph was to turn control of the school, including all of its assets and debts, over to the Brotherhood of the Christian Churches of Texas, the state governing body, in hope that the move would bring the financial resources needed to erase the school's debt and increase its operating revenue.

ABOVE
Nellie Howard, professor in the Primary Department at Add-Ran Christian University. "Nellie Howard," 1892-1893. TCU Photograph Collection, RU 53. Photo Number: 1328. https://repository.tcu.edu:443/handle/116099117/3646. Courtesy of TCU Special Collections. Mary Couts Burnett Library. Texas Christian University.

ABOVE
Mary E. Wideman, dean of women at Add-Ran Christian University. "Mary E. Wideman," 1892. TCU Photograph Collection, RU 53. Photograph Number: 260. https://repository.tcu.edu:443/handle/116099117/2865. Courtesy of TCU Special Collections. Mary Couts Burnett Library. Texas Christian University.

ABOVE
William B. Parks, professor of natural science at Add-Ran Christian University. "William B. Parks," 1892–1893. TCU Photograph Collection, RU 53. Photo Number: 1321. https://repository.tcu.edu:443/handle/116099117/3742. Courtesy of TCU Special Collections. Mary Couts Burnett Library. Texas Christian University.

ABOVE
Portrait of Addison Clark. "Addison Clark," 1897. TCU Photograph Collection, RU 53. Photo Number: 43, PN Number: 15. https://repository.tcu.edu:443/handle/116099117/2510. Courtesy of TCU Special Collections. Mary Couts Burnett Library. Texas Christian University.

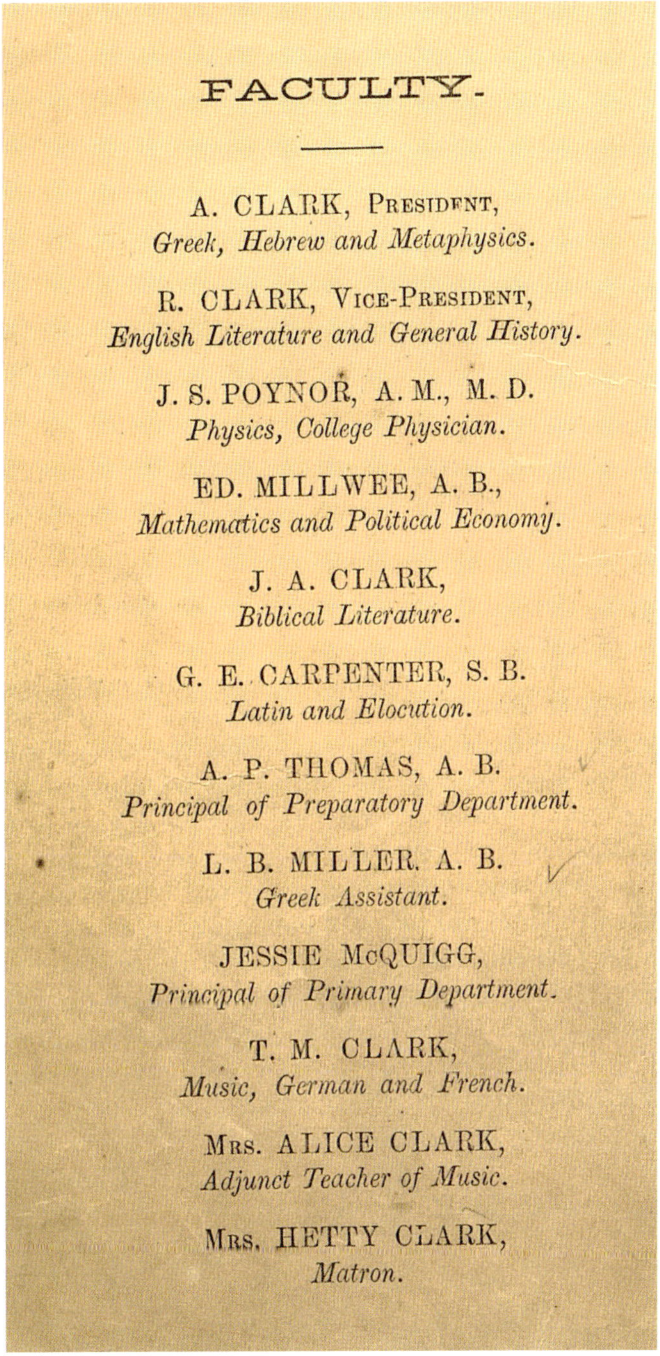

FACULTY.

A. CLARK, PRESIDENT,
Greek, Hebrew and Metaphysics.

R. CLARK, VICE-PRESIDENT,
English Literature and General History.

J. S. POYNOR, A. M., M. D.
Physics, College Physician.

ED. MILLWEE, A. B.,
Mathematics and Political Economy.

J. A. CLARK,
Biblical Literature.

G. E. CARPENTER, S. B.
Latin and Elocution.

A. P. THOMAS, A. B.
Principal of Preparatory Department.

L. B. MILLER, A. B.
Greek Assistant.

JESSIE McQUIGG,
Principal of Primary Department.

T. M. CLARK,
Music, German and French.

MRS. ALICE CLARK,
Adjunct Teacher of Music.

MRS. HETTY CLARK,
Matron.

ABOVE
List of Add-Ran College Faculty in 1881 Catalogue. "Catalogue of the Officers and Students of Add-Ran College, for the 8th Session ending April 28, 1881." Pdf image 4. (Hood County: Printed by Student Office of Add-Ran College, 1881), 2. TCU Catalogs Collection. https://repository.tcu.edu/handle/116099117/41570. Courtesy of TCU Special Collections. Mary Couts Burnett Library. Texas Christian University.

ABOVE
Portrait of Randolph Clark. "Randolph Clark," 1874. TCU Photograph Collection, RU 53. Photo Number: 1146. https://repository.tcu.edu:443/handle/116099117/2335. Courtesy of TCU Special Collections. Mary Couts Burnett Library. Texas Christian University.

ABOVE
Portrait of Mrs. M. E. Huston, who served as the Boy's Matron at AddRan Christian University. "Mrs. Huston," n.d. TCU Photograph Collection, RU 53. Photo Number: 507. https://repository.tcu.edu:443/handle/116099117/3056. Courtesy of TCU Special Collections. Mary Couts Burnett Library. Texas Christian University.

ABOVE
Robert Holloway, professor of mathematics at Add-Ran Christian University, and Randolph Clark's son-in-law. "Robert Holloway," 1890s. TCU Photograph Collection, RU 53. Photo Number: 1162. https://repository.tcu.edu:443/handle/116099117/3298. Courtesy of TCU Special Collections. Mary Couts Burnett Library. Texas Christian University.

RIGHT
A. C. Easley, professor of business at Add-Ran Christian University. "A. C. Easley," 1892–1893. TCU Photograph Collection, RU 53. Photo Number: 1160. https://repository.tcu.edu:443/handle/116099117/2498. Courtesy of TCU Special Collections. Mary Couts Burnett Library. Texas Christian University.

ABOVE
Background: Building at Thorp Spring Campus. "Add-Ran Christian University," 1891–1892. TCU Photograph Collection, RU 53. Photo Number: 2402. https://repository.tcu.edu:443/handle/116099117/3465. Courtesy of TCU Special Collections. Mary Couts Burnett Library. Texas Christian University.

Music Row in the Church

The Disciples' debate over musical instruments in worship services began in 1860, and by the end of the century, few Disciples escaped the debate, including the Clark family and the students of AddRan. Although it never threatened to tear the close-knit family apart, the dispute over music did raise tensions among family members, leading to the infamous "Organ Incident."

The instrument in question was a small Etsy organ, which the AddRan students had used in their private worship services the year prior to the community debate. Its presence on campus probably would have remained unremarkable had Addison not promised the students they would use the instrument for Religious Emphasis Week, a community-oriented revival held on campus, in February 1894.

As the revival approached, lines were drawn, with those opposed to the use of the organ labeled "antis," while those who did not oppose use of the organ were simply considered part of the more progressive Disciples. Joseph Clark, father of Addison and Randolph, was one of the more outspoken antis. His opposition to use of the organ lay in his belief that it represented Disciples' straying from their traditional use of the Bible as the ultimate authority in all matters of worship. Because the Bible does not specifically mention mechanical instruments, many Disciples did not endorse their use, especially in worship services. Although they sought to maintain unity, Addison and Randolph were not opposed to the organ.

At the opening service, Addison gave a prayer calling for unity within the church and community. Joseph likewise gave prayer, though he and others maintained they would not participate in any service that included mechanical music. When Addison announced the first hymn, Joseph and the rest of the antis rose and marched out of the service. At that instant, Addison raised his right hand and pointed to the school's organist, Bertha Mason, and spoke the phrase that became associated with the episode: "Play on, Miss Bertha."

RIGHT
"State Historical Marker at former AddRan Campus," 1973. TCU Photograph Collection, RU 53. Photo Number: 939. https://repository.tcu.edu:443/handle/116099117/3387. Courtesy of TCU Special Collections. Mary Couts Burnett Library. Texas Christian University.

RIGHT
Add-Ran University Faculty in front of Main Building at Thorp Spring Campus. "Add-Ran Christian University Faculty," 1891–1892. TCU Photograph Collection, RU 53. Photo Number: 2403. https://repository.tcu.edu:443/handle/116099117/3705. Courtesy of TCU Special Collections. Mary Couts Burnett Library. Texas Christian University.

ABOVE
Add-Ran faculty seated and standing in front of Main Building at Thorp Spring Campus. "Add-Ran College Faculty," 1890. Joseph Lynn Clark Papers, MS 156. Box 4, File 15. https://repository.tcu.edu/handle/116099117/7022. Courtesy of TCU Archives and Special Collections. Mary Couts Burnett Library. Texas Christian University.

ABOVE
Add-Ran Art Department students and faculty displaying projects in front of Main Building at Thorp Spring Campus. "Students and Faculty," 1890. TCU Photograph Collection, RU 53. Photo Number: 1344, PN Number: 632. https://repository.tcu.edu:443/handle/116099117/3102. Courtesy of TCU Special Collections. Mary Couts Burnett Library. Texas Christian University.

CHAPTER 2

The Waco Years: 1896-1910

EDUCATIONAL INSTITUTIONS
ADD-RAN UNIVERSITY.

AddRan Relocates to Waco

During the fall of 1893 AddRan University enrolled 445, its largest student body, but problems soon wracked the school. Doctrinal debates regarding the use of organs in church abruptly split the school and faith into a conservative faction, which became the Church of Christ, and a more progressive faction, which became the Christian Church. These doctrinal divisions also created intense financial problems for the school as enrollment declined in 1894 to only 294 students, the lowest number in sixteen years.

The Waco Christian Church and the Waco Commercial Club offered to purchase the former Waco Female College building and give it to AddRan if the school would relocate to the bustling city of twenty thousand. The Waco faction also offered $5,000 and fifteen acres of land as well as other inducements including transportation for faculty, students, and other personnel from Thorp Spring to Waco, if the move occurred before 1896. Even though AddRan President Addison Clark objected, in September 1895 the board of directors approved the move. Once relocated to Waco, the institution would be sustained by the Christian Church and would officially open on January 1, 1897.

On Christmas Day, 1896, about one hundred faculty, students, and others, including Addison Clark, alighted from the train at the MK&T depot in Waco. They formed a procession and marched in parade through the business section of downtown toward a formal welcoming and reception ceremony at First Baptist Church, attended by local politicians, club leaders, and religious representatives. The minister of First Baptist Church and the president of Baylor, Rufus Burleson, gave speeches welcoming AddRan University to Waco. After the festivities, the AddRan body marched three miles to North Eighteenth Street to a lone brick building standing atop a grassy hill. They were home!

LEFT
Students and faculty on parade float promoting Add-Ran Christian University in Waco. "Students and Faculty," 1897. TCU Photograph Collection, RU 53. Photo Number: 2239, PN Number 564. https://repository.tcu.edu:443/handle/116099117/2147. Courtesy of TCU Special Collections, Mary Couts Burnett Library. Texas Christian University.

ABOVE
Photograph of faculty and students at Waco campus. One of the first photographs taken after the move to Waco. "Add-Ran Christian University Faculty and Student Body," 1895. TCU Photograph Collection, RU 53. Photo Number: 481. https://repository.tcu.edu/handle/116099117/46013. Courtesy of TCU Special Collections. Mary Couts Burnett Library. Texas Christian University.

BELOW
Clipping from Sanborn Fire Map showing Add-Ran Christian University in Waco. Sanborn Map Company, Sanborn Fire Insurance Maps. "Waco, Texas, 1899, Sheet 21." Sanborn Fire Insurance Maps Collection. https://collections.lib.utexas.edu/catalog/utlmaps:24403e37-be5f-457d-84cc-fa7f168edd96. Courtesy of Perry-Castañeda Library Maps. University of Texas Libraries, University of Texas at Austin.

Football Comes to Texas!

Football came to Texas during the 1890s, but Addison Clark had no interest in the sport. Instead, he promoted military drill and hard work rather than frivolity. When his son, Addison Jr., (Addie) returned from the University of Michigan in 1896 to teach at AddRan University, he brought a steadfast interest in football. He had an ally in AddRan graduate Aaron C. (A. C.) Easley, who studied during the summer of 1896 at the University of Chicago, where he met Amos Alonzo Stagg. Easley secured a new football rulebook from Stagg and returned to Waco during the fall to help Addie organize the first AddRan University football game, played on Thanksgiving Day, November 26, 1896. Colby D. Hall, a 124-pound quarterback, played with and against other AddRan students in an intramural game. They completed the 1896 season with three games against opponents, compiling a record of 1-1-1.

With a field on the southwest corner of campus, the "Boys from the Heights," or north Waco, formed the school's first intercollegiate team in 1897. Winning 6-0 in Dallas against a noncollegiate team, they later also beat Texas A&M and Fort Worth University. Concluding the season with a record of 3-1-0, the team's only loss came in Waco on November 3, 1897, to the University of Texas, 16-10. Apparently, AddRan University was one of the first college teams to ever score on the University of Texas, as left halfback M. R. Sharp dove into the end zone for the school's first touchdown against Texas. The 1897 season record would be the school's best mark for a decade, and TCU would score only two more touchdowns before finally beating the University of Texas in Austin during their fifteenth meeting on November 16, 1929.

RIGHT (OPPOSITE)
1904 Horned Frog Football Team in practice. Photo is included in a collage of TCU Baseball photos. "TCU Baseball Team," 1905. Group Photos of Sports Teams. TCU Photograph Collection, RU 53. Photo Number: 317. https://repository.tcu.edu:443/handle/116099117/2347. Courtesy of TCU Special Collections, Mary Couts Burnett Library. Texas Christian University.

RIGHT
Photo of Charles Edwin Bull who attended and played football at AddRan Christian University. "Charles Edwin Bull," 1898. TCU Photograph Collection, RU 53. Photo Number: 2242, PN Number: 536. https://repository.tcu.edu:443/handle/116099117/2160. Courtesy of TCU Special Collections, Mary Couts Burnett Library. Texas Christian University.

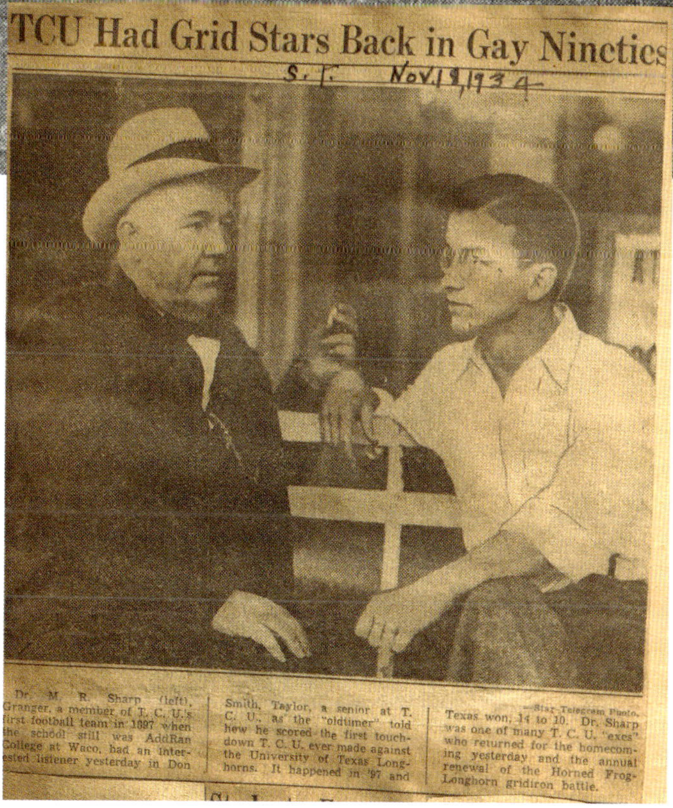

TCU Had Grid Stars Back in Gay Nineties

S. T. Nov 19, 1934

—Star-Telegram Photo.

Dr. M. R. Sharp (left), Granger, a member of T. C. U.'s first football team in 1897 when the school still was AddRan College at Waco, had an interested listener yesterday in Don Smith, Taylor, a senior at T. C. U., as the "oldtimer" told how he scored the first touchdown T. C. U. ever made against the University of Texas Longhorns. It happened in '97 and Texas won, 14 to 10. Dr. Sharp was one of many T. C. U. "exes" who returned for the homecoming yesterday and the annual renewal of the Horned Frog-Longhorn gridiron battle.

RIGHT
Newspaper clipping showing M. R. Sharp, who scored the first touchdown against the University of Texas-Austin in 1898. TCU Scrapbook Collection, RU 8. Box 24, Folder 19; "Society, 1934-35." Nov. 18, 1934, *Fort Worth Star-Telegram* clipping "TCU Had Grid Stars back in the Gay Nineties." Courtesy of TCU Archives and Special Collections, Mary Couts Burnett Library. Texas Christian University.

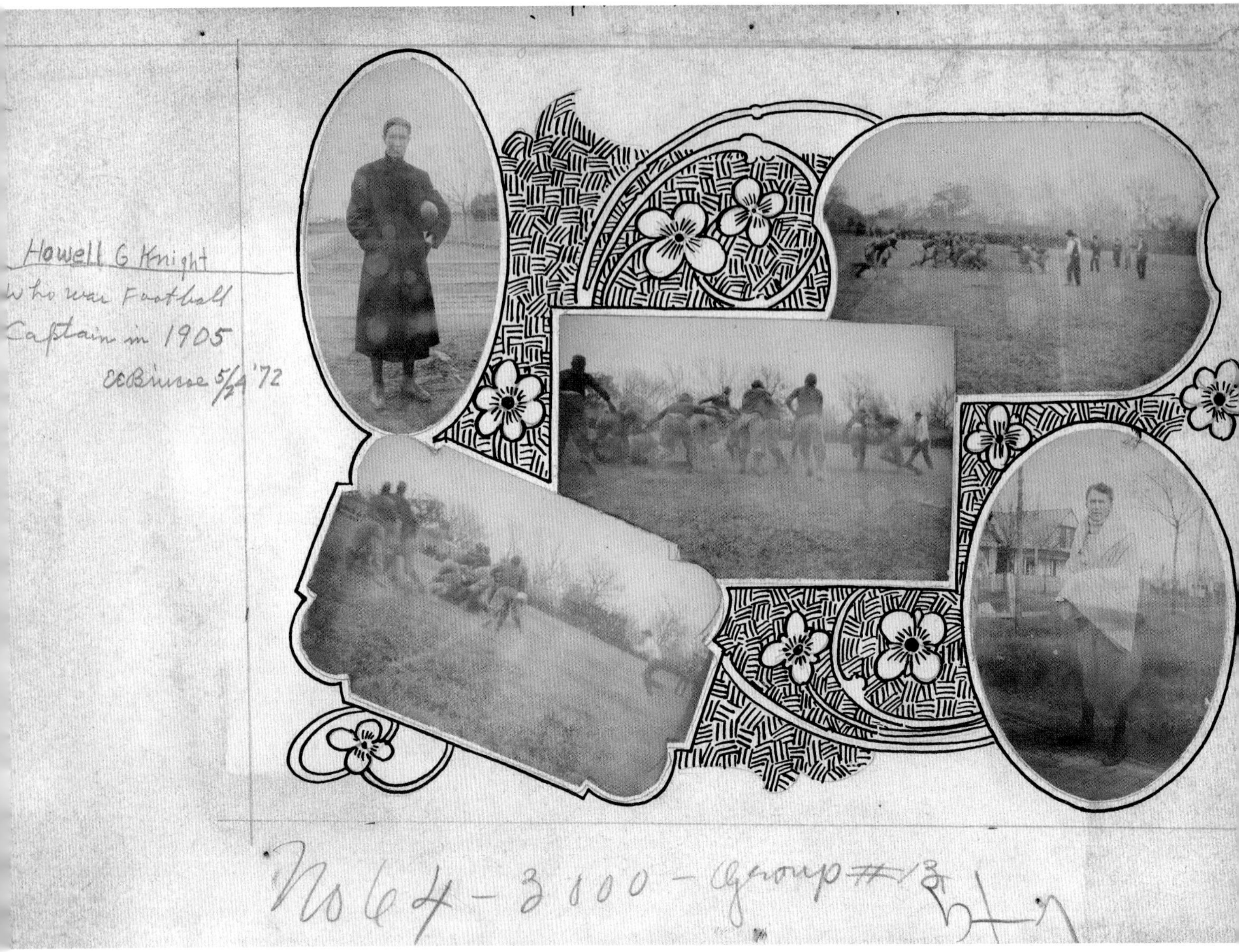

ABOVE
Photograph of TCU Thanksgiving Football Game in 1905. Photo is part of a collage documenting the game. "1905 Football Team," 1905. TCU Photograph Collection, RU 53. Photo Number: 1382. https://repository.tcu.edu:443/handle/116099117/2895. Courtesy of TCU Special Collections, Mary Couts Burnett Library. Texas Christian University.

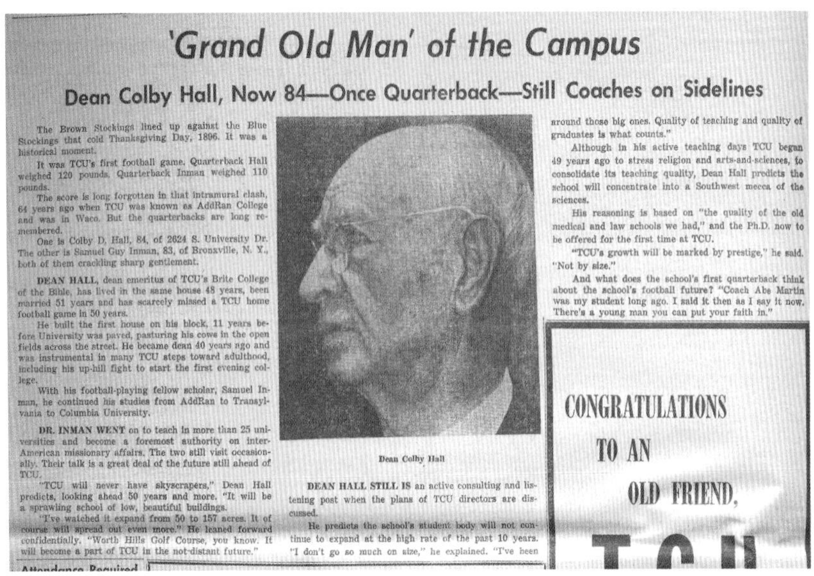

'Grand Old Man' of the Campus

Dean Colby Hall, Now 84—Once Quarterback—Still Coaches on Sidelines

The Brown Stockings lined up against the Blue Stockings that cold Thanksgiving Day, 1896. It was a historical moment.

It was TCU's first football game. Quarterback Hall weighed 120 pounds. Quarterback Inman weighed 110 pounds.

The score is long forgotten in that intramural clash, 64 years ago when TCU was known as AddRan College and was in Waco. But the quarterbacks are long remembered.

One is Colby D. Hall, 84, of 2624 S. University Dr. The other is Samuel Guy Inman, 83, of Bronxville, N. Y., both of them crackling sharp gentlement.

DEAN HALL, dean emeritus of TCU's Brite College of the Bible, has lived in the same house 48 years, been married 51 years and has scarcely missed a TCU home football game in 50 years.

He built the first house on his block, 11 years before University was paved, pasturing his cows in the open fields across the street. He became dean 40 years ago and was instrumental in many TCU steps toward adulthood, including his up-hill fight to start the first evening college.

With his football-playing fellow scholar, Samuel Inman, he continued his studies from AddRan to Transylvania to Columbia University.

DR. INMAN WENT on to teach in more than 25 universities and become a foremost authority on inter-American missionary affairs. The two still visit occasionally. Their talk is a great deal of the future still ahead of TCU.

"TCU will never have skyscrapers," Dean Hall predicts, looking ahead 50 years and more. "It will be a sprawling school of low, beautiful buildings.

"I've watched it expand from 50 to 157 acres. It of course will spread out even more." He leaned forward confidentially. "Worth Hills Golf Course, you know. It will become a part of TCU in the not-distant future."

Dean Colby Hall

DEAN HALL STILL IS an active consulting and listening post when the plans of TCU directors are discussed.

He predicts the school's student body will not continue to expand at the high rate of the past 10 years. "I don't go so much on size," he explained. "I've been around those big ones. Quality of teaching and quality of graduates is what counts."

Although in his active teaching days TCU began 49 years ago to stress religion and arts-and-sciences, to consolidate its teaching quality, Dean Hall predicts the school will concentrate into a Southwest mecca of the sciences.

His reasoning is based on "the quality of the old medical and law schools we had," and the Ph.D. now to be offered for the first time at TCU.

"TCU's growth will be marked by prestige," he said. "Not by size."

And what does the school's first quarterback think about the school's football future? "Coach Abe Martin was my student long ago. I said it then as I say it now. There's a young man you can put your faith in."

CONGRATULATIONS
TO AN
OLD FRIEND,

LEFT (OPPOSITE)

Newspaper clipping showing Colby Hall who played in first football game held at Add-Ran Christian University on Thanksgiving Day in 1896. TCU Scrapbook Collection, RU 8. Box 21, Folder 52; "Public Relations, 1960." Sunday, Oct 2, 1960, *Fort Worth Press*, page 8, "'Grand Old Man' of the Campus" newspaper clipping. Courtesy of TCU Archives and Special Collections, Mary Couts Burnett Library. Texas Christian University.

ABOVE

Team photo of 1897 Horned Frog Football Team. "1897 Football Team," 1897. TCU Photograph Collection, RU 53. Photo Number: 56. https://repository.tcu.edu:443/handle/116099117/2153. Courtesy of TCU Special Collections, Mary Couts Burnett Library. Texas Christian University.

The Clarks Take Leave

Though the Clarks handed control of AddRan Christian College over to the Disciples of Christ in 1889, they remained invaluable leaders within the institution itself. The move to Waco proved difficult for Addison, Randolph, and their families. As early as the spring of 1896, Randolph devised a plan in which he would return to his family in Thorp Spring that autumn. Once there he planned to open and administer a sister school named the Jarvis Institute. He hoped that this school could serve as a feeder to the main campus in Waco. However, the school actually caused both campuses to languish, as they recruited from the same pool of students, with negative financial and enrollment consequences. Jarvis Institute proved short-lived, as it closed its doors in 1898.

Meanwhile, Addison continued to serve as the university president in Waco until 1899, when he offered his resignation to the board of trustees. He believed that the school needed new leadership. The board ultimately convinced Addison to remain as a professor until a suitable replacement could be found. During this period, financial strains weighed heavily on the institution, and the school experienced a mass exodus of experienced faculty between 1898 and 1900. The exodus included Addison Clark Jr. (principal of School of History and English Literature), J. B. Sweeney (dean of Bible College), W. B. Parks (principal of School of Natural Science), and J. W. Froley (principal of School of Mathematics). Addison Clark Sr. continued to serve as a professor of philosophy and dean of the Bible College until 1901, when he accepted a position as pastor at the Central Christian Church in Waco. When Addison left the institution, no official connections remained between the Clark family and AddRan Christian University. These developments ensured a future overhaul of campus faculty and leadership.

OPPOSITE
Photograph of Assembly Hall at Add-Ran Christian University Campus in 1900. "Assembly Hall," 1900s. TCU Photograph Collection, RU 53. Photo Number: 485. https://repository.tcu.edu:443/handle/116099117/3445. Courtesy of TCU Special Collections, Mary Couts Burnett Library. Texas Christian University.

ABOVE
Photograph of TCU professor working in his office at Waco campus during early 1900s. "Office of a Professor," 1900s. TCU Photograph Collection, RU 53. Photo Number: 484, PN Number: 573. https://repository.tcu.edu:443/handle/116099117/3347. Courtesy of TCU Special Collections, Mary Couts Burnett Library. Texas Christian University.

ABOVE
Photograph of TCU Spanish class on steps of Main Building in 1904. "Spanish Class on Steps of Main Building," 1904–1905. TCU Photograph Collection, RU 53. Photo Number: 1346. https://repository.tcu.edu:443/handle/116099117/3240. Courtesy of TCU Special Collections, Mary Couts Burnett Library. Texas Christian University.

RIGHT
Photograph of TCU Orchestra taken by W. D. Smith of Fort Worth in 1907. "Orchestra Group," 1907. TCU Photograph Collection, RU 53. Photo Number: 1901. https://repository.tcu.edu:443/handle/116099117/3125. Courtesy of TCU Special Collections, Mary Couts Burnett Library. Texas Christian University.

ABOVE
Primary Department class with students seated at desks. "Primary Department Class," 1903. TCU Photograph Collection, RU 53. Photo Number: 2422. https://repository.tcu.edu:443/handle/116099117/2644. Courtesy of TCU Special Collections, Mary Couts Burnett Library. Texas Christian University.

LEFT
Add-Ran Christian University Faculty including Charles Ivan Alexander, W. T. Hammer, and others, taken in 1900. "Add-Ran Christian University Faculty," 1900. TCU Photograph Collection, RU 53. Photo Number: 338. https://repository.tcu.edu:443/handle/116099117/2159. Courtesy of TCU Special Collections, Mary Couts Burnett Library. Texas Christian University.

ABOVE
Photograph of Latin class standing at front of classroom at TCU in 1903. "Latin Class," 1903. TCU Photograph Collection, RU 53. Photo Number: 2420. https://repository.tcu.edu:443/handle/116099117/3285. Courtesy of TCU Special Collections, Mary Couts Burnett Library. Texas Christian University.

RIGHT
Photograph of J. A. Dacus and business class at TCU in 1907. "College of Business," 1907. TCU Photograph Collection, RU 53. https://repository.tcu.edu/handle/116099117/12239. Courtesy of TCU Special Collections, Mary Couts Burnett Library. Texas Christian University.

ABOVE
Photograph of President Ely Zollars in his office. “President Zollars,” 1909. TCU Photograph Collection, RU 53. Photo Number: 2133. https://repository.tcu.edu/handle/116099117/6659. Courtesy of TCU Special Collections. Mary Couts Burnett Library. Texas Christian University.

Name, Colors, and Mascot

For three years, the AddRan Board of Trustees conducted a wide-ranging search to find a successor to Addison Clark Sr. The board offered the position of president to four candidates without success before finally selecting Ely Vaughn Zollars on March 14, 1902. Zollars arrived at the university after serving thirteen years as president of Hiram College in Hiram, Ohio. His appointment marked a transition into a period of relative stability that stood in stark contrast to the instability that marred the school between 1896 and 1901. As one of his first tasks, he sought to redefine the public image of the school and chart a new era for the institution. He recommended a name change and the adoption of official university colors and mascot.

On the morning of March 15, 1902, the board of trustees, at President Zollars's request, officially renamed the school Texas Christian University. The trustees then resolved that the College of Science, Literature, and Arts be renamed AddRan College of Arts and Sciences to honor the contributions of the Clark family in founding the university. Zollars also pushed the school to formally adopt purple and white as the official school colors. Sporting teams and fans had already been utilizing these colors, but the school had not declared them official until this time. Finally, the school officially adopted the "Horned Frog" as the university mascot, as previously suggested by "Little Addie" Clark Jr. in 1898. According to local observers, the "Horned Frogs" sounded a bit more intimidating than the "Fightin' Preacher Boys."

LEFT
Portrait of Addison Clark Jr. "Addison Clark, Jr." 1897. TCU Photograph Collection, RU 53. Photo Number: 1218. https://repository.tcu.edu:443/handle/116099117/2601. Courtesy of TCU Special Collections. Mary Couts Burnett Library. Texas Christian University.

ABOVE
TCU women's basketball players lying in a circle around a ball. "Women in a circle around basketball, with TCU 07." Waco—Schools and Colleges. Texas Christian University. Item no. 2388. Negative No. PR-T547. Courtesy of The Texas Collection, Baylor University.

ABOVE
Purple and white ribbon found in the Amboline Tyson scrapbook. Amboline Tyson Scrapbook, Page 8. TCU Scrapbook Collection. RU 8. Box 34, Folder 3. https://repository.tcu.edu/handle/116099117/4610. Courtesy of TCU Archives and Special Collections. Mary Couts Burnett Library. Texas Christian University.

RIGHT (ABOVE)
Portrait of T. E. Shirley. "Thorton E. Shirley," n.d. TCU Photograph Collection, RU 53. Photo Number: 209, PN Number: 92. https://repository.tcu.edu:443/handle/116099117/2185. Courtesy of TCU Special Collections. Mary Couts Burnett Library. Texas Christian University.

RIGHT
Cover of *The Horned Frog*, 1906. (Waco: J.S. Hill & Co., 1906.) https://repository tcu.edu/handle/116099117/11033. Courtesy of TCU Archives and Special Collections. Mary Couts Burnett Library. Texas Christian University.

Olive Leaman McClintic, Head of Oratory

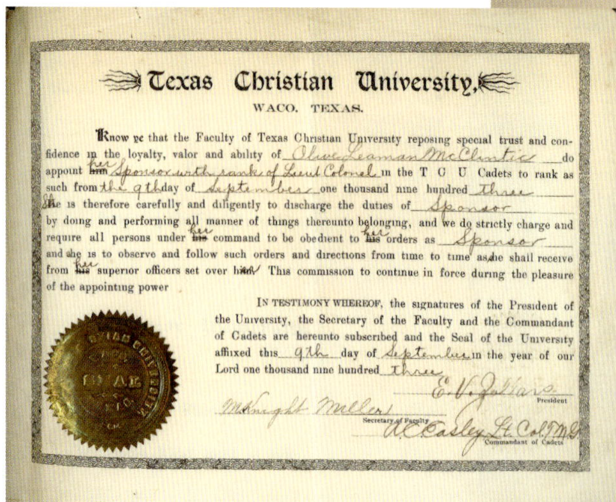

Texas Christian University,

WACO, TEXAS.

Know ye that the Faculty of Texas Christian University reposing special trust and confidence in the loyalty, valor and ability of Olive Leaman McClintic do appoint her Sponsor with rank of Lieut Colonel in the T C U Cadets to rank as such from the 9th day of September one thousand nine hundred three She is therefore carefully and diligently to discharge the duties of Sponsor by doing and performing all manner of things thereunto belonging, and we do strictly charge and require all persons under her command to be obedient to her orders as Sponsor and she is to observe and follow such orders and directions from time to time as she shall receive from her superior officers set over her This commission to continue in force during the pleasure of the appointing power

In Testimony Whereof, the signatures of the President of the University, the Secretary of the Faculty and the Commandant of Cadets are hereunto subscribed and the Seal of the University affixed this 9th day of September in the year of our Lord one thousand nine hundred three

E. V. Zollars
President

McKnight Miller
Secretary of Faculty

A. C. Easley Lt. Col. T.M.G.
Commandant of Cadets

Olive Leaman McClintic matriculated at AddRan University in January 1898, studying oratory and literature before graduating in the spring of 1901. Spending the following summer and winter gaining further education at Northwestern University's School of Oratory and Emerson College of Oratory in Boston, she returned to Waco in March 1902 to teach oratory for the remainder of the spring term.

The youthful and erudite McClintic quickly became one of the most popular instructors at the university. In February 1903 she served as one of three editors (along with Colby D. Hall and Ed S. McKinney) of the university newspaper, the *Skiff*. Later that same year she was promoted to sole editor. President Zollars capitalized on her popularity in September 1903, appointing her Lt. Colonel and Sponsor of the TCU Cadets. Despite her other duties, McClintic focused on teaching elocution/speech. She required every student to take oral reading courses, not necessarily to make entertainers, but to read and speak better. As the director of the Department of Reading and Expression from 1902–1907, her program became one of the largest areas of study at the university. Her students were in high demand for theatrical performances, to offer presentations, and to serve as speakers and masters of ceremony, and her male and female debaters brought recognition to the university. She, herself, became recognized as a popular artist and performer.

McClintic, however, did not remain at TCU. She married in 1908, becoming Olive McClintic Johnson, and accepted a teaching position at the newly created Oklahoma College for Women, where she started a degree program in expression. Still a popular teacher, her OCW students named the literary society after her. By 1911 she had returned to Texas to become a prolific writer, and as late as December 1942 she served as the director of speech at North Texas Agricultural College.

ABOVE (RIGHT)
Miss Olive Leaman McClintic scrapbook. Sept 9, 1903, McClintic appointed Lt. Col. Sponsor of TCU Cadets. Page 41. TCU Scrapbook Collection, Record Unit 8, Box 32, Folder 51; "Speech and Drama, 1898-1908". https://repository.tcu.edu/handle/116099117/4609. Courtesy of TCU Archives and Special Collections. Mary Couts Burnett Library. Texas Christian University.

OPPOSITE (LOWER)
Notecard with portrait and biographical information of Olive Leaman McClintic. TCU Scrapbook Collection, RU 8. Box 32, Folder 51. Second Image. https://repository.tcu.edu/handle/116099117/4609. Courtesy of TCU Archives and Special Collections. Mary Couts Burnett Library. Texas Christian University.

OLIVE LEAMAN McCLINTIC, A. B.,

Principal School of Oratory.

Miss McClintic entered Texas Christian University January, 1898, was graduated in both Oratory and Literature in the class of 1901. She spent the following winter in Emerson College of Oratory, Boston; was called home in March to teach the remainder of the term. Has held the position until now, and her work has been most enthusiastically received.

Miss McClintic is in the fortunate position of the artist who has achieved applause and distinction in what might be termed the first flush of youth. Her abilities as a teacher and reader indicate both character and strength. She is recognized as a most gifted and popular reader by all who have heard her, and her teaching has given great satisfaction.

ABOVE
Photograph of TCU Campus with Olive Leaman McClintic on horseback in front of Main Building. "TCU Waco Campus," 1905. Olive Leaman McClintic, director of the Department of Oratory. TCU Photograph Collection, RU 53. Photo Number. 1379, PN Number. 600. https://repository.tcu.edu:443/handle/116099117/2628. Courtesy of TCU Special Collections. Mary Couts Burnett Library. Texas Christian University.

The *Skiff*

Beginning in December 1895, AddRan Christian University began the publication of a student-edited university magazine, *The Collegian*. *The Collegian* succeeded an earlier, inconsistent publication known as *The Student* from the Thorp Spring era. Unfortunately, faculty editors co-opted *The Collegian* to issue their own editorials, which represented "unwarranted attacks upon Baylor University, upon the students of the State University, upon preachers generally, and that the same are construed to ridicule and hold in contempt the religious services of both Baylor and AddRan Universities, and furthermore to cast a slur upon the ladies of Waco who are members of the Shakespeare Club and upon citizens generally for not attending football games." The board of trustees demanded apologies from the faculty sponsor and faculty editorial staff, which they received in December 1898.

Due to these circumstances, in 1902 TCU students requested that the school sponsor a weekly student newspaper under greater student control. Emerging faculty leaders and students combined their efforts to ensure that the newspaper succeeded. Professors Olive McClintic, Ed McKinney, and Colby Hall served as faculty editors. Everett Jones and E. King Lavender reported on university and local news. Mary Taliaferro and Pocahontas Jones provided coverage related to the Girls' Home. Lastly, West Parker and Colby Smith reported on religious activities and athletics. The first volume of the *Skiff* rolled off the presses on September 19, 1902. For a mere fifty cents, one could purchase a yearly subscription. Local businesses in Waco demonstrated their support by purchasing advertisement to help fund the paper's publication. Stories about campus events, sporting contests, student pranks, and national or international events have populated the pages in every issue since. To this day, TCU student reporters and writers publish the *Skiff* on a weekly basis during the fall and spring semesters.

RIGHT
Photograph of Colby Dixon Hall in his office. "Colby Dixon Hall," 1923. TCU Photograph Collection, RU 53. Photo Number: 618. https://repository.tcu.edu:443/handle/116099117/2608. Courtesy of TCU Special Collections. Mary Couts Burnett Library. Texas Christian University.

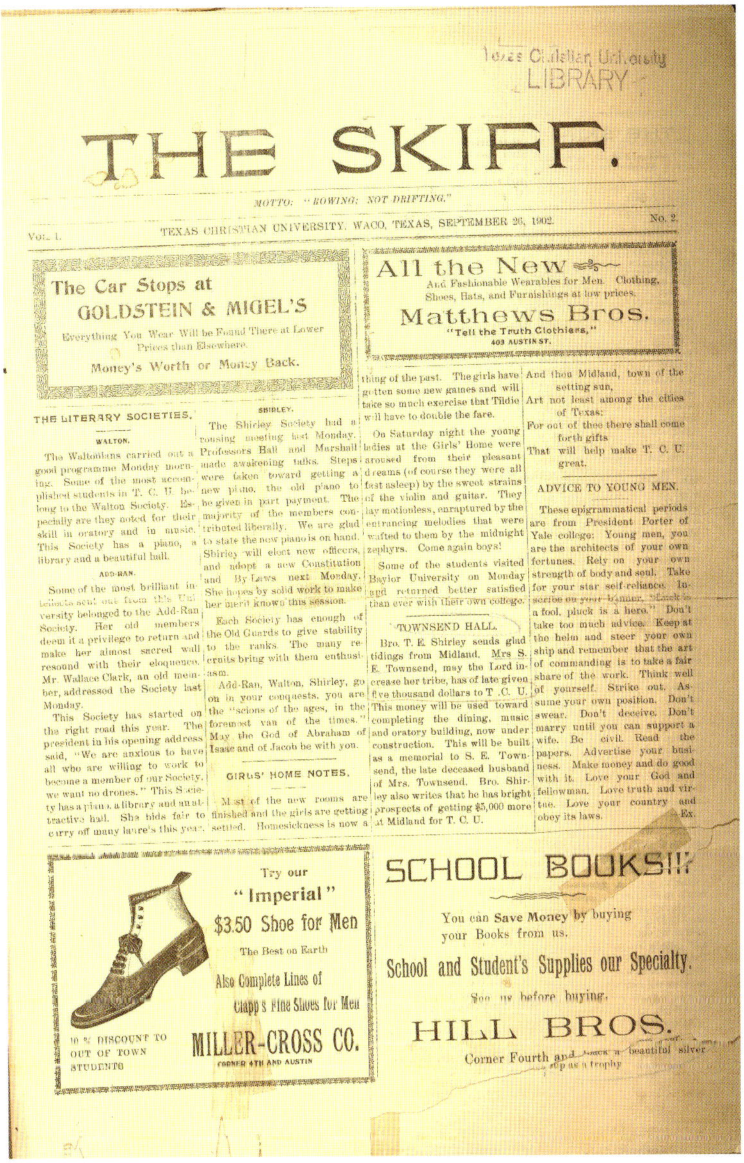

THE SKIFF.

MOTTO: "ROWING; NOT DRIFTING."

VOL. 1. TEXAS CHRISTIAN UNIVERSITY, WACO, TEXAS, SEPTEMBER 26, 1902. No. 2.

THE LITERARY SOCIETIES.

WALTON.

The Waltonians carried out a good programme Monday morning. Some of the most accomplished students in T. C. U. belong to the Walton Society. Especially are they noted for their skill in oratory and in music. This Society has a piano, a library and a beautiful hall.

ADD-RAN.

Some of the most brilliant intellects sent out from this University belonged to the Add-Ran Society. Her old members deem it a privilege to return and make her almost sacred wall resound with their eloquence. Mr. Wallace Clark, an old member, addressed the Society last Monday.

This Society has started on the right road this year. The president in his opening address said, "We are anxious to have all who are willing to work to become a member of our Society, we want no drones." This Society has a piano, a library and an attractive hall. She bids fair to carry off many laurels this year.

SHIRLEY.

The Shirley Society had a rousing meeting last Monday. Professors Ball and Marshall made awakening talks. Steps were taken toward getting a new piano, the old piano to be given in part payment. The majority of the members contributed liberally. We are glad to state the new piano is on hand. Shirley will elect new officers, and adopt a new Constitution and By-Laws next Monday. She hopes by solid work to make her merit known this session.

Each Society has enough of the Old Guards to give stability to the ranks. The many recruits bring with them enthusiasm.

Add-Ran, Walton, Shirley, go on in your conquests, you are the "scions of the ages, in the foremost van of the times." May the God of Abraham of Isaac and of Jacob be with you.

GIRLS' HOME NOTES.

Most of the new rooms are finished and the girls are getting settled. Homesickness is now a thing of the past. The girls have gotten some new games and will take so much exercise that Tildie will have to double the fare.

On Saturday night the young ladies at the Girls' Home were aroused from their pleasant dreams (of course they were all fast asleep) by the sweet strains of the violin and guitar. They lay motionless, enraptured by the entrancing melodies that were wafted to them by the midnight zephyrs. Come again boys!

Some of the students visited Baylor University on Monday and returned better satisfied than ever with their own college.

TOWNSEND HALL.

Bro. T. E. Shirley sends glad tidings from Midland. Mrs S. E. Townsend, may the Lord increase her tribe, has of late given five thousand dollars to T. C. U. This money will be used toward completing the dining, music and oratory building, now under construction. This will be built as a memorial to S. E. Townsend, the late deceased husband of Mrs. Townsend. Bro. Shirley also writes that he has bright prospects of getting $5,000 more at Midland for T. C. U.

And thou Midland, town of the setting sun,
Art not least among the cities of Texas;
For out of thee there shall come forth gifts
That will help make T. C. U. great.

ADVICE TO YOUNG MEN.

These epigrammatical periods are from President Porter of Yale college: Young men, you are the architects of your own fortunes. Rely on your own strength of body and soul. Take for your star self-reliance. Inscribe on your banner, "Luck is a fool, pluck is a hero." Don't take too much advice. Keep at the helm and steer your own ship and remember that the art of commanding is to take a fair share of the work. Think well of yourself. Strike out. Assume your own position. Don't swear. Don't deceive. Don't marry until you can support a wife. Be civil. Read the papers. Advertise your business. Make money and do good with it. Love your God and fellowman. Love truth and virtue. Love your country and obey its laws. —Ex.

ABOVE

Portrait of Martha Taliaferro, Dean of Women. "Martha Taliaferro," 1902–1903. TCU Photograph Collection, RU 53. Photo Number: 1201. https://repository.tcu.edu:443/handle/116099117/3725. Courtesy of TCU Special Collections. Mary Couts Burnett Library. Texas Christian University.

ABOVE (LEFT)

Front page of the *Skiff* vol. 1, no. 2 (Waco, TX). Sept. 26, 1902. https://repository.tcu.edu/handle/116099117/12512. Courtesy of TCU Archives and Special Collections. Mary Couts Burnett Library. Texas Christian University.

LEFT

Photograph of Manless Wedding held in 1904. "Manless Wedding," 1904. TCU Photograph Collection, RU 53. Photo Number: 1387. https://repository.tcu.edu:443/handle/116099117/3735. Courtesy of TCU Special Collections. Mary Couts Burnett Library. Texas Christian University.

ABOVE
Photograph of 1910 TCU Baseball Team in Waco. "TCU Baseball Team," c. 1910. TCU Photograph Collection, RU 53. Photo Number: 2302, PN Number: 650. https://repository.tcu.edu:443/handle/116099117/3189. Courtesy of TCU Special Collections. Mary Couts Burnett Library. Texas Christian University.

OPPOSITE (LOWER)
Photograph of students dancing at the Girls' Home Ball in 1904. "Girls' Home Ball after Manless Wedding," 1904. TCU Photograph Collection, RU 53. Photo Number: 1403. https://repository.tcu.edu:443/handle/116099117/2374. Courtesy of TCU Special Collections. Mary Couts Burnett Library. Texas Christian University.

ABOVE
Photograph of students sitting on steps outside of Main Building. "Students in Waco," 1898. TCU Photograph Collection, RU 53. Photo Number: 2235. https://repository.tcu.edu:443/handle/116099117/2526. Courtesy of TCU Special Collections. Mary Couts Burnett Library. Texas Christian University.

Summer School and Year-Round Education

Most collegiate students utilize summer courses to either catch up or get ahead in their degree programs. One may wonder when summer sessions became a part of TCU's yearly calendar. AddRan College initially pioneered summer school in 1880, over twenty years before it became commonplace. In 1881 and 1882, the school catalogue listed a ten-week program. By 1888, school leaders reduced the term to an eight-week program. During these initial years, it seems that the summer school programs did not achieve sustainable enrollment, and they disappeared from the school calendar by 1894.

In March 1903, the board of trustees formally approved plans to restart summer sessions. Faculty and students hailed the decision as "another step in our progress toward a complete modern university." The first summer outlined seven weeks of courses in which students would complete a rapid review of foundational content. These reviews aimed to prepare students for more advanced courses in the traditional fall and spring semesters. All involved imagined a future in which the summer school would evolve into "a full and regular session of the college year." With the advent of "systemic exercise" in the 1890s, including calisthenics and regimented physical activities, educational leaders believed that students could now meet the mental and physical demands of a yearly educational calendar. Today, every college at TCU offers summer courses designed to help students stay engaged year-round.

LEFT
Library at Waco campus. "Library," 1900. TCU Photograph Collection, RU 53. Photo Number: 947. https://repository.tcu.edu:443/handle/116099117/2862. Courtesy of TCU Special Collections. Mary Couts Burnett Library. Texas Christian University.

ABOVE
Students seated next to bed in dorm room at Waco campus. "dormitory room," 1900s. TCU Photograph Collection, RU 53. Photo Number: 479. https://repository.tcu.edu:443/handle/116099117/2893. Courtesy of TCU Special Collections. Mary Couts Burnett Library. Texas Christian University.

RIGHT
Three students wading in water near Waco campus. "Wading," 1902. TCU Photograph Collection, RU 53. Photo Number: 2545. https://repository.tcu.edu/handle/116099117/6711. Courtesy of TCU Special Collections. Mary Couts Burnett Library. Texas Christian University.

ABOVE
Students having a picnic near TCU campus in Waco. "Picnic," 1902. TCU Photograph Collection, RU 53. Photo Number: 2546. https://repository.tcu.edu/handle/116099117/6710. Courtesy of TCU Special Collections. Mary Couts Burnett Library. Texas Christian University.

ABOVE
"Male Students in Dorm Room," 1900s. TCU Photograph Collection, RU 53. Photo Number: 1279, PN Number 574. https://repository.tcu.edu:443/handle/116099117/2341. Courtesy of TCU Special Collections. Mary Couts Burnett Library. Texas Christian University.

RIGHT
TCU campus in Waco in 1903. "Waco Campus," 1903. TCU Photograph Collection, RU 53. Photo Number: 2417. https://repository.tcu.edu:443/handle/116099117/3607. Courtesy of TCU Special Collections. Mary Couts Burnett Library. Texas Christian University.

Student Employment on Campus

Student employment serves as a vital cog of any higher educational institution. Student workers perform key roles that enable the seamless function of many university events and operations. During TCU's years in Waco, opportunities for student employment greatly expanded. The construction of a heating and lighting plant in 1902–03 and a laundry plant in September 1904 created many of these positions. Prior to this development, students could only find employment on TCU's campus by performing dining or janitorial work. Students could now pick up shifts at the heating and lighting plant and the laundry plant. The laundry plant created a "practical method for the purpose of aiding students who wish to work their way through school." Writers for the *Skiff* estimated that the plant would provide employment for twenty-five or thirty students. Progressive Era thinkers believed that the "industrial student" learned invaluable lessons through work that could not be acquired in the classroom. This belief has continued to inform our perceptions of student development and preparation in the form of internships and student employment. Today, hundreds of students hold on-campus employment at TCU that helps them fund their education and living expenses. These workers ensure the operations of many vital university functions and events.

BELOW
Academic procession at the Waco Campus in 1908. "TCU Waco Campus," 1908-1909. TCU Photograph Collection, RU 53. Photo Number: 245, PN Number: 580. https://repository.tcu.edu:443/handle/116099117/2298. Courtesy of TCU Special Collections. Mary Couts Burnett Library. Texas Christian University.

ABOVE
Wade Hampton Shumate, a TCU football player, with roommate in boy's dorm room. "Wade Hampton Shumate," 1902. TCU Photograph Collection, RU 53. Photo Number: 499, PN Number: 198. https://repository.tcu.edu:443/handle/116099117/2258. Courtesy of TCU Archives and Special Collections. Mary Couts Burnett Library. Texas Christian University.

RIGHT
1908 TCU graduates on Waco campus. "Student Life," 1908. TCU Photograph Collection, RU 53. Photo Number: 497, PN Number: 565. https://repository.tcu.edu:443/handle/116099117/2890. Courtesy of TCU Special Collections. Mary Couts Burnett Library. Texas Christian University.

ABOVE
"TCU, Gymnasium and Powerhouse in Waco." Waco—Schools and Colleges. Texas Christian University. Item no. 2369. Courtesy of The Texas Collection, Baylor University.

LEFT
"Main Building, Waco," 1903. TCU Photograph Collection, RU 53. Photo Number: 2418. https://repository.tcu.edu:443/handle/116099117/2965. Courtesy of TCU Special Collections. Mary Couts Burnett Library. Texas Christian University.

ABOVE
Two students lying in snow at Waco campus. "Students," 1896–1897. TCU Photograph Collection, RU 53. Photo Number: 2234. https://repository.tcu.edu:443/handle/116099117/3458. Courtesy of TCU Special Collections. Mary Couts Burnett Library. Texas Christian University.

RIGHT
Heating and Lighting plant at Waco campus. In "Pictorial Presentation of Texas Christian University with Biographic Sketches of its Faculty." TCU Scrapbook Collection, Record Unit 8, Box 32, Folder 51; "Speech and Drama, 1898-1908." https://repository.tcu.edu/handle/116099117/4609. Courtesy of TCU Archives and Special Collections. Mary Couts Burnett Library. Texas Christian University.

THE CENTRAL HEATING AND LIGHTING PLANT.

The building in this pictvre is constructed of iron. In contains two 60-horse power tubular boilers and from it the three large buildings of the University are heated. The boiler capacity is sufficient for the heating of additional buildings as they may be erected from time to time.

The east end of the building is to be occupied by an electric lighting plant during coming the summer. The building is situated at the rear of the ain buildlng.

ABOVE
TCU's Main Building during fire on March, 22, 1910. "Main Building During the Fire—When Roof Fell In, 1910." Waco—Schools and Colleges. Texas Christian University. Item no. 2362. Courtesy of The Texas Collection, Baylor University.

The Night that Changed TCU!

The evening of Tuesday, March 22, 1910, changed the history of TCU forever. Shortly after 8:00 p.m., as students returned to campus for their mandated study session, Roy Tomlinson and Dibrell "Carl" Melton discovered fire in the ceiling of the northwest wing of the campus's Main Building, the largest educational structure in the southwest.

As they tried to extinguish it, other students suddenly smelled smoke. Someone from the fourth floor, according to Buford Isaacks, screamed "fire, fire, the building is on fire. The whole roof is ablaze." Panic ensued!

Students and faculty on the lower floors scrambled to remove their valuables, but those on the fourth floor lost everything. Within two hours, the fire had gutted the entire building and the roof collapsed. All the students and townspeople could do was watch the flames.

"The catastrophe had drawn the students and townspeople together as they never had been before. Even our [TCU's] 'hate' for Baylor was turned to admiration and love by the kindness and generosity of Baylor University in our hour of need."

Returning to Fort Worth?

The fire foretold great things for TCU. A week after the disaster, March 29, 1910, the university board of trustees held a special meeting to decide whether to rebuild in Waco or relocate.

During the following weeks proposals came from several communities, including Waco, Dallas, Fort Worth, McKinney, and Gainesville. Each seemed to offer certain benefits, but ultimately Dallas and Fort Worth emerged as the front-runners. At the same time Dallas civic boosters were also negotiating for the establishment of a Methodist University (SMU opened in 1910) in the city, which greatly influenced TCU trustees. The Convention of Christian Churches meeting in Dallas on May 11 announced Fort Worth would be TCU's new home.

Fort Worth civic leaders made a genuine and generous offer. The contract, signed on May 10, 1910, by TCU trustees and a group of Fort Worth businessmen operating under the charter of the Fairmount Land Company, defined the benefits:

1. University would receive 50 acres of land with utility and sewer service; paved roads would not come until 1923.

2. North Texas Traction Company would construct a streetcar line to the location; arrived in 1916.

3. $200,000 to be paid to TCU; half provided jointly by the Chamber of Commerce, Fort Worth Christian churches, and the other half derived from sale of 400 lots provided by the Fairmount Land Company.

4. Additional lands around the campus to be sold by the company and the proceeds split between the company and TCU.

The union between Fort Worth civic boosters and TCU represented the beginnings of profitable relationships for both.

RIGHT (ABOVE)
Postcard of Main Building before fire. Waco—Schools and Colleges. Texas Christian University. Postcard Collection. Courtesy of The Texas Collection, Baylor University.

RIGHT
1910 postcard after fire with horse and buggy in front of building. Gildersleeve postcard. Waco—Schools and Colleges. Texas Christian University. Postcard Collection. Courtesy of The Texas Collection, Baylor University.

LEFT
Texas State Historical Marker denoting the former location of Texas Christian University in Waco, Texas. Photo by the authors.

ABOVE
Main Building ruins the day after the fire. "Ruins after the Fire," March 23, 1910. Photo taken by C. F. McCall (Waco, Tex.). TCU Photograph Collection, RU 53. Photo Number 1089; Box 11. https://repository.tcu.edu/handle/116099117/7024. Courtesy of TCU Special Collections. Mary Couts Burnett Library. Texas Christian University.

CHAPTER 3

Return to Fort Worth: 1910–1923

Return to Fort Worth!

Returning to Fort Worth after the fire in Waco and a thirty-seven-year sojourn, TCU found a much different city from what it left in 1873. Among other changes, streetcars traversed the city, and the Armour and Swift Companies in the Stockyards provided employment and brought different ethnicities to a city of more than seventy-three thousand.

As the TCU campus underwent feverish construction on "the hill," TCU began its 1910–11 academic year in a series of two-story rented buildings on the corner of Weatherford and Commerce Streets, diagonally across from the Tarrant County Courthouse. Generally called Ingram Flats, the leased buildings provided classrooms, a dining room, and dormitory space, but were cramped from the beginning. Offices, classrooms, a chapel, a dining room, and a print shop were on lower floors, with dormitories upstairs. Other TCU students and faculty lived in houses rented nearby. Despite less-than-desirable conditions in the rented buildings, enrollment dropped only very little when the university relocated to Fort Worth, and fifteen faculty members even relocated from Waco.

On September 23, the thirty-eighth annual opening of TCU, students, faculty, and townspeople held a convocation in the auditorium of City Hall. Mayor W. D. Davis, city and county school superintendents, and the chairman of the Fort Worth Board of Trade gave rousing addresses welcoming TCU home. Addison Clark also traveled from Thorp Spring to bless the school's return to the city he had originally chosen for the institution. It was a hearty welcome for this return.

Meanwhile, city and county officials rushed to get roads and utilities stretched to the grass-covered hilly home for TCU. Construction began on the new administration building (Reed Hall) and women's dorm (Jarvis Hall), and renderings of a ten-building campus vision appeared in the *Skiff* in January 1911. On May 16, 1911, TCU ceremoniously laid its cornerstone for the Administration Building. There was no microphone, and the event attracted so many people that most of the crowd could not hear or see the ceremony. Construction of Goode Hall (men's dorm), which also began that spring, was ready at the opening of the school year—September 19, 1911.

RIGHT
Image of business class at downtown campus. "College of Business Class," 1910. From *1911 Horned Frog*. (Fort Worth: Exline-Reimers Co., 1911), 127. https://repository.tcu.edu/handle/116099117/12236. Courtesy of TCU Archives and Special Collections. Mary Couts Burnett Library. Texas Christian University.

ABOVE
Photograph of downtown Administration Building after TCU moved to Fort Worth. "Administration building, 1910-1911." TCU Photograph Collection, RU 53. Photo Number: 2303, PN Number 652.https://repository.tcu.edu:443/handle/116099117/3758. Courtesy of TCU Special Collections. Mary Couts Burnett Library. Texas Christian University.

The Girl Graduate: Amboline Tyson, 1915

Eighteeen-year-old Amboline Tyson, of Santa Anna, Texas, was attending TCU as a prep-school student when fire destroyed the Waco campus. For the remainder of the spring, she recalled, students took classes on the lawn, in the dining halls, and the girls' home. She had attended TCU because her brother, Paul Tyson, had played football and baseball there, graduating in 1908; he ultimately became a Waco high school football coaching legend, winning four Texas state championships and one national championship during the 1920s. He also coached at Stanford University with Pop Warner, and influenced Knute Rockne of Notre Dame University.

Amboline relocated to Fort Worth, graduating TCU in the spring of 1915. Writing in her scrapbook that "Service is the Measure of Life" and serving as vice president of her class, Tyson admitted to having contrary opinions but not fussing or openly disputing her classmates. She concluded that her class "never disagreed and we were a happy bunch."

During the last few weeks of her senior year at TCU, she and other students attended a series of social engagements. At a party on Saturday night (June 5) before Sunday graduation, and escorted by John P. Cox, they played cards, had punch and cake, and sat on the front porch swing, before riding the streetcar back to TCU. She remarked that during the walk back to campus what happened after midnight belongs to "frolics."

A few nights earlier, on Monday (May 31, 1915) evening, the thirteen seniors dressed in cap and gown "cut the fine arts recital" and gathered at their class advisor Dr. Egbert Cockrell's house for a final get-together, so they could find themselves "closer to one another." The five girls of the class gathered in a circle in an upstairs bedroom where each offered a farewell talk. It was a night to remember, and although Tyson lamented that "I have no souvenirs of the party . . . I shall never forget this and many other enjoyable times I have had at dear old T.C.U." She "verily believed the words of the old song, When I am an old lady, with children ten and two, I'll teach them the alphabet begins with 'T.C.U.'"

After her June 6, 1915, graduation Amboline taught in a one-room schoolhouse near her native Santa Anna, and married S. A. Mahaffey of Sterling, TX.

RIGHT
Portrait of Amboline Tyson. "Amboline Tyson," 1915. TCU Photograph Collection, RU 53. Photo Number 2578. https://repository.tcu.edu/handle/116099117/6694. Courtesy of TCU Special Collections. Mary Couts Burnett Library. Texas Christian University.

RIGHT
TCU graduates after commencement. "Amboline Tyson Scrapbook," Page 8. TCU Scrapbook Collection, RU 8. Box 34, Folder 3. https://repository.tcu.edu/handle/116099117/4610. Courtesy of TCU Archives and Special Collections. Mary Couts Burnett Library. Texas Christian University.

ABOVE
Portrait of Amboline Tyson's brother. "Paul Tyson," n.d. TCU Photograph Collection, RU 53. Photo Number 358. https://repository.tcu.edu:443/handle/116099117/3118. Courtesy of TCU Special Collections. Mary Couts Burnett Library. Texas Christian University.

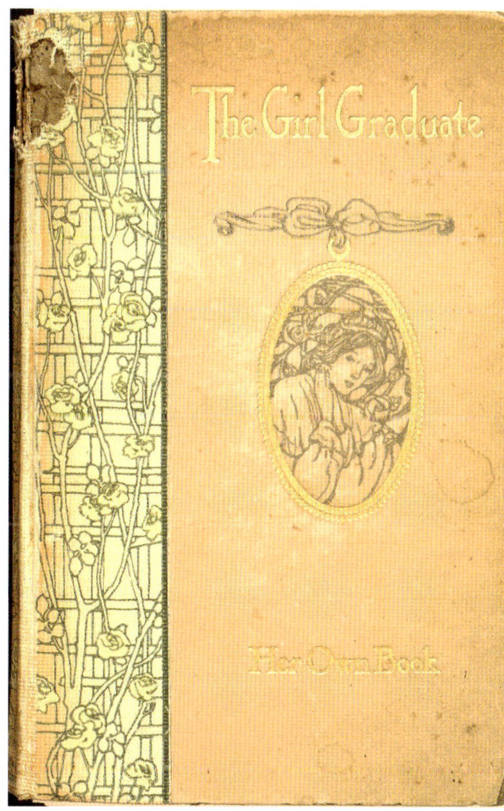

RIGHT
Cover of *The Girl Graduate* booklet. "Amboline Tyson Scrapbook," Page 2. TCU Scrapbook Collection, RU 8. Box 34, Folder 3. https://repository.tcu.edu/handle/116099117/4610. Courtesy of TCU Archives and Special Collections. Mary Couts Burnett Library. Texas Christian University.

One Tree Hill

In 1911, when builders hauled the first bricks onto TCU's new fifty-acre Fort Worth campus, the setting featured rolling grasslands without a single tree.

The first students to study on South University Drive had lived through a calamitous fire in Waco and then makeshift classrooms in downtown Fort Worth. Perhaps desiring to add something permanent to the transient experience of university life, the senior class of 1912 decided to purchase a mature live oak tree and plant it in front of what would later become Dave Reed Hall.

Joe Murray, chairman of the committee of the Class of 1912, hired the Texas Shade Tree Co. to uproot an approximately fifty-year-old live oak tree from the vague "neighboring woodlands" and dig it a new home on University Drive.

On March 22, 1912, students and administrators gathered for the official planting ceremony, where soon-to-be TCU graduates dubbed the new campus addition the "Senior Tree."

As TCU grew, arborists planted more live oak trees along University Drive, and the canopy of shiny green leaves became part of the university's trademark look. The original tree, presumably more than fifty years older than its neighbors, became an anonymous part of the crowd.

In the early twenty-first century, an environmental science class measured all of the live oak trees in the center of campus and discovered that the one in front of Reed Hall was thicker, thus older, than the others. An archival photograph revealed that indeed the campus once featured a single tree.

To honor the tree's history, the university installed a plaque in 2011 that reads: "The only tree present on the new TCU campus was this Live Oak transplanted 'from the forest' by the class of 1912."

RIGHT
The original oak tree at TCU in front of Jarvis Hall. Courtesy of *TCU Magazine*.

RIGHT (OPPOSITE)
The small tree in front of recently constructed TCU buildings. The original oak is in the background. "Early Campus," 1913. TCU Photograph Collection, RU 53. Photo Number 1867. https://repository.tcu.edu:443/handle/116099117/3133. Courtesy of TCU Special Collections. Mary Couts Burnett Library. Texas Christian University.

RIGHT
Photograph of granite marker denoting the original oak tree at TCU. Courtesy of *TCU Magazine*.

Braxton B. Wade Prohibition Library

The Mary Couts Burnett Library represents a centerpiece of today's TCU campus. Prior to its construction in 1925, the library was housed across the street on the second floor of the Administration Building (Reed Hall). It also had a different name: the Braxton B. Wade Memorial Prohibition Library.

Braxton B. Wade arrived at TCU in 1906. He studied oratory under the stewardship of Olive McClintic and represented both AddRan's Debate Team in campus contests and TCU in numerous local and state-wide oratory competitions, largely centered on the issue of Prohibition. He also helped charter a chapter of the Intercollegiate Prohibition Association at TCU, and he served as treasurer for the state chapter. During this period, Prohibition had become a major plank for Progressive moral reformers who hoped to "clean up" the nation. The Prohibition Party had even nominated Randolph Clark to run as their candidate for governor in 1896.

Wade attended TCU until 1911 before leaving and completing a law degree at the University of Texas in 1913. After graduation, he embarked on a brief career as an attorney in Elgin, Texas. His career proved to be short-lived, as he felt compelled to continue the fight for prohibition. In 1914, he campaigned unsuccessfully for state representative as a nominee of the Prohibitionist Party. Not one to give up easily, Wade then accepted employment as a traveling secretary for the Intercollegiate Prohibition Association. He began an extensive traveling agenda to help universities across Texas start local IPA chapters. His persistent, exhausting travel schedule combined with lingering injuries suffered in a streetcar accident in Waco eventually took a toll on his health. His condition steadily deteriorated until his death on January 11, 1916.

Wade's family, friends, colleagues, and TCU faculty and students felt compelled to honor his persistent efforts for Prohibition. By May 1916, their efforts coalesced in the creation of the Braxton B. Wade Memorial Prohibition Library at TCU. Former classmates and friends remembered his constant complaints that the library only had seventeen books on Prohibition and of these, only three were not common circulars. They began a campaign to create the largest collection of books on Prohibition in the Southwest. Wade's family donated the first one hundred dollars and his entire personal collection to kick-start the drive. By December 1916, groups such as the National Temperance Society, Anti-Saloon Leagues of Texas, Mississippi, and Arkansas, and numerous authors all contributed books and pamphlets in Wade's memory. Head librarian Nell Andrews featured the expanding Prohibitionist collection on several glass bookshelves throughout the library. Despite its promising start, Wade Memorial Library was lost to time after the construction of Mary Couts Burnett Library in 1925.

ABOVE
The Administration Building that contained the third floor library. "Administration Building," 1910s. TCU Photograph Collection, RU 53. Photo Number: 578, PN Number: 613. https://repository.tcu.edu:443/handle/116099117/2112. Courtesy of TCU Special Collections. Mary Couts Burnett Library. Texas Christian University.

ABOVE
Braxton Wade pictured in *The Horned Frog*, vol. 12. (Fort Worth: The Reimers Company, 1916), 39. https://repository.tcu.edu/handle/116099117/11042. Courtesy of TCU Archives and Special Collections. Mary Couts Burnett Library. Texas Christian University.

LEFT
Prohibition Association Officers in *The Horned Frog*, vol. 13. (Fort Worth: The Reimers Company, 1917), 140. https://repository.tcu.edu/handle/116099117/11043. Courtesy of TCU Archives and Special Collections. Mary Couts Burnett Library. Texas Christian University.

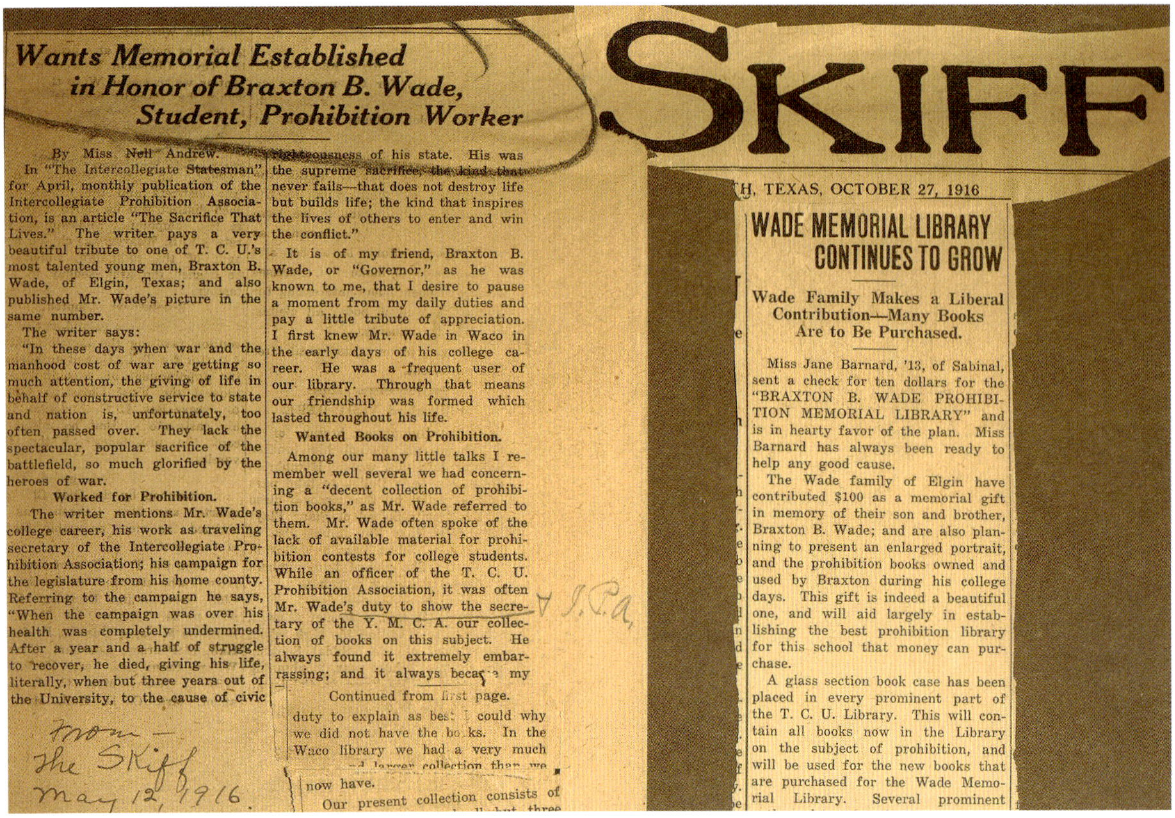

Wants Memorial Established in Honor of Braxton B. Wade, Student, Prohibition Worker

By Miss Nell Andrew.

In "The Intercollegiate Statesman" for April, monthly publication of the Intercollegiate Prohibition Association, is an article "The Sacrifice That Lives." The writer pays a very beautiful tribute to one of T. C. U.'s most talented young men, Braxton B. Wade, of Elgin, Texas; and also published Mr. Wade's picture in the same number.

The writer says:

"In these days when war and the manhood cost of war are getting so much attention, the giving of life in behalf of constructive service to state and nation is, unfortunately, too often passed over. They lack the spectacular, popular sacrifice of the battlefield, so much glorified by the heroes of war.

Worked for Prohibition.

The writer mentions Mr. Wade's college career, his work as traveling secretary of the Intercollegiate Prohibition Association; his campaign for the legislature from his home county. Referring to the campaign he says, "When the campaign was over his health was completely undermined. After a year and a half of struggle to recover, he died, giving his life, literally, when but three years out of the University, to the cause of civic righteousness of his state. His was the supreme sacrifice, the kind that never fails—that does not destroy life but builds life; the kind that inspires the lives of others to enter and win the conflict."

It is of my friend, Braxton B. Wade, or "Governor," as he was known to me, that I desire to pause a moment from my daily duties and pay a little tribute of appreciation. I first knew Mr. Wade in Waco in the early days of his college career. He was a frequent user of our library. Through that means our friendship was formed which lasted throughout his life.

Wanted Books on Prohibition.

Among our many little talks I remember well several we had concerning a "decent collection of prohibition books," as Mr. Wade referred to them. Mr. Wade often spoke of the lack of available material for prohibition contests for college students. While an officer of the T. C. U. Prohibition Association, it was often Mr. Wade's duty to show the secretary of the Y. M. C. A. our collection of books on this subject. He always found it extremely embarrassing; and it always became my

Continued from first page.

duty to explain as best I could why we did not have the books. In the Waco library we had a very much ... larger collection than we now have.

Our present collection consists of ...

from — The Skiff May 12, 1916.

SKIFF

...H, TEXAS, OCTOBER 27, 1916

WADE MEMORIAL LIBRARY CONTINUES TO GROW

Wade Family Makes a Liberal Contribution—Many Books Are to Be Purchased.

Miss Jane Barnard, '13, of Sabinal, sent a check for ten dollars for the "BRAXTON B. WADE PROHIBITION MEMORIAL LIBRARY" and is in hearty favor of the plan. Miss Barnard has always been ready to help any good cause.

The Wade family of Elgin have contributed $100 as a memorial gift in memory of their son and brother, Braxton B. Wade; and are also planning to present an enlarged portrait, and the prohibition books owned and used by Braxton during his college days. This gift is indeed a beautiful one, and will aid largely in establishing the best prohibition library for this school that money can purchase.

A glass section book case has been placed in every prominent part of the T. C. U. Library. This will contain all books now in the Library on the subject of prohibition, and will be used for the new books that are purchased for the Wade Memorial Library. Several prominent

The Horned Frog — Vol. vii

M. E. Daniels, Vice-President — True Strong, Treasurer — B. B. Wade, President — W. C. Ferguson, Secretary

THE Prohibition Association has accomplished better work this year than it has ever accomplished in any previous year. Heretofore, the only aim has been to win the State Prohibition Contest, but this year a new insight has been gained and every effort and purpose is to train men and women to meet and try to overcome that great monster, the liquor problem, that is so vile in its ravishings. Our orators have all expressed a desire to be of some assistance in the coming campaign in the State, and it is easy to see that the efforts of the club have not been in vain, for some of its members will some day serve their people by attacking this nefarious detriment and wiping its stain from the lives of their fellowmen.

Mr. Braxton B. Wade, of Elgin, was our representative to the State Contest, at Decatur, last Spring, and made a remarkable showing. Mr. Wade has at all times shown himself a thorough student of the liquor problem and will become a public worker immediately after leaving college.

116]

ABOVE

Skiff newspaper article that headlines "TCU Wants Memorial Established in Honor of Braxton B. Wade Prohibition Worker." TCU Scrapbook Collection, RU 8. Box 30, Folder 6. Scrapbook no. 35, "Braxton B. Wade Memorial Prohibition Library, 1916-1922." Courtesy of TCU Archives and Special Collections. Mary Couts Burnett Library. Texas Christian University.

LEFT

Braxton B. Wade and Prohibition Association at TCU. *The Horned Frog*, vol. 7. (Fort Worth: Exline-Reimers Company, 1911), pg. 116. https://repository.tcu.edu/handle/116099117/11037. Courtesy of TCU Archives and Special Collections. Mary Couts Burnett Library. Texas Christian University.

OPPOSITE

Article from *Intercollegiate Statesman* about Braxton B. Wade. TCU Scrapbook Collection, RU 8. Box 30, Folder 6. Scrapbook no. 35, "Braxton B. Wade Memorial Prohibition Library, 1916-1922." Courtesy of TCU Archives and Special Collections. Mary Couts Burnett Library. Texas Christian University.

The Intercollegiate Statesman

VOL. XIII APRIL, 1916 NO. 6

LEADERSHIP REQUIRES SACRIFICE

A course in the study of the liquor problem under the Department of Economics continuing five days a week for three weeks is scheduled this year at Friends University, Wichita, Kans.

Aurora College (Ill.) students took a vigorous part in the spring campaign against saloons in that vigorous but wet city. They furnished singers, speakers, canvassers and clerical helpers for the office of the city dry federation. Last year their services won the highest commendation of leading men of Aurora.

BRAXTON B. WADE

Mark R. Shaw, New England Traveling Secretary, did special work among the colleges of Vermont during the recent "state-wide" campaign. It was not the fault of the students that Vermont did not win, this time.

Two deputation teams have been going out weekly in prohibition work at State College, Pennsylvania, during the winter; the arrangement is to continue thruout the spring. The plan involves two experienced men and one new man on each team each trip. The local league is working in co-operation with the local option campaign committee.

THE SACRIFICE THAT LIVES

In these days, when war and the manhood cost of war are getting so much attention, the giving of life in behalf of constructive service to state and nation is, unfortunately, too often passed over. They lack the spectacular, popular, sacrifice of the battlefield, so much glorified by the heroes of war.

Braxton B. Wade, a college man of Texas, was one of those who has recently given his life to the prohibition movement. Wade was a T. C. U. man of 1911, and a law graduate of the University of Texas, two years later. Keen, ambitious, earnest, of an old Southern family with standing and influence, he had, oddly enough to some, an intense desire to be a Christian force in politics.

On finishing law he took up its practice in his home city, gaining, in a few months, a very promising practice. This he laid aside, in the fall of 1913, to present the claims of the prohibition movement to the college men of the Southwest, as traveling secretary of the I. P. A., at a salary scarcely more than half of what he had been getting.

The next spring he was engaged in a three or four months' struggle with the liquor traffic in his home county—one of the "wettest" of the "wet" in that nearly "dry" state. He ran as dry candidate for the legislature, where dry candidate had never been elected. He threw himself into the campaign with tremendous earnestness and abandon, running 400 ahead of his ticket but being defeated by 20 votes, so strong was the grip of the liquor traffic on the county. When the campaign was over his health was completely undermined. After a year and a half of struggle to recover he died—giving his life, literally, when but three years out of the university, to the cause of civic righteousness of his state.

His was the supreme sacrifice, the kind that never fails—that does not destroy life but that builds life, the kind that inspires the lives of others to enter and win the conflict.

WHY NATIONAL CONSTITUTIONAL PROHIBITION WILL WIN

LEFT
Students walking in Forest Park. "Students Strolling," 1911–1912. TCU Photograph Collection, RU 53. Photo Number: 992. https://repository.tcu.edu:443/handle/116099117/3280. Courtesy of TCU Special Collections. Mary Couts Burnett Library. Texas Christian University.

BELOW
"Texas Christian University Frog Car," 1927. *North Texas Traction Company: Activities and Accomplishments for the Year Ending December 31, 1927.* Page 119. Northern Texas Traction Company Scrapbook Collection, Box 1. Courtesy of the Genealogy, History and Archives Unit, Fort Worth Public Library.

LEFT
"Safety Car," 1927. *North Texas Traction Company: Activities and Accomplishments for the Year Ending December 31, 1927.* Pg. 277. Northern Texas Traction Company Scrapbook Collection, Box 1. Courtesy of the Genealogy, History and Archives Unit, Fort Worth Public Library.

BELOW (RIGHT)
TCU coeds shooting basketball in front of streetcar in "1912-1916 Student Life Scrapbook." TCU Scrapbook Collection RU 8. Box 25, Folder 4. Scrapbook no. 34. https://repository.tcu.edu/handle/116099117/6420. Courtesy of TCU Archives and Special Collections. Mary Couts Burnett Library. Texas Christian University.

BELOW
Students waiting on the streetcar. "Waiting on the Green Bug." *The Horned Frog*, vol. 15. (Fort Worth: The Reimers Company, 1919), 103. https://repository.tcu.edu/handle/116099117/11045. Courtesy of TCU Archives and Special Collections. Mary Couts Burnett Library. Texas Christian University.

Let's Take the Streetcar

When the first three buildings of the TCU campus opened for students during the fall of 1911, a single gravel street (Forest Park Blvd.) connected the campus with the city. Although civic leaders had promised land, money, utility hookups, and streetcar service connecting campus to downtown, there was not yet a streetcar line to campus. Finally in 1916 the North Texas Traction Company fulfilled this promise, completing a line that ran directly in front of campus, along the current University Avenue. Most wide roads in Fort Worth today had streetcar lines running in the middle of them.

Streetcar trips were cheap and easily accessible, as students could take "The Green Bug" and make the one-way trip downtown in about thirty minutes. This convenience did not provide any opportunity for study or meditation. Instead, once boarded, the trip began with a "whirr and bang," clanging, lurching, and stopping. Each turn tossed the crowded standing passengers from side to side. Even so, trips from campus became so popular that the company encouraged TCU students to reserve streetcars and interurban trains for special occasions, even decorating them with streamers, banners, and purple horned frogs.

Unfortunately, by November 1929 buses had begun replacing streetcar lines, and within three years the NTTC streetcar lines went into receivership. By the mid-1930s auto and bus travel boasted a convenience that rail lines could not offer. With inexpensive gasoline, relatively cheap automobiles, and improved roads, city rail travel could no longer compete. An advanced and extensive rail system that serviced almost the entirety of North Texas had disappeared, even though streetcar access had bolstered the university, contributed to housing and commercial development in the area, and helped to shape TCU and the southwestern portion of the city.

Professional Schools Come and Go

The Medical Department of Fort Worth University, organized in 1894, conferred its first degree in 1895. Dr. Bacon Saunders, surgeon and president of the medical school faculty, had been elected to the TCU Board of Trustees in 1910. By 1911, Fort Worth University merged with Epworth University in Guthrie, Oklahoma, to create Oklahoma City University, and with its departure—and because of Saunders's influence—the Medical School affiliated with TCU. From 1911–1918 the medical school was linked to AddRan College, and students could complete a four-year program to earn an MD degree, or a six-year program, with three years in AddRan College, to earn a BA and an MD degree. But by 1917 TCU could not guarantee the financial expenditures required by the American Medical Association, and the school was facing probation. During the spring of 1918, the board of trustees closed the school, and the students and their records transferred to the Baylor College of Medicine in Dallas.

From 1915–1920 TCU also had a School of Law affiliated with AddRan College. Dr. Egbert R. Cockrell initially tried to establish a law school at AddRan University in 1898, but the project closed its doors in 1900. Cockrell did not give up on the project, and he reestablished the Department of Law in 1915. For two years it trained students for admittance to the bar. After 1917 students could get a BA in law through AddRan in three years or the LLB from AddRan and the School of Law in six years. Convinced the American Bar Association would impose financial standards on the school that the university would be unable and unwise to meet (included among the standards was bolstering the law library to more than ten thousand volumes, which would require at least $25,000), TCU closed the school in the summer of 1920. During the time of TCU's Centennial in Fort Worth, the university unsuccessfully negotiated to secure a law school in downtown.

The medical school, however, became a reality. By 2019—a century after TCU shut down its degree program—the TCU-UNTHSC School of Medicine opened to train a new generation of medical professionals.

ABOVE
Postcard with image of Fort Worth Medical College which later became TCU Medical School. Fort Worth Postcards Collection, Box 1. Courtesy of the Genealogy, History and Archives Unit, Fort Worth Public Library.

T.C.U.

DEAN S. A. WOODWARD, M. D.

MEDICAL DEPARTMENT OF T. C. U.

The Medical Department of Texas Christian University was organized in 1894. It has had, therefore, twenty-three years of splendid service. The organization of the school of medicine grew out of a desire on the part of a body of strong, earnest, progressive physicians and surgeons to elevate the standards of the medical profession, to provide better physicians and better facilities for practice, and to assist the local profession to a greater efficiency. The school has always stood for progress, and has an alumni of nearly one thousand physicians, who are doing an efficient service for humanity throughout the entire Southwest. It was one of the first colleges of the South to become a member of the Southern Medical Association. Its faculty has led in securing better medical practice acts and medical laws in Texas. Dean S. A. Woodward has done a conspicuous service in the business management of this department during the last year. The school has, upon its faculty, fifty members, many of whom are distinguished in their professions at home and abroad. The school is recognized by the State Medical Association and the American Medical Association as doing work of a standard character.

T.C.U.

MEDICAL COLLEGE LIBRARY

This large, spacious, well lighted room is on the third floor of the Administration Building, and contains 2,215 bound volumes and 216 duplicates, including the most modern texts and reference books with the Index Medicus. In addition there are 200 unbound volumes and 60 current journals placed at the disposition of the student.

ABOVE (TOP)

Image and description of Dean S. A. Woodward and Medical College. *Texas Christian University Pictorial Bulletin*. (Fort Worth: Texas Christian University, 1917), 50. https://repository.tcu.edu/handle/116099117/7081. Courtesy of TCU Archives and Special Collections. Mary Couts Burnett Library. Texas Christian University.

ABOVE

"Medical College Library." *Texas Christian University Pictorial Bulletin*. (Fort Worth: Texas Christian University, 1917), 52. https://repository.tcu.edu/handle/116099117/7081. Courtesy of TCU Archives and Special Collections. Mary Couts Burnett Library. Texas Christian University.

RIGHT
New Law Department article in the yearbook. *The Horned Frog*, vol. 12. (Fort Worth: Reimers Company, 1916), 87. https://repository.tcu.edu/handle/116099117/11042. Courtesy of TCU Archives and Special Collections. Mary Couts Burnett Library. Texas Christian University.

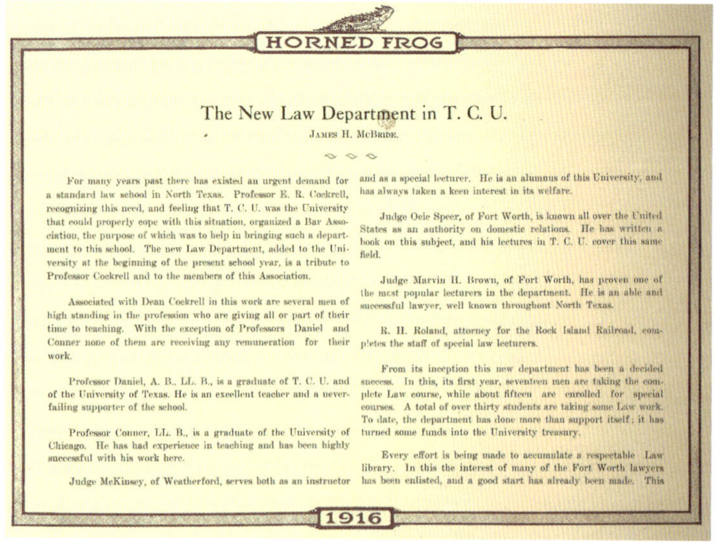

HORNED FROG

The New Law Department in T. C. U.

James H. McBride.

For many years past there has existed an urgent demand for a standard law school in North Texas. Professor E. R. Cockrell, recognizing this need, and feeling that T. C. U. was the University that could properly cope with this situation, organized a Bar Association, the purpose of which was to help in bringing such a department to this school. The new Law Department, added to the University at the beginning of the present school year, is a tribute to Professor Cockrell and to the members of this Association.

Associated with Dean Cockrell in this work are several men of high standing in the profession who are giving all or part of their time to teaching. With the exception of Professors Daniel and Conner none of them are receiving any remuneration for their work.

Professor Daniel, A. B., LL. B., is a graduate of T. C. U. and of the University of Texas. He is an excellent teacher and a never-failing supporter of the school.

Professor Conner, LL. B., is a graduate of the University of Chicago. He has had experience in teaching and has been highly successful with his work here.

Judge McKinsey, of Weatherford, serves both as an instructor and as a special lecturer. He is an alumnus of this University, and has always taken a keen interest in its welfare.

Judge Ocie Speer, of Fort Worth, is known all over the United States as an authority on domestic relations. He has written a book on this subject, and his lectures in T. C. U. cover this same field.

Judge Marvin H. Brown, of Fort Worth, has proven one of the most popular lecturers in the department. He is an able and successful lawyer, well known throughout North Texas.

R. H. Roland, attorney for the Rock Island Railroad, completes the staff of special law lecturers.

From its inception this new department has been a decided success. In this, its first year, seventeen men are taking the complete Law course, while about fifteen are enrolled for special courses. A total of over thirty students are taking some Law work. To date, the department has done more than support itself; it has turned some funds into the University treasury.

Every effort is being made to accumulate a respectable Law library. In this the interest of many of the Fort Worth lawyers has been enlisted, and a good start has already been made. This

1916

RIGHT
The TCU Bar Association. *The Horned Frog*, vol. 15. (Fort Worth: Reimers Company, 1919), 49. https://repository.tcu.edu:443/handle/116099117/2149. Courtesy of TCU Archives and Special Collections. Mary Couts Burnett Library. Texas Christian University.

THE BAR ASSOCIATION

Row 1: Upton, Douglas, Ogilvie, Bailey, Crunk, Lawrence.
Row 2: Faulkner, Billingsley, Martin, McBride, Harrold, Brittian, Sturgeon, Hudson.
Row 3: Scardino, Kemble, Jones, Lowry, Hamlin, McCutcheon.

1919

RIGHT
TCU Law School Faculty. *The Horned Frog*, vol. 15. (Fort Worth: Reimers Company, 1919), 48. https://repository.tcu.edu:443/handle/116099117/2149. Courtesy of TCU Archives and Special Collections. Mary Couts Burnett Library.Texas Christian University.

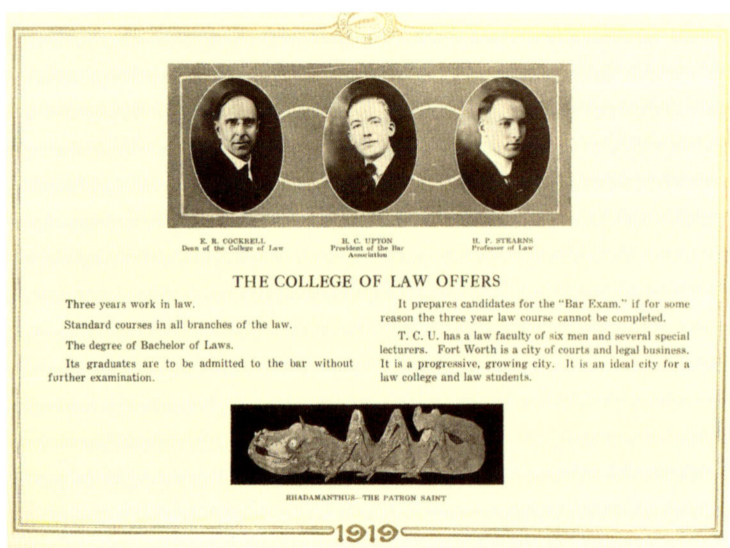

E. R. COCKRELL
Dean of the College of Law

H. C. UPTON
President of the Bar Association

H. P. STEARNS
Professor of Law

THE COLLEGE OF LAW OFFERS

Three years work in law.

Standard courses in all branches of the law.

The degree of Bachelor of Laws.

Its graduates are to be admitted to the bar without further examination.

It prepares candidates for the "Bar Exam." if for some reason the three year law course cannot be completed.

T. C. U. has a law faculty of six men and several special lecturers. Fort Worth is a city of courts and legal business. It is a progressive, growing city. It is an ideal city for a law college and law students.

RHADAMANTHUS—THE PATRON SAINT

1919

Airplanes and CRASHES!

The first airplane arrived in Fort Worth during January 1911, when Frenchman Roland Garros landed his Bleriot monoplane near the current-day Montgomery Plaza off West Seventh Street. TCU had returned to Fort Worth only a few months earlier. By 1914 World War I had begun, and airplanes frequently circled local skies, with the area serving as a training base for Allied troops. The US joined the war in April 1917, and Camp Bowie officially opened as a US Army base in late August, training men to fight "over there." The Canadian Royal Flying Corps leased three airfields—Taliaferro (Hicks) Field #1 in North Richland Hills; Taliaferro (Carruthers) Field #2 in Benbrook; Taliaferro (Barron) Field #3 in Everman—believing Texas's temperate climate would permit year-round training. An especially cold winter in 1917–18 and the emergent Spanish Influenza epidemic frustrated expectations.

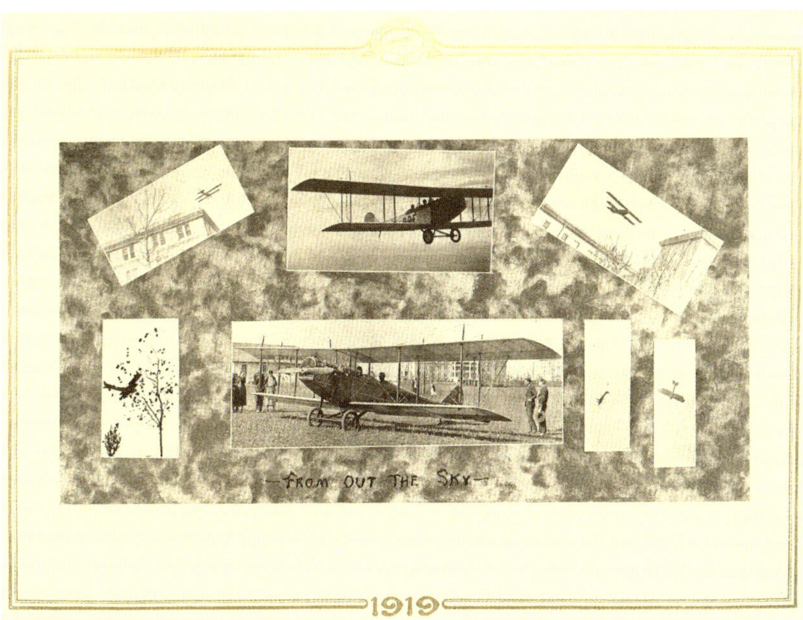

ABOVE
Soldiers supporting plane standing on its front. Image D in *Benbrook Airfield Collection Scrapbook*. Scrapbook Collection. Courtesy of Tarrant County Archives.

LEFT
Images of airplanes and TCU during 1918. *The Horned Frog* (Fort Worth: The Reimers Company,1919), 102. https://repository.tcu.edu/handle/116099117/11045. Courtesy of TCU Archives and Special Collections. Mary Couts Burnett Library. Texas Christian University.

Canadian pilots training in Benbrook frequently flew their Curtiss "Jenny" biplanes over the TCU campus, a reference point atop a grassy knoll southwest of downtown. On Monday, March 27, 1917, a pilot flying near campus about 1:00 p.m. experienced a problem when his elevator cables broke, leaving the plane unable to rise above the flagpole in front of Main (Reed Hall) Building. Hitting the pole with his left wing, bending the pole to the ground, the plane swerved left with the propeller striking the northwest corner of the building and damaging the vestibule over the northern door; several girls in the revolving door narrowly escaped injury. The rear of the plane swooped around and hit the iron-frame arbor leading into the south entrance of Jarvis Hall. Badly damaged, the plane landed upside down, but the pilot survived unscathed. Later that evening Canadian soldiers arrived on campus to clean up the debris, including twenty-eight feet of brick knocked off the building.

A second incident occurred in November 1917, when a pilot from Benbrook crashed on campus after the Carruthers Field-TCU football game. Apparently, the 1917 game had ended with the Canadians winning, and as the pilot attempted to land, his landing gear caught on a barbed wire fence! The plane spun around and dove into the ground. The pilot was not hurt, but he had to face a frustrated crowd until a repair truck arrived to retrieve the damaged plane.

ABOVE
Painting of Main Building after the plane crash. The painting is framed in wood fragments form the building damaged by the plane. "Image of TCU Framed in Building Fragments" by S. P. Ziegler. TCU Permanent Art Collection. https://repository.tcu.edu/handle/116099117/19764. Courtesy of TCU Archives and Special Collections. Mary Couts Burnett Library. Texas Christian University.

RIGHT
Soldiers standing next to upside down airplane. Image D in *Benbrook Airfield Collection Scrapbook*. Scrapbook Collection. Courtesy of Tarrant County Archives.

RIGHT
A football game at TCU in 1918. Image C in *Benbrook Airfield Collection Scrapbook*. Scrapbook Collection. Courtesy of Tarrant County Archives.

RIGHT
View of clouds from airplane. Image A in *Benbrook Airfield Collection Scrapbook*. Scrapbook Collection. Courtesy of Tarrant County Archives.

The Epidemic—Spanish Influenza and TCU Nurses

In 1918 the Spanish Flu swept across the United States and the world, carried by soldiers across the country, across the Atlantic Ocean, and ultimately killing more than fifty million people worldwide. Soldiers at Camp Bowie became a local source of the epidemic, and some 1,900 were treated in makeshift structures. Soldiers frequently slept outside because they had to remain five feet apart to avoid infection. African American Army Private Louis Warren became Camp Bowie's first victim, and shortly thereafter, camp commander Colonel Albert Hall died as well. Even the base's clerical assistant and nurses began succumbing to the virus.

By the end of October, more than 1,200 DFW residents had died, and a *Star-Telegram* article pronounced, "Quarantine Is Placed on T.C.U. By Influenza." President Edwards McShane Waits quarantined the school and mandated students to wear masks and distance themselves to prevent the disease from spreading. Additionally, the administration proactively instructed student beds to be taken outside and given fresh air, which was believed to mitigate the spread of the virus. By the end of October, both Fort Worth and Dallas had closed all schools, theaters, streetcars, and even churches. Since the virus was so difficult to contain, community people even wore masks so they would not contract or spread the virus.

ABOVE
"Clark Hall," 1927. TCU Photograph Collection, RU 53. Photo Number: 598. https://repository.tcu.edu:443/handle/116099117/2121. Courtesy of TCU Special Collections. Mary Couts Burnett Library. Texas Christian University.

As the virus began to abate, TCU nursing students boldly volunteered at Camp Bowie to serve ailing soldiers because of the scarcity of nurses. Art professor Dura Brokaw Cockrell began training students to work in convalescent homes for soldiers, teaching weaving, pottery, basketry, tool making, woodworking, modeling, and metal work; she also offered free rag rug (Hospital Rug) making classes for teachers working with the Junior Red Cross. TCU rose to the occasion to assist in this crisis, even transforming the third floor of Clark Hall into a makeshift hospital for students and the community. President Waits and the administration independently acted in the best interest of the institution, faculty, staff, students, and community.

INFLUENZA AND AFTER-EFFECTS INCREASE WORK OF NURSES OF RELIEF ASSOCIATION FOR WINTER

These groups of tots have been patients at various times this Winter of the Relief Association nurses. They're well and healthy now. Note their smiles. Most of them were in the "tonsil" party, given two weeks ago by the Association to its proteges, who consented to have their tonsils and adenoids removed.

LEFT
Newspaper Article on "Spanish Influenza and Increased Nurse Work." TCU Scrapbook Collection, RU 8. Box 34, Folder 2. "Art Department, 1911-1920." Courtesy of TCU Archives and Special Collections. Mary Couts Burnett Library. Texas Christian University.

ABOVE
"Clark Hall," 1923. TCU Photograph Collection, RU 53. Photo Number: 568. https://repository.tcu.edu:443/handle/116099117/3764. Courtesy of TCU Special Collections. Mary Couts Burnett Library. Texas Christian University.

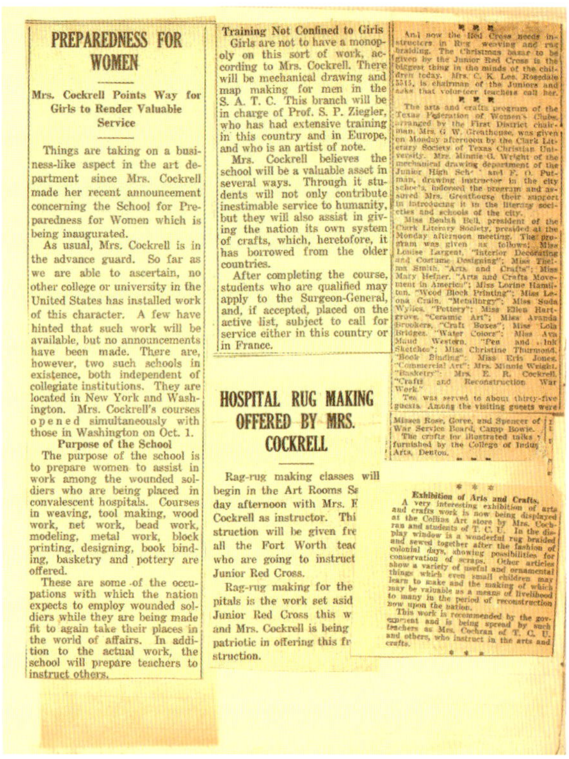

PREPAREDNESS FOR WOMEN

Mrs. Cockrell Points Way for Girls to Render Valuable Service

Things are taking on a business-like aspect in the art department since Mrs. Cockrell made her recent announcement concerning the School for Preparedness for Women which is being inaugurated.

As usual, Mrs. Cockrell is in the advance guard. So far as we are able to ascertain, no other college or university in the United States has installed work of this character. A few have hinted that such work will be available, but no announcements have been made. There are, however, two such schools in existence, both independent of collegiate institutions. They are located in New York and Washington. Mrs. Cockrell's courses opened simultaneously with those in Washington on Oct. 1.

Purpose of the School

The purpose of the school is to prepare women to assist in work among the wounded soldiers who are being placed in convalescent hospitals. Courses in weaving, tool making, wood work, net work, bead work, modeling, metal work, block printing, designing, book binding, basketry and pottery are offered.

These are some of the occupations with which the nation expects to employ wounded soldiers while they are being made fit to again take their places in the world of affairs. In addition to the actual work, the school will prepare teachers to instruct others.

Training Not Confined to Girls

Girls are not to have a monopoly on this sort of work, according to Mrs. Cockrell. There will be mechanical drawing and map making for men in the S. A. T. C. This branch will be in charge of Prof. S. P. Ziegler, who has had extensive training in this country and in Europe, and who is an artist of note.

Mrs. Cockrell believes the school will be a valuable asset in several ways. Through it students will not only contribute inestimable service to humanity, but they will also assist in giving the nation its own system of crafts, which, heretofore, it has borrowed from the older countries.

After completing the course, students who are qualified may apply to the Surgeon-General, and, if accepted, placed on the active list, subject to call for service either in this country or in France.

HOSPITAL RUG MAKING OFFERED BY MRS. COCKRELL

Rag-rug making classes will begin in the Art Rooms Sa[illegible] day afternoon with Mrs. E[illegible] Cockrell as instructor. Thi[illegible] struction will be given fre[illegible] all the Fort Worth teac[illegible] who are going to instruct [illegible] Junior Red Cross.

Rag-rug making for the [illegible] pitals is the work set asid[illegible] Junior Red Cross this w[illegible] and Mrs. Cockrell is being [illegible] patriotic in offering this fr[illegible] struction.

And now the Red Cross needs instructors in Rug weaving and rug braiding. The Christmas bazar to be given by the Junior Red Cross is the biggest thing in the minds of the children today. Mrs. C. K. Lee, Rosedale 5515, is chairman of the Juniors and asks that volunteer teachers call her.

The arts and crafts program of the Texas Federation of Women's Clubs, arranged by the First District chairman, Mrs. G. W. Greathouse, was given on Monday afternoon by the Clark Literary Society of Texas Christian University. Mrs. Minnie G. Wright of the mechanical drawing department of the Junior High Sch[illegible] and F. O. Putman, drawing instructor in the city schools, indorsed the program and assured Mrs. Greathouse their support in introducing it in the literary societies and schools of the city.

Miss Beulah Bell, president of the Clark Literary Society, presided at the Monday afternoon meeting. The program was given as follows: Miss Louise Largent, "Interior Decorating and Costume Designing"; Miss Thelma Smith, "Arts and Crafts"; Miss Mary Hefner, "Arts and Crafts Movement in America"; Miss Lorine Hamilton, "Wood Block Printing"; Miss Leona Crain, "Metallurgy"; Miss Suda Wylies, "Pottery"; Miss Ellen Hartgrove, "Ceramic Art"; Miss Avanda Brookers, "Craft Boxes"; Miss Lola Bridges, "Water Colors"; Miss Ava Maud Western, "Pen and Ink Sketches"; Miss Christine Thurmond, "Book Binding"; Miss Eris Jones, "Commercial Art"; Mrs. Minnie Wright, "Basketry"; Mrs. E. R. Cockrell, "Crafts and Reconstruction War Work."

Tea was served to about thirty-five guests. Among the visiting guests were Misses Rose, Goree, and Spencer of War Service Board, Camp Bowie.

The crafts for illustrated talks [illegible] furnished by the College of Indus[illegible] Arts, Denton.

Exhibition of Arts and Crafts.

A very interesting exhibition of arts and crafts work is now being displayed at the Collins Art store by Mrs. Cochran and students of T. C. U. In the display window is a wonderful rug braided and sewed together after the fashion of colonial days, showing possibilities for conservation of scraps. Other articles show a variety of useful and ornamental things which even small children may learn to make and the making of which may be valuable as a means of livelihood to many in the period of reconstruction now upon the nation.

This work is recommended by the government and is being spread by such teachers as Mrs. Cochran of T. C. U. and others, who instruct in the arts and crafts.

ABOVE (TOP)

Mattresses drying in sunlight. "Photo of Beds Sunning Outside of Clark Hall." TCU Scrapbook Collection, RU 8. Box 30, Folder 7. Scrapbook "Student Life, 1919-1924." Courtesy of TCU Archives and Special Collections. Mary Couts Burnett Library. Texas Christian University.

ABOVE

"Newspaper article on Hospital Rug Making and Preparedness of Women." TCU Scrapbook Collection, RU 8. Box 34, Folder 2. "Art Department, 1911-1920." Courtesy of TCU Archives and Special Collections. Mary Couts Burnett Library. Texas Christian University.

ABOVE

"Photo of TCU Nurses in back of Truck." Image 103 in 1919 *Horned Frog* pdf file. *The Horned Frog*, vol. 15. (Fort Worth: The Reimers Company,1919), 103. https://repository.tcu.edu/handle/116099117/11045. Courtesy of TCU Archives and Special Collections. Mary Couts Burnett Library. Texas Christian University.

ABOVE
The Cockrell family (Egbert, Dura, Vardaman, and Dura Louise) sitting in their parlor in Fort Worth. "Cockrell Family," 1915. TCU Photograph Collection, RU 53. Photo Number 503. https://repository.tcu.edu:443/handle/116099117/2434. Courtesy of TCU Special Collections. Mary Couts Burnett Library. Texas Christian University.

A TCU Power Couple: The Cockrells

Many families have illustrious, generational histories at TCU, but none played as integral a role as the Cockrell family in building and supporting TCU during its time in Waco and its subsequent move to Fort Worth. Dr. Egbert Railey Cockrell served TCU as a professor of history, political science, and law from 1897 to 1924. His wife, esteemed TCU Professor Dura Brokaw Cockrell, served as head of the Art Department from 1899–1924.

Egbert Cockrell accepted a position teaching history and political science and arrived at AddRan University in 1897. He attempted to begin a law school in 1898, but the venture closed its doors by 1900. As the department head of History and Political Science, Cockrell established a robust curriculum that featured summer tours of the Western United States (open to students, staff, and local citizens). He later established the TCU Law School, which operated from 1915 to 1920.

Dura Cockrell arrived at TCU in 1899 after she earned prestigious graduate training in Chicago, New York, Scotland, Holland, London, and Paris. She won numerous awards in local, state, and regional art competitions with her painting and pottery. Her experiences and talent led her to influence numerous TCU students. By 1914, TCU's Art Department boasted the largest art program enrollment in the state. The couple frequently hosted such student organizations as Shirley and Clark Literary Societies, the "Brushes," and class officers at their home on Forest Park Boulevard. As noted by Amboline Tyson, they fostered a sense of family and belonging for students.

LEFT
"The Brushes" student club photograph. "The Brushes" in *The Horned Frog*. (Reimers Company, 1917), 64. https://repository.tcu.edu/handle/116099117/11043. Courtesy of TCU Archives and Special Collections. Mary Couts Burnett Library. Texas Christian University.

This TCU power couple not only provided excellent mentorship and education to students, they also served as important local community leaders. Dura Cockrell became a leader for the women's suffrage movement in Fort Worth during the 1910s and 1920s. She also supported local institutions during the Spanish influenza epidemic with her hospital rug drive. Egbert Cockrell won the election as Fort Worth's seventeenth mayor in 1921. During his tenure, he expanded the mileage of paved roads in the city, including the TCU area. He also instituted a city manager form of government for the city.

In 1924, the Cockrells resigned their positions at TCU to accept employment at William Woods College in Missouri, Egbert as the president and Dura as the chair of art department. Next time you walk, drive, or ride around campus, be on the lookout for Cockrell Street, just behind the campus bookstore, and remember the couple that played a pivotal role in shaping both Fort Worth and TCU's history.

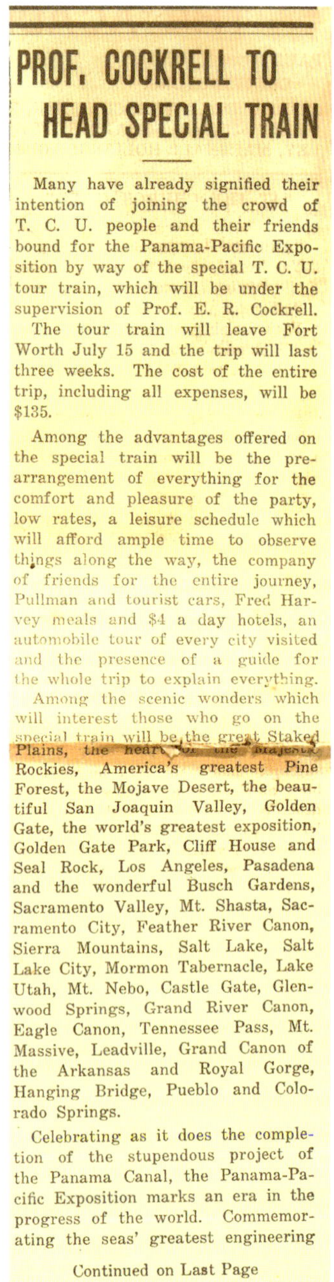

PROF. COCKRELL TO HEAD SPECIAL TRAIN

Many have already signified their intention of joining the crowd of T. C. U. people and their friends bound for the Panama-Pacific Exposition by way of the special T. C. U. tour train, which will be under the supervision of Prof. E. R. Cockrell. The tour train will leave Fort Worth July 15 and the trip will last three weeks. The cost of the entire trip, including all expenses, will be $135.

Among the advantages offered on the special train will be the prearrangement of everything for the comfort and pleasure of the party, low rates, a leisure schedule which will afford ample time to observe things along the way, the company of friends for the entire journey, Pullman and tourist cars, Fred Harvey meals and $4 a day hotels, an automobile tour of every city visited and the presence of a guide for the whole trip to explain everything.

Among the scenic wonders which will interest those who go on the special train will be the great Staked Plains, the heart [illegible] Rockies, America's greatest Pine Forest, the Mojave Desert, the beautiful San Joaquin Valley, Golden Gate, the world's greatest exposition, Golden Gate Park, Cliff House and Seal Rock, Los Angeles, Pasadena and the wonderful Busch Gardens, Sacramento Valley, Mt. Shasta, Sacramento City, Feather River Canon, Sierra Mountains, Salt Lake, Salt Lake City, Mormon Tabernacle, Lake Utah, Mt. Nebo, Castle Gate, Glenwood Springs, Grand River Canon, Eagle Canon, Tennessee Pass, Mt. Massive, Leadville, Grand Canon of the Arkansas and Royal Gorge, Hanging Bridge, Pueblo and Colorado Springs.

Celebrating as it does the completion of the stupendous project of the Panama Canal, the Panama-Pacific Exposition marks an era in the progress of the world. Commemorating the seas' greatest engineering

Continued on Last Page

RIGHT
Newspaper article on "Professor Cockrell to head Special Western Train." TCU Scrapbook Collection, RU 8. Box 25, Scrapbook no. 34. "Student Life, 1912-1916." Courtesy of TCU Archives and Special Collections. Mary Couts Burnett Library. Texas Christian University.

ABOVE
The parlor in the Cockrells' home with paintings by Mrs. Cockrell and her pupils. "Parlor with Pictures by Mrs. Cockrell and her Pupils," 1908. TCU Photograph Collection, RU 53. Photo Number 778, PN Number: 200. https://repository.tcu.edu:443/handle/116099117/3352. Courtesy of TCU Special Collections. Mary Couts Burnett Library. Texas Christian University.

ABOVE
Portrait of Dura L. Cockrell. "Dura L. Cockrell," 1925. TCU Photograph Collection, RU 53. Photo Number: 2110. https://repository.tcu.edu:443/handle/116099117/2932. Courtesy of TCU Special Collections. Mary Couts Burnett Library. Texas Christian University.

ABOVE
Portrait of Mayor E. R. Cockrell. Fort Worth Mayors Collection, Box I. Courtesy of the Genealogy, History and Archives Unit, Fort Worth Public Library.

Expanding Opportunities for Women's Sports

With the expansion of collegiate athletics in the decades after 1890, men's football and baseball typically receive the most attention. What about TCU women's clubs of the same period? During the Thorp Spring era, female students participated in recreational tennis, croquet, aquatic sports, and the occasional equestrian outing. These activities seem to be limited to weekend exercise. After the move to Waco, opportunities for women to compete in athletics began to expand. By 1904, female students who lived in "The Home" elected officers to manage the tennis club on campus. The club secured a space on campus to create new and improved courts. They also formed a women's basketball team, captained by I. V. Purcell, to compete against local teams. By 1908, the women's athletic club also organized a swimming club.

With the move to Fort Worth, opportunities for women's athletics continued to expand. The construction of an outdoor basketball and tennis court on campus in 1913 generated buzz and excitement among the students. Competing tennis clubs "the Scorpions" and "The Never Nets" allowed students to compete against one another and local schools. Meanwhile, the Lady Frogs Basketball team of 1912–1913 earned a reputation as the "best girl athletes in the State." The team, led by Senior Libbie Wade and Sophomore Irene Carson, won all its contests that season. The depth and talent of the Lady Frogs rendered practice games between the first and second teams as must-see action, and reportedly, the toughest test for the first team all year. Despite the continued participation and popularity of women's sports on campus, editors of *The Horned Frog* ended its annual review of women's athletics by 1917. Instead, they emphasized the participation and successes of female students enrolled in the domestic sciences.

OPPOSITE
TCU women's basketball team photo on outdoor courts. "1912-1916 Student Life Scrapbook." TCU Scrapbook Collection, RU 8. Box 25, Scrapbook no. 34. Courtesy of TCU Archives and Special Collections. Mary Couts Burnett Library. Texas Christian University.

RIGHT
Outdoor courts built in front of academic buildings in 1910s. "Tennis Courts," 1919. TCU Photograph Collection, RU 53. Photo Number: 1094. https://repository.tcu.edu:443/handle/116099117/2149. Courtesy of TCU Special Collections. Mary Couts Burnett Library. Texas Christian University.

ABOVE
Team photo of 1912 Women's Tennis Club. "Women's Tennis," 1912. TCU Photograph Collection, RU 53. Photo Number: 983. https://repository.tcu.edu:443/handle/116099117/3405. Courtesy of TCU Special Collections. Mary Couts Burnett Library. Texas Christian University.

RIGHT
TCU students seated on branch over the Trinity River. "TCU Swimming Hole." TCU Scrapbook Collection, RU 8. Box 34, Folder 3. "Student Life, 1912-1916." https://repository.tcu.edu/handle/116099117/4610. Courtesy of TCU Archives and Special Collections. Mary Couts Burnett Library. Texas Christian University.

LEFT
TCU women's basketball player shooting ball toward basket while other players watch. "1912-1916 Student Life Scrapbook." TCU Scrapbook Collection, RU 8. Box 25, Scrapbook no. 34. Courtesy of TCU Archives and Special Collections. Mary Couts Burnett Library. Texas Christian University.

LEFT
TCU women's basketball players contesting a jump ball. "1912-1916 Student Life Scrapbook." TCU Scrapbook Collection, RU 8. Box 25, Scrapbook no. 34. Courtesy of TCU Archives and Special Collections. Mary Couts Burnett Library. Texas Christian University.

LEFT
Waterfall on Trinity River in Forest Park. "TCU Waterfall." TCU Scrapbook Collection, RU 8. Box 34, Folder 3. "Student Life, 1912-1916." https://repository.tcu.edu/handle/116099117/4610. Courtesy of TCU Archives and Special Collections. Mary Couts Burnett Library. Texas Christian University.

Mary Couts Burnett: Savior of TCU!

Born in 1856, Mary Couts Burnett was one of five daughters sired by Parker County banker and rancher Colonel James Robertson Couts, who admired Addison Clark's educational mission and donated money to the school while it was in Thorp Spring.

After Mary's first husband died, she married the cattle baron Samuel Burk Burnett in September 1892. Burnett's Four Sixes Ranch had partnered with Quanah Parker to lease grazing lands on Comanche and Kiowa reservations in Oklahoma, making him incredibly wealthy. The couple built their home in Fort Worth, and had one child, son Samuel Burk Burnett Jr., who died in 1916, shortly before his twenty-first birthday. The marriage suddenly became contentious because of Burnett's relationship with his granddaughter Anne Burnett (Tandy). By 1920 Mary believed, and told others, that Burk was trying to murder her. Burk had Mary declared legally insane and committed her to an asylum in a private Weatherford home, where she was virtually a prisoner. On the day of Burk's death, June 26, 1922, Mary escaped. Her personal physician, Charles Harris (who later founded Harris College of Nursing), assisted Mary in getting the insanity ruling reversed. Challenging her husband's will, which left his entire $6 million estate to his granddaughter, the court ruled that Mary should receive half of the estate.

After winning the legal battle, in December 1923 she made a $3 million bequest to TCU. She had no connection with TCU, and her husband had reportedly said none of his money would ever go to a religious or academic institution. But the influence of her physician and recollection of her father's support of AddRan College convinced her to make the bequest, which was used to replace TCU's existing library, then housed in the university's administration building. And in accordance with the will, $150,000 was immediately allocated to the construction of a new library building. Adjusted for inflation, the $3 million equates to more than $46 million today. That bequest saved TCU from impending financial disaster.

ABOVE
Oil painting of Mary Couts Burnett. "Portrait of Mary Couts Burnett," by Emily Guthrie Smith (1984). TCU Permanent Art Collection. https://repository.tcu.edu/handle/116099117/14076. Courtesy of TCU Archives and Special Collections. Mary Couts Burnett Library. Texas Christian University.

OPPOSITE
Main reading room in Mary Couts Burnett Library in 1930. "Mary Couts Burnett Library," 1930s. TCU Photograph Collection, RU 53. Photo Number 160. https://repository.tcu.edu:443/handle/116099117/2620. Courtesy of TCU Special Collections. Mary Couts Burnett Library. Texas Christian University.

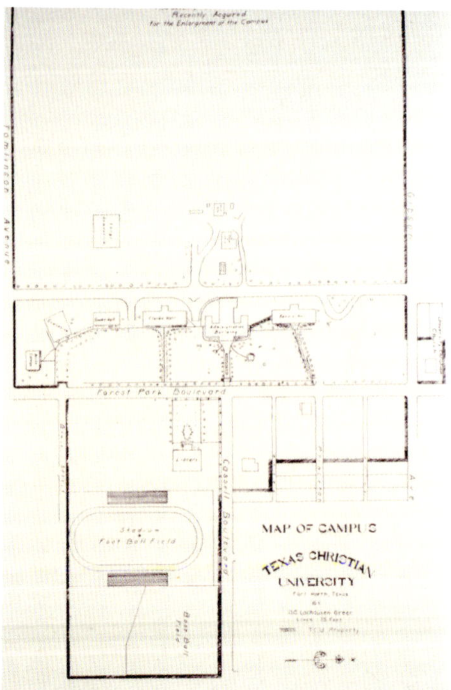

ABOVE
Mary Couts Burnett Library after construction in the 1920s. "Mary Couts Burnett Library," 1920s. TCU Photograph Collection, RU 53. Photo Number: 147. https://repository.tcu.edu:443/handle/116099117/2599. Courtesy of TCU Special Collections. Mary Couts Burnett Library. Texas Christian University.

RIGHT
Drawn plan of TCU campus with Mary Couts Burnett as the only academic building on east side of Forest Park Drive in 1924. "TCU Campus," 1924. TCU Photograph Collection (RU 53). Photo Number: 2103. https://repository.tcu.edu:443/handle/116099117/3852. Courtesy of TCU Special Collections. Mary Couts Burnett Library. Texas Christian University.

THE SKIFF

TEXAS CHRISTIAN UNIVERSITY

LIBRARY TO BE READY FALL OF '24

MRS. BURNETT'S GIFT MAKES T. C. U.

ONE OF BIGGEST SCHOOLS IN U. S. FUTURE OF T. C. U.

TO HER

(Mrs. Mary Couts Burnett)

For her love of T. C. U.,
For her gift dearer than myrrh,
For her generosity so true—
Our praise to her.
For the joy that she has brought

ABOVE

"Construction of Mary Couts Burnett Library," 1924. TCU Photograph Collection, RU 8. Photo Number 2170, PN Number 527. https://repository.tcu.edu:443/handle/116099117/2129. Courtesy of TCU Special Collections. Mary Couts Burnett Library. Texas Christian University.

LEFT

Front page of the *Skiff* estimated the completion of Mary Couts Burnett Library and celebrated Mrs. Burnett's gift as TCU's savior. The *Skiff* vol. 22, no. 14 (Fort Worth), Dec. 18, 1923. TCU Scrapbook Collection, RU 8. Box 26, Folder 12. Scrapbook no. 4, "Mary Couts Burnett Gift to TCU Library, 1923-1924." Courtesy of TCU Archives and Special Collections. Mary Couts Burnett Library. Texas Christian University.

CHAPTER 4

Strengthening the Foundation: 1923–1941

1923—The Golden Jubilee

On Tuesday, June 5, 1923, TCU conferred an honorary degree on Randolph Clark. When the aging founder mounted the temporary platform to accept this honor, he was guided to the podium because his eyes were bandaged because of a recent surgery. Before he began speaking, the crowd erupted with a rousing ovation to the man who had founded the school and who was still alive to see his hopes fulfilled.

This commencement for the class of 1923 highlighted a week of programs celebrating the Golden Jubilee—fifty years. From June 1 through June 4 the convention of Christian churches met in Fort Worth, and the TCU celebration spanned from June 3 to June 5. On the evening of June 4, as the church convention opened, delegates, TCU students, and others gathered near First Christian Church on Throckmorton for the TCU Jubilee Parade. Afterward, Sam J. McFarland, president of the board of trustees, served as the toastmaster for the Jubilee Banquet at the Hotel Texas. Later that evening the TCU Footlights Club presented a play in the university chapel.

The 1923 commencement, held on campus in an area in front of the Honeysuckle Arbor between Main (Reed Hall) and Jarvis Hall, began a tradition that lasted until 1949 and the completion of Landreth Hall with its auditorium. The event saw the granting of earned degrees and the awarding of eleven honorary degrees to men, including Clark, who were all distinguished by their contributions to the Christian Church. Following commencement, all were invited to a lunch on campus in which class president Edwin A. Elliott announced that with funds collected from the class and other university friends, they were erecting a Memorial Arch in memory of TCU students who died in World War I.

Other events followed, including alumni meetings by class as well as a baseball game between the 1923 team and alumni players. The following morning the jubilee concluded with a pageant depicting the history of TCU titled "These Fifty Years." The celebration was a momentous occasion.

RIGHT
Oil painting of TCU campus by Samuel P. Ziegler. "View of Campus," 1919. Oil on canvas by Samuel P. Ziegler. Art in Special Collections, TCU Permanent Collection. https://repository.tcu.edu/handle/116099117/14018. Courtesy of TCU Archives and Special Collections. Mary Couts Burnett Library. Texas Christian University.

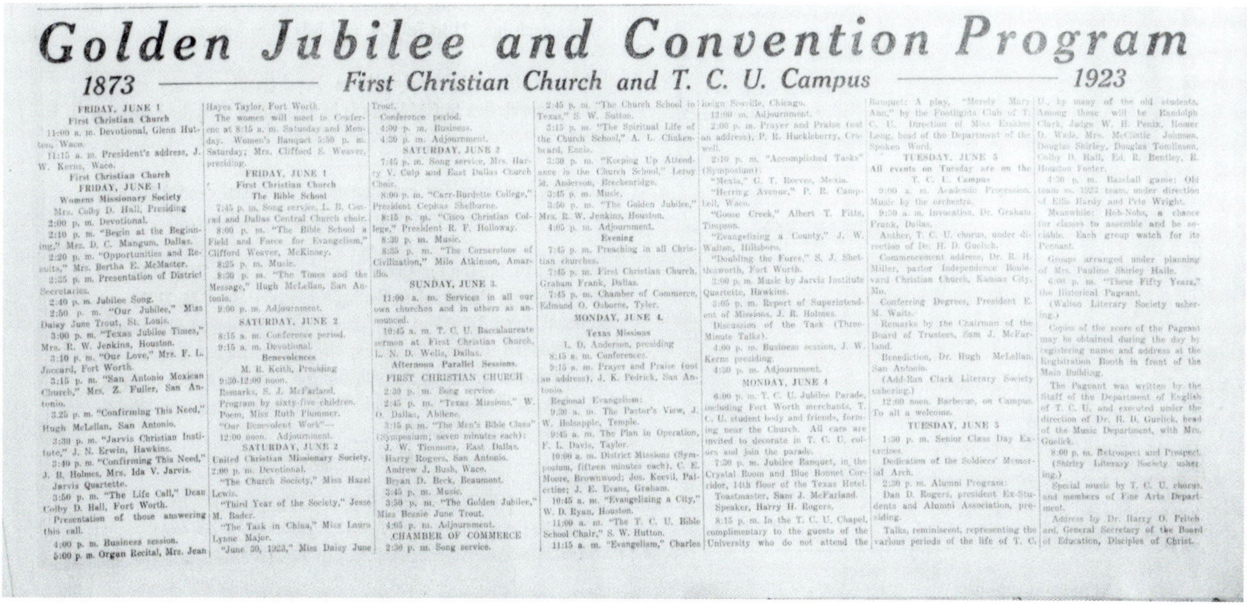

Golden Jubilee and Convention Program

1873 — First Christian Church and T. C. U. Campus — 1923

FRIDAY, JUNE 1
First Christian Church

11:00 a. m. Devotional, Glenn Hutton, Waco.

11:15 a. m. President's address, J. W. Kerns, Waco.

First Christian Church
FRIDAY, JUNE 1
Womens Missionary Society
Mrs. Colby D. Hall, Presiding

2:00 p. m. Devotional.

2:10 p. m. "Begin at the Beginning," Mrs. D. C. Mangum, Dallas.

2:20 p. m. "Opportunities and Results," Mrs. Bertha E. McMaster.

2:35 p. m. Presentation of District Secretaries.

2:40 p. m. Jubilee Song.

2:50 p. m. "Our Jubilee," Miss Daisy June Trout, St. Louis.

3:00 p. m. "Texas Jubilee Times," Mrs. R. W. Jenkins, Houston.

3:10 p. m. "Our Love," Mrs. F. L. Jaccard, Fort Worth.

3:15 p. m. "San Antonio Mexican Church," Mrs. Z. Fuller, San Antonio.

3:25 p. m. "Confirming This Need," Hugh McLellan, San Antonio.

3:30 p. m. "Jarvis Christian Institute," J. N. Erwin, Hawkins.

3:40 p. m. "Confirming This Need," J. B. Holmes, Mrs. Ida V. Jarvis. Jarvis Quartette.

3:50 p. m. "The Life Call," Dean Colby D. Hall, Fort Worth.

Presentation of those answering this call.

4:00 p. m. Business session.

5:00 p. m. Organ Recital, Mrs. Jean Hayes Taylor, Fort Worth.

The women will meet in Conference at 8:15 a. m. Saturday and Monday. Women's Banquet 5:50 p. m. Saturday; Mrs. Clifford S. Weaver, presiding.

FRIDAY, JUNE 1
First Christian Church
The Bible School

7:45 p. m. Song service, L. B. Conrad and Dallas Central Church choir.

8:00 p. m. "The Bible School a Field and Force for Evangelism," Clifford Weaver, McKinney.

8:25 p. m. Music.

8:30 p. m. "The Times and the Message," Hugh McLellan, San Antonio.

9:00 p. m. Adjournment.

SATURDAY, JUNE 2

8:15 a. m. Conference period.

9:15 a. m. Devotional.

Benevolences
M. E. Keith, Presiding

9:30-12:00 noon.

Remarks, S. J. McFarland.

Program by sixty-five children.

Poem, Miss Ruth Plummer.

"Our Benevolent Work"—

12:00 noon. Adjournment.

SATURDAY, JUNE 2
United Christian Missionary Society.

2:00 p. m. Devotional.

"The Church Society," Miss Hazel Lewis.

"Third Year of the Society," Jesse M. Bader.

"The Task in China," Miss Laura Lynne Major.

"June 30, 1923," Miss Daisy June Trout.

Conference period.

4:00 p. m. Business.

4:30 p. m. Adjournment.

SATURDAY, JUNE 2

7:45 p. m. Song service, Mrs. Harry V. Culp and East Dallas Church Choir.

8:00 p. m. "Carr-Burdette College," President Cephas Shelburne.

8:15 p. m. "Cisco Christian College," President R. F. Holloway.

8:30 p. m. Music.

8:35 p. m. "The Cornerstone of Civilization," Milo Atkinson, Amarillo.

SUNDAY, JUNE 3.

11:00 a. m. Services in all our own churches and in others as announced.

10:45 a. m. T. C. U. Baccalaureate sermon at First Christian Church, L. N. D. Wells, Dallas.

Afternoon Parallel Sessions.
FIRST CHRISTIAN CHURCH

2:30 p. m. Song service.

2:45 p. m. "Texas Missions," W. O. Dallas, Abilene.

3:15 p. m. "The Men's Bible Class" (Symposium; seven minutes each):

J. W. Timmons, East Dallas.
Harry Rogers, San Antonio.
Andrew J. Bush, Waco.
Bryan D. Beck, Beaumont.

3:45 p. m. Music.

3:50 p. m. "The Golden Jubilee," Miss Bessie June Trout.

4:05 p. m. Adjournment.

CHAMBER OF COMMERCE

2:30 p. m. Song service.

2:45 p. m. "The Church School in Texas," S. W. Sutton.

3:15 p. m. "The Spiritual Life of the Church School," A. L. Chalkenbeard, Ennis.

3:30 p. m. "Keeping Up Attendance in the Church School," Leroy M. Anderson, Breckenridge.

3:45 p. m. Music.

3:50 p. m. "The Golden Jubilee," Mrs. R. W. Jenkins, Houston.

4:05 p. m. Adjournment.

Evening

7:45 p. m. Preaching in all Christian churches.

7:45 p. m. First Christian Church, Graham Frank, Dallas.

7:45 p. m. Chamber of Commerce, Edmund O. Osborne, Tyler.

MONDAY, JUNE 4.
Texas Missions
L. D. Anderson, presiding

8:15 a. m. Conferences.

9:15 a. m. Prayer and Praise (not an address), J. K. Peirick, San Antonio.

Regional Evangelism:

9:30 a. m. The Pastor's View, J. W. Holsapple, Temple.

9:45 a. m. The Plan in Operation, F. L. Davis, Taylor.

10:00 a. m. District Missions (Symposium, fifteen minutes each), C. E. Moore, Brownwood; Jos. Keevil, Palestine; J. E. Evans, Graham.

10:45 a. m. "Evangelizing a City," W. D. Ryan, Houston.

11:00 a. m. "The T. C. U. Bible School Chair," S. W. Hutton.

11:15 a. m. "Evangelism," Charles Reign Scoville, Chicago.

12:00 m. Adjournment.

2:00 p. m. Prayer and Praise (not an address), P. R. Huckleberry, Crowell.

2:10 p. m. "Accomplished Tasks" (Symposium):

"Mexia," G. T. Reeves, Mexia.

"Herring Avenue," P. R. Campbell, Waco.

"Goose Creek," Albert T. Fitts, Timpson.

"Evangelizing a County," J. W. Walton, Hillsboro.

"Doubling the Force," S. J. Shettlesworth, Fort Worth.

3:00 p. m. Music by Jarvis Institute Quartette, Hawkins.

3:05 p. m. Report of Superintendent of Missions, J. R. Holmes.

Discussion of the Task (Three-Minute Talks).

4:00 p. m. Business session, J. W. Kerns presiding.

4:30 p. m. Adjournment.

MONDAY, JUNE 4

6:00 p. m. T. C. U. Jubilee Parade, including Fort Worth merchants, T. C. U. student body and friends, forming near the Church. All cars are invited to decorate in T. C. U. colors and join the parade.

7:30 p. m. Jubilee Banquet, in the Crystal Room and Blue Bonnet Corridor, 14th floor of the Texas Hotel.

Toastmaster, Sam J. McFarland.

Speaker, Harry H. Rogers.

8:15 p. m. In the T. C. U. Chapel, complimentary to the guests of the University who do not attend the Banquet: A play, "Merely Mary Ann," by the Footlights Club of T. C. U. Direction of Miss Erskine Long, head of the Department of the Spoken Word.

TUESDAY, JUNE 5

All events on Tuesday are on the T. C. U. Campus

9:00 a. m. Academic Procession. Music by the orchestra.

9:30 a. m. Invocation, Dr. Graham Frank, Dallas.

Anthem, T. C. U. chorus, under direction of Dr. H. D. Guelick.

Commencement address, Dr. R. H. Miller, pastor Independence Boulevard Christian Church, Kansas City, Mo.

Conferring Degrees, President E. M. Waits.

Remarks by the Chairman of the Board of Trustees, Sam J. McFarland.

Benediction, Dr. Hugh McLellan, San Antonio.

(Add-Ran Clark Literary Society ushering.)

12:00 noon. Barbecue, on Campus. To all a welcome.

TUESDAY, JUNE 5

1:30 p. m. Senior Class Day Exercises.

Dedication of the Soldiers' Memorial Arch.

2:30 p. m. Alumni Program:

Dan D. Rogers, president Ex-Students and Alumni Association, presiding.

Talks, reminiscent, representing the various periods of the life of T. C. U., by many of the old students. Among these will be Randolph Clark, Judge W. H. Penix, Homer D. Wade, Mrs. McClintic Johnson, Douglas Shirley, Douglas Tomlinson, Colby D. Hall, Ed. R. Bentley, R. Houston Foster.

4:30 p. m. Baseball game: Old team vs. 1923 team, under direction of Ellis Hardy and Pete Wright.

Meanwhile: Hob-Nobs, a chance for classes to assemble and be sociable. Each group watch for its Pennant.

Groups arranged under planning of Mrs. Pauline Shirley Halle.

6:00 p. m. "These Fifty Years," the Historical Pageant.

(Walton Literary Society ushering.)

Copies of the score of the Pageant may be obtained during the day by registering name and address at the Registration Booth in front of the Main Building.

The Pageant was written by the Staff of the Department of English of T. C. U., and executed under the direction of Dr. H. D. Guelick, head of the Music Department, with Mrs. Guelick.

8:00 p. m. Retrospect and Prospect.

(Shirley Literary Society ushering.)

Special music by T. C. U. chorus, and members of Fine Arts Department.

Address by Dr. Harry O. Pritchard, General Secretary of the Board of Education, Disciples of Christ.

ABOVE

Schedule and list of events conducted during TCU's Golden Jubilee celebration in 1923. "Golden Jubilee and Convention Program," front page. The *Skiff* 21, no. 34 (June, 1923). https://repository.tcu.edu/handle/116099117/13219. Courtesy of TCU Archives and Special Collections. Mary Couts Burnett Library. Texas Christian University.

LEFT

Randolph Clark sitting on a bench at TCU campus during the Golden Jubilee celebration. "Randolph Clark," 1920s. TCU Photograph Collection. RU 53, Photo Number: 1143. https://repository.tcu.edu:443/handle/116099117/2886. Courtesy of TCU Special Collections. Mary Couts Burnett Library. Texas Christian University.

RIGHT
The arbor walk behind the TCU Administration Building. "Arbor on Campus," 1926. TCU Photograph Collection. RU 53, Photo Number: 2363. https://repository.tcu.edu:443/handle/116099117/2325. Courtesy of TCU Special Collections. Mary Couts Burnett Library. Texas Christian University.

RIGHT
Program for the Golden Jubilee Celebration on June 5, 1923. "These Fifty Years Program." RU 32, Class Reunions Folder. https://repository.tcu.edu/handle/116099117/11726. Courtesy of TCU Archives and Special Collections. Mary Couts Burnett Library. Texas Christian University.

1873 1923

TEXAS
CHRISTIAN UNIVERSITY

FIFTIETH ANNIVERSARY
PAGEANT

"These Fifty Years"

Contributed by the
ENGLISH DEPARTMENT *of* T. C. U.
TO THE
Golden Jubilee Celebration
June 5, 1923

Presented by the
STUDENTS of the UNIVERSITY
Mrs. H. D. GUELICK, Pageant Director
Miss CHARLOTTE OWSLEY, in Charge of Costumes
Mr. H. D. GUELICK, in Charge of Music

ABOVE
Amon G. Carter leading TCU band in parade before TCU versus Rice football game in 1946. Photo taken in 1946. AR406-6 Carter Files. Courtesy, *Fort Worth Star-Telegram Collection*, Special Collections, The University of Texas at Arlington Libraries.

Amon Carter, Fort Worth, and TCU

Amon Giles Carter Sr., born December 11, 1879, in Crafton, Texas, spent much of his early life in Bowie. By May 1905, Carter had accepted a job in Fort Worth selling advertising for a newspaper. Working for the *Fort Worth Star*, he quickly secured financial control over the paper and soon thereafter purchased its competitor, the *Fort Worth Telegram*. By January 1, 1909, he combined the two papers, forming the *Fort Worth Star-Telegram*, which by the mid-1920s had the largest circulation in the south. The paper's financial success permitted Carter to start WBAP (1922), the oldest radio station in Fort Worth, and Texas's first television station WBAP TV (1948).

Carter became Fort Worth's most important booster. He drummed up business and government spending for his home region, including persuading Southern Air Transport (now American Airlines) to move its headquarters from Dallas to nearby Fort Worth. He convinced several oil companies to move to or keep their headquarters in Fort Worth after personal interventions. Additionally, Carter helped obtain for Fort Worth the construction of Air Force Plant 4 (now the headquarters of Lockheed Martin Aeronautics) and the relocation of Bell Aircraft (now Bell Helicopter Textron). Finally, Carter would become an avid proponent of Fort Worth's university, TCU.

Carter understood that TCU's football success during the late 1920s brought attention to Fort Worth. In 1929 he helped raise money for the construction of a new TCU football stadium, arranging for Fort Worth citizens to contribute 60 percent of the construction costs for the stadium that ultimately carried Amon G. Carter's name. He later served on the TCU Board of Trustees and supported the construction of several campus buildings during the 1940s and early 1950s, including Foster Hall, Landreth Hall, and Winton-Scott Hall. Since his death on June 23, 1955, the Amon Carter Foundation has continued to be a major financial supporter of TCU.

OPPOSITE
Amon G. Carter in front of a tree on TCU campus. "Amon Giles Carter, Sr.," 1955. TCU Photograph Collection, RU 53. Photo Number: 922. https://repository.tcu.edu:443/handle/116099117/2726. Courtesy of TCU Special Collections. Mary Couts Burnett Library. Texas Christian University.

ABOVE
Leo R. "Dutch" Meyer receiving a trophy from Amon G. Carter for twenty years of service at TCU. "Leo R. 'Dutch' Meyer," 1938–1939. TCU Photograph Collection, RU 53. Photo Number: 366. https://repository.tcu.edu:443/handle/116099117/3191. Courtesy of TCU Special Collections. Mary Couts Burnett Library. Texas Christian University.

ABOVE (TOP)
Amon G. Carter with TCU baseball players and a mule team. "Amon Carter with Baseball Players," 1920s. TCU Photograph Collection, RU 53. Photo Number: 534. https://repository.tcu.edu:443/handle/116099117/2634. Courtesy of TCU Special Collections. Mary Couts Burnett Library. Texas Christian University.

ABOVE
Colby Hall standing with the TCU football team at the St. Louis train station in 1940. "TCU Football Team," 1940. TCU Photograph Collection, RU 53. Photo Number: 1051. https://repository.tcu.edu:443/handle/116099117/3765. Courtesy of TCU Special Collections. Mary Couts Burnett Library. Texas Christian University.

RIGHT
Will Rogers and Amon G. Carter at the Texas and Pacific Station in Fort Worth, Texas. Photo taken on January 24, 1931. AR406-6 Carter Files. Courtesy, *Fort Worth Star-Telegram Collection*, Special Collections, The University of Texas at Arlington Libraries.

ABOVE
"Amon G. Carter Stadium," 1936. TCU Photograph Collection, RU 53. Photo Number: 529, PN Number: 604. https://repository.tcu.edu:443/hadle/116099117/2656. Courtesy of TCU Special Collections. Mary Couts Burnett Library. Texas Christian University.

Fort Worth (TCU) School of Art

Born in Lancaster, Pennsylvania, on January 4, 1882, Samuel P. Ziegler enjoyed his student years at the Pennsylvania Academy of the Fine Arts, studying with William Merritt Chase, Thomas Anschutz, and Hugh Breckenridge. He also studied music at the Philadelphia Musical Academy from 1905 to 1912, when he traveled to Europe on a six-month scholarship to tour museums. Returning in 1913 for his final year of study, he operated a painting studio in Philadelphia and taught cello at the Musical Academy.

Ziegler relocated to Texas in 1917 to teach cello and music theory at TCU. After two years he left to become the head of the art department across town at Texas Wesleyan College. Returning to TCU in 1925 as head (and only member until 1946) of the art department, he gained attention as a portrait and figure painter and lithographer, focusing his work on Fort Worth and neighboring ranches and oil fields. Winning a series of prestigious competitions in art and lithography at the State Fair in Dallas, the West Texas Exposition in San Angelo, and the Southern States Arts League, Ziegler had his work mounted in solo exhibitions at the Museum of Fine Arts Houston and the Elizabeth Ney Museum in Austin in 1931.

Ziegler expanded the art curriculum to a four-year degree program in Add-Ran College. He also created a popular two-year program for earning a teacher's certificate, and a three-year program for earning a certificate in art. Inspired by his talent, his students regularly placed in the Texas State Fair and other competitions. Increased enrollment after World War II permitted the department to hire a second full-time teacher in 1946; by 1954 the department had four members, by 1958 five, and by the TCU centennial the department boasted nine members. Ziegler retired in 1953, and today his work is represented in collections at the Modern Art Museum of Fort Worth, the Carnegie Library in Fort Worth, and at Texas Christian University.

OPPOSITE
"The TCU Library," 1932. Engraving by Samuel P. Ziegler. Art in Special Collections, TCU Permanent Collection. https://repository.tcu.edu/handle/116099117/14040. Courtesy of TCU Archives and Special Collections. Mary Couts Burnett Library. Texas Christian University.

OPPOSITE
Oil painting by Samuel P. Ziegler illustrating the pink sky west of the TCU campus. "The Pink Cloud," 1922/23. Oil on canvas by Samuel P. Ziegler. Art in Special Collections, TCU Permanent Collection. https://repository.tcu.edu/handle/116099117/14093. Courtesy of TCU Archives and Special Collections. Mary Couts Burnett Library. Texas Christian University.

RIGHT
Portrait of Professor Samuel P. Ziegler. "Samuel P. Ziegler," 1934. TCU Photograph Collection. RU 53, Photo Number: 960. https://repository.tcu.edu:443/handle/116099117/2399. Courtesy of TCU Special Collections. Mary Couts Burnett Library. Texas Christian University.

S.P. ZIEGLER

Colby Hall, a Building or a Person?

Walking across campus today, people see the dorm Colby Hall and often ask Colby's first name. They are surprised to learn his full name was really Colby Hall.

Hall, born in Madisonville, Kentucky, on December 29, 1875, studied at the AddRan Preparatory School before matriculating at AddRan Christian University in Waco (1889–1899). On Thanksgiving Day, 1896, the 124-pound Hall played quarterback in the first AddRan University football game. Leaving Waco, he attended an older Disciples of Christ institution, Transylvania College in Lexington, Kentucky, where he received a BA in 1902. He also earned a classical diploma from the College of the Bible (Lexington Theological Seminary). Returning to Waco, he served as an acting professor of Latin for the 1902–03 year before attending Columbia University, earning his MA in 1904.

Hall returned to Texas and began serving as a pastor in Hillsboro until 1906, when he became the educational secretary for TCU. In 1909, the new University Christian Church in Waco asked Hall to be their first full-time pastor. That same year he also married Beatrice Tomlinson, the daughter of TCU Trustee member T. E. Tomlinson, and they remained together until his death in 1963; she passed the following year, 1964.

After TCU returned to Fort Worth, Hall became a professor of Latin in 1912 and professor of English Bible in 1913; he also served as the part-time pastor of University Christian Church from 1912 to 1917. With the creation of Brite College of the Bible in 1914, Hall became the first dean, holding that position until 1947; Transylvania University awarded him the LLD degree in 1935. He also served as dean of the university from 1920 to 1943, and he continued as a professor of religion until his 1950 retirement. During his career, Hall wrote several religious books, but perhaps his most important work is the first history of TCU, *History of Texas Christian University: a College of the Cattle Frontier*, published by TCU Press in 1947.

In 1957 TCU built a women's dorm and named it in honor of Colby Hall. By 2015, it had been renovated and reopened in style, as the last renovated dorm on campus.

ABOVE
"Colby Dixon Hall," 1946. TCU Photgraph Collection, RU 53. Photo Number: 948. https://repository.tcu.edu:443/handle/116099117/3121. Courtesy of TCU Special Collections. Mary Couts Burnett Library. Texas Christian University.

OPPOSITE
Aerial view of campus taken in 1960 that shows Colby Hall. "Aerial View of Campus," 1960. TCU Photograph Collection. RU 53, Photo Number: 417. https://repository.tcu.edu:443/handle/116099117/2901. Courtesy of TCU Special Collections. Mary Couts Burnett Library. Texas Christian University.

OPPOSITE
"Image of Colby Hall in 1958," *The Horned Frog*, vol. 54. (Fort Worth: University Supply and Equipment Co., 1958), 36. https://repository.tcu.edu/handle/116099117/11084. Courtesy of TCU Archives and Special Collections. Mary Couts Burnett Library. Texas Christian University.

Colby D. Hall, the newest women's dormitory, is the home of TCU's ten sororities. Twelve kitchens, an elevator, a laundry room, and air-conditioning make the dorm a dream home for TCU co-eds.

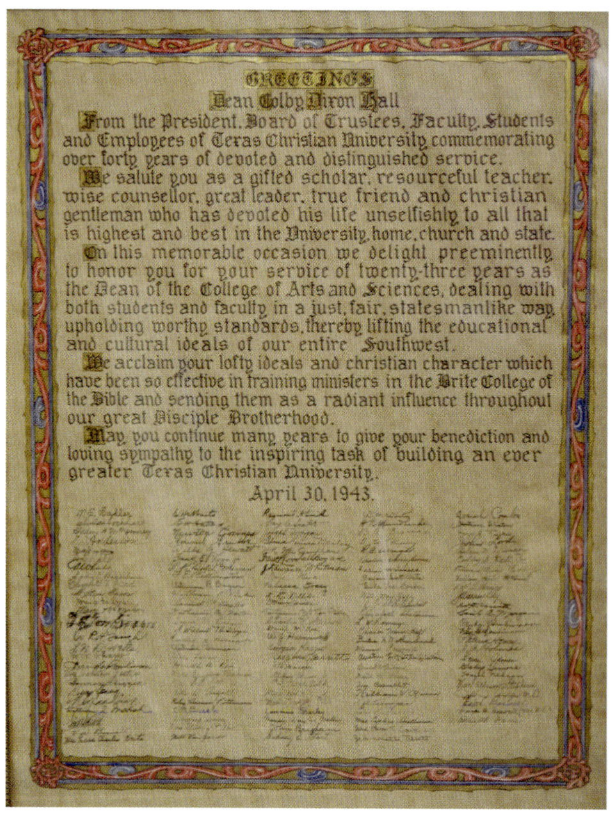

Greetings

Dean Colby Dixon Hall

From the President, Board of Trustees, Faculty, Students and Employees of Texas Christian University commemorating over forty years of devoted and distinguished service.

We salute you as a gifted scholar, resourceful teacher, wise counsellor, great leader, true friend and christian gentleman who has devoted his life unselfishly to all that is highest and best in the University, home, church and state.

On this memorable occasion we delight preeminently to honor you for your service of twenty-three years as the Dean of the College of Arts and Sciences, dealing with both students and faculty in a just, fair, statesmanlike way, upholding worthy standards, thereby lifting the educational and cultural ideals of our entire Southwest.

We acclaim your lofty ideals and christian character which have been so effective in training ministers in the Brite College of the Bible and sending them as a radiant influence throughout our great Disciple Brotherhood.

May you continue many years to give your benediction and loving sympathy to the inspiring task of building an ever greater Texas Christian University.

April 30, 1943.

ABOVE

Colby Hall seated behind his desk. "Colby Dixon Hall," 1943. TCU Photograph Collection, RU 53. Photo Number 1024. https://repository.tcu.edu:443/handle/116099117/2571. Courtesy of TCU Special Collections. Mary Couts Burnett Library. Texas Christian University.

RIGHT

Framed statement declaring "A Day to Honor the Contributions of Dean Colby Hall" on April 30, 1943. Day to Honor Contributions of Dean Colby Hall, "Dean Colby Hall with Signatures." TCU Permanent Collection. https://repository.tcu.edu/handle/116099117/14118. Courtesy of TCU Archives and Special Collections. Mary Couts Burnett Library. Texas Christian University.

ABOVE
"Brite College of the Bible," 1919. TCU Photograph Collection, RU 53. Photo Number: 548. https://repository.tcu.edu:443/handle/116099117/3064. Courtesy of TCU Special Collections. Mary Couts Burnett Library. Texas Christian University.

Brite College of the Bible

J. B. Sweeney received a BA from AddRan Christian University in 1885, then attended the College of the Bible in Lexington, Kentucky. After a successful pastorate in Taylor, Texas, he returned to AddRan in 1895 to create a Bible department in the university. From 1896 to 1900 it was listed as the Bible College in catalogs; from 1900 to 1914 it was listed as the College of the Bible; from 1914 to 1964 as the Brite College of the Bible; and after 1964 as the Brite Divinity School.

Brite College of the Bible was named after Marfa cattleman Lucas Charles Brite and his wife, who in 1911 donated $25,000 to the College of the Bible to create a Bible chair and build a suitable Bible building. Elected to the TCU Board of Trustees in 1912, Brite prepared a proposal for the education of ministerial students and a proposal that the College of the Bible be chartered as a separate corporation and receive a deed to the building to be constructed on the south end of campus. By 1914 the Brites had donated an additional $34,000 for the construction of the Bible building, which became the fifth building constructed on the modern TCU Fort Worth campus. Known as the Brite College of the Bible and built on the southeast corner of campus, perpendicular to Jarvis and Reed Halls, this facility represents the first TCU building to house a single academic program. For thirty-nine years—from its construction in 1914 until 1954—this building accommodated students who attended TCU to pursue degrees in religion and preaching. Designed by architects Sanguinet and Staats, who modeled the facility after the College of the Bible in Lexington, Kentucky, the building was constructed with traditional TCU buff-colored brick and cast stone and sported a flat roof with Tuscan columns. In 1954, Brite College of the Bible began the process of relocating into the newly constructed Robert Carr Chapel complex on the east side of University Drive. In 1963, it was renamed the Brite Divinity School.

ABOVE
The 1924 Girls' Glee Club at TCU in front of the TCU Administration Building. "Girls' Glee Club," 1924. TCU Photograph Collection, RU 53. Photograph Number: 990, PN Number: 595. https://repository.tcu.edu:443/handle/116099117/2167. Courtesy of TCU Special Collections. Mary Couts Burnett Library. Texas Christian University.

ABOVE (TOP)
"Brite College of the Bible," 1939. TCU Photograph. RU 53, Photo Number: 20. https://repository.tcu.edu/handle/116099117/6775. Courtesy of TCU Special Collections. Mary Couts Burnett Library. Texas Christian University.

ABOVE
Photo looking out through the door of Brite College of the Bible building. "Campus View," 1940.TCU Photograph Collection, RU 53. Photo Number: 523. https://repository.tcu.edu:443/handle/116099117/2885. Courtesy of TCU Special Collections. Mary Couts Burnett Library. Texas Christian University.

ABOVE
"Brite College of the Bible Faculty & Staff," 1937–1938. TCU Photograph Collection, RU 53. Photograph Number: 36. https://repository.tcu.edu/handle/116099117/6805. Courtesy of TCU Special Collections. Mary Couts Burnett Library. Texas Christian University.

RIGHT
"Bandstand and Jarvis Hall," 1923. TCU Photograph Collection, RU 53. Photo Number: 540, PN Number: 703. https://repository.tcu.edu:443/handle/116099117/2161. Courtesy of TCU Special Collections. Mary Couts Burnett Library. Texas Christian University.

RIGHT
"Memorial Arch," 1938. TCU Photograph Collection, RU 53. Photo Number: 530. https://repository.tcu.edu:443/handle/116099117/2238. Courtesy of TCU Special Collections. Mary Couts Burnett Library. Texas Christian University.

PAGE 116 (TOP)
The Memorial Columns after the expansion of University Drive that led to the relocation of the Memorial Arch. "Memorial Columns," 1947. TCU Photograph Collection, RU 53. Photo Number: 1905. https://repository.tcu.edu:443/handle/116099117/3817. Courtesy of TCU Special Collections. Mary Couts Burnett Library. Texas Christian University.

Memorial Arch

World War I began in June 1914 with the assassination of Austrian Archduke Franz Ferdinand in Sarajevo. While the war quickly enveloped Europe, the United States did not join the conflict until April 1917. "Uncle Sam" then recruited a generation of soldiers, including many enrolled in colleges like TCU, to go "Over There."

In September 1917 students started training under the War Department plan for the Students Army Training Corps (SATC). Clark Hall and a part of the Brite building served the SATC, and the only curriculum change included a course in European history listed as "War Aims." TCU men accepted into the program received free college tuition, room and board, uniforms, and the pay of a private.

Some 625 TCU alumni and students served in the American Expeditionary Force during the war, and six died in service to their country. Milus Little Jr., Herndon (Dick) Hardwick, and Aubrey Cooper died in combat, while Burton

Carpenter, Oscar Johnson, and Berthold E. Goebel died from training camp illnesses (likely Spanish Flu). Cooper became the first Fort Worth soldier to die in France on July 19, 1918; the 1916 TCU graduate's tombstone in Greenwood Cemetery includes a statement from Commander-in-Chief John J. Pershing, noting that Cooper received the "Distinguished Service Cross."

The Class of 1923 raised funds for a memorial arch in memory of those who served, dedicating it "to the men and women who served humanity" during World War I. The arch originally included two limestone Ionic columns supporting a flat, bricked arch embellished with an entablature containing relief panels of an eagle and cartouches. It also included special reference to three TCU students who died in combat.

When the city widened University Drive in 1949, the arch was relocated and redesigned into two columns (without the flat brick arch). The Memorial Arch has since been rededicated to all TCU students and alumni who have died during war. Special bronze plaques include the names of the dead from World Wars I and II, along with the names of the 1923 senior class.

BELOW
The TCU honor roll flag in 1919. "Honor Roll," *The Horned Frog*, vol. 15. (Reimers Company, 1919), 109. https://repository.tcu.edu/handle/116099117/11045. Courtesy of TCU Archives and Special Collections. Mary Couts Burnett Library. Texas Christian University.

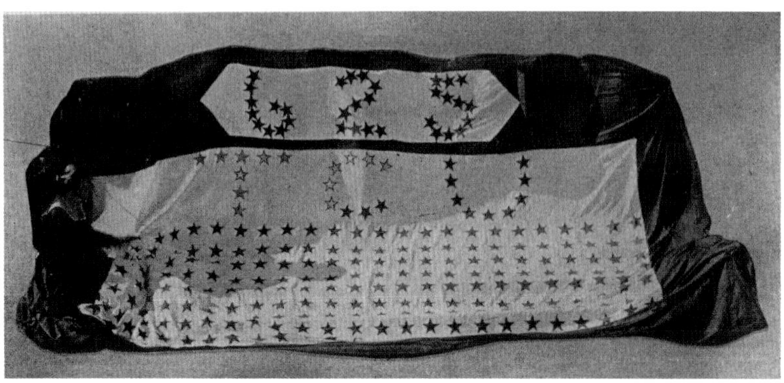

LEFT
The Memorial Arch with flagpole and TCU Administration Building in the background. "Memorial Arch," 1928. TCU Photograph Collection, RU 53. Photo Number: 2536. Sue Harvey Album. https://repository.tcu.edu/handle/116099117/6701. Courtesy of TCU Special Collections. Mary Couts Burnett Library. Texas Christian University.

PAGE 10 FORT WORTH STAR-TELEGRAM

—Star-Telegram Staff Photo.
NEW TCU MEMORIAL — Replacing the old Texas Christian University arch at the campus' main entrance on University Dr. is this new memorial, dedicated to the school's dead of both World Wars. Shown are Miss Pat Wilson, 2609 Frazier, junior student, and Reuben Batoon, graduate religion student and native of Luzon, Philippines.

ABOVE
The Memorial Column after the relocation of the Memorial Arch. "Article re: Memorial Columns," 1949. TCU Vertical Files, RU 32. September 2, 1949, *Fort Worth Star-Telegram* Article. https://repository.tcu.edu/handle/116099117/11989. Courtesy of TCU Archives and Special Collections. Mary Couts Burnett Library. Texas Christian University.

ABOVE
The Memorial Arch with Mary Couts Burnett Library in the background. "Memorial Arch," n.d. TCU Photograph Collection, RU 53. Photo Number: 958. https://repository.tcu.edu:443/handle/116099117/2580. Courtesy of TCU Special Collections. Mary Couts Burnett Library. Texas Christian University.

Literary Societies and Student Organizations

Literary Societies formed a vital part of TCU student experiences beginning with the university's inception. These student-led and faculty-sponsored groups offered students a chance to engage in intellectual expression outside of the classroom. The AddRan Literary Society (1874) and the Walton Literary Society (1877) represented the first two student clubs on campus. The clubs limited membership to only junior or senior men with faculty recommendations until 1886, when faculty leaders requested that these groups be open to both men and women.

In 1907, TCU literary societies again defined membership based on sex. Men could join either the AddRan or Shirley Societies, while women could join either the Clark or Walton Societies. The societies sponsored most intellectual activities and events on campus from the 1870s to the early 1920s. These groups collaborated and competed in debates, oratorical performances, plays, and musical performances, with each society vying for bragging rights.

By 1925, the literary societies voted to disband, and in their place a plethora of other student organizations expanded their membership and operations. The Brite College of the Bible Association, Timothy Club, YMCA, and YWCA represented religious organizations on campus. The academic honor societies Sigma Tau Delta (English), Pi Gamma Mu (Social Science), Alpha Zeta Pi (Romance Languages), and Parabola (Mathematics) all expanded membership to sponsor content-related contests. The Bio-Geo Club, Brushes, Bryson Literary Club, Dramatic Club, Debate and Oratory Clubs, and Dana Press Club replaced the literary societies as sponsors of art, debate, oratory, writing, and dramas on campus. The "T" Club and Women's Athletic Association established clubs for Horned Frog athletes. Students also organized a formal student government association during this period. Most consequentially, the Student Council forced TCU's administrators to sanction the first official school dance on May 26, 1934. The next year, over one hundred social events dotted student calendars. Today, numerous student organizations and societies continue to provide unique opportunities for student engagement and development.

OPPOSITE
"TCU T Association," 1920s. TCU Photograph Collection, RU 53. Photo Number: 2231, PN Number: 591. https://repository.tcu.edu:443/handle/116099117/3143. Courtesy of TCU Special Collections. Mary Couts Burnett Library. Texas Christian University.

RIGHT
Newton Bell, operating camera, and Gaines Sparks taking photographs for the Parabola Club. "Parabola Student Organization." *The Horned Frog*, vol. 30. (Fort Worth: Stafford-Lowdon Co., 1934), 196. https://repository.tcu.edu/handle/116099117/11060. Courtesy of TCU Archives and Special Collections. Mary Couts Burnett Library. Texas Christian University.

LEFT
1934 student body officers, from left to right: Mary Jarvis, secretary-treasurer; Roy O'Brien, president; and Lynn Brown, vice president. "Student Body Officers: Miss Mary Jarvis, Roy O'Brien, and Lynn Brown," *The Horned Frog*, vol. 30. (Fort Worth: Stafford-Lowdon Co., 1934), 34. https://repository.tcu.edu/handle/116099117/11060. Courtesy of TCU Archives and Special Collections. Mary Couts Burnett Library. Texas Christian University.

ABOVE (TOP)
"The Outcast Student Organization." *The Horned Frog*, vol. 30. (Fort Worth: Stafford-Lowdon Co., 1934), 189. https://repository.tcu.edu/handle/116099117/11060. Courtesy of TCU Archives and Special Collections. Mary Couts Burnett Library. Texas Christian University.

ABOVE
The Sixth Annual Popularity Revue Dance. "Horned Frog Sixth Annual Popularity Revue," *The Horned Frog*, vol. 32. (Fort Worth: Stafford-Lowdon Co., 1936), 158. https://repository.tcu.edu/handle/116099117/11062. Courtesy of TCU Archives and Special Collections. Mary Couts Burnett Library. Texas Christian University.

ABOVE
The south entrance to the TCU Administration Building blocked with a car by students celebrating the school's football victory over Temple at Philadelphia. Photo taken on October 7, 1938. AR406-6-793. Courtesy, *Fort Worth Star-Telegram Collection*, Special Collections, The University of Texas at Arlington Libraries.

ABOVE
The Brushes student organization, from left to right: Professor Samuel P. Ziegler, Mary Jo Merkt, Izzy Ackerman, Helen Woods, Helen Woolery, and others. "The Brushes Student Organization." *The Horned Frog*, vol. 30. (Fort Worth: Stafford-Lowdon Co., 1934), 193. https://repository.tcu.edu/handle/116099117/11060. Courtesy of TCU Archives and Special Collections. Mary Couts Burnett Library. Texas Christian University.

History Professor and Mayor of Fort Worth

Born in Red Oak, Texas, on October 21, 1896, William Jackson (Jack) Hammond (1896–1966) enrolled at TCU in 1915. When the US entered World War I, Hammond enlisted in the army and served in France from 1917–1919. While there, he studied at the Sorbonne for a year before returning to study at TCU. While completing his coursework at TCU, Hammond served as a student pastor in Christian Churches in Dallas, Iowa Park, and Fort Worth. Graduating with his BA and MA, he became an instructor of history at TCU before completing his PhD in 1929 at the University of California in Berkeley.

Hammond returned to Fort Worth in 1929 to teach Latin American and American Indian history at TCU. He became a full professor in 1934 and was chairman of the History Department until 1963.

Hammond also participated in local politics. From 1935–1937 he served as a Fort Worth Councilman for the Progressive Democratic Party. A self-described FDR "New Dealer," he sought and won the office of city mayor in 1937, serving but one year in office. His term in office was fraught with controversy over his social and liberal programs, which stressed human values. Interested in civic issues such as public housing, jail reform, and crime prevention, he challenged Fort Worth's corrupt politics. He successfully advocated for the creation of a city hospital and public library, but his tenure ended with a political dispute over parking meter prices in Fort Worth. This dispute forced Hammond to choose between teaching and politics.

He chose to teach, resigning as mayor in 1938, although he remained active in the American Legion, Tarrant County Democratic Club, and Roosevelt Democrats in Texas. Returning to TCU, as a faculty mentor he sponsored student organizations like Young Democrat and Young Republican Clubs. Known as a very compassionate and knowledgeable teacher, he remained at TCU until he died of a heart attack in June 1966.

In 1973 the TCU Board of Trustees passed a resolution preventing faculty and staff from holding political office without taking an unpaid leave of absence. Undoubtedly, history professors Cockrell and Hammond serving as mayor of Fort Worth influenced that decision.

ABOVE
"Mayor W. J. Hammond," 1930–1939. Fort Worth Mayors, Box 1. Courtesy of the Genealogy, History and Archives Unit, Fort Worth Public Library.

ABOVE
Fort Worth parking meter. Photo taken on December 12, 1939. AR406-6-1088. Courtesy, *Fort Worth Star-Telegram Collection*, Special Collections, The University of Texas at Arlington Libraries.

RIGHT
"Downtown Fort Worth," 1928 or 1929. Historic Photograph Collection, Street Scenes. Courtesy of the Genealogy, History and Archives Unit, Fort Worth Public Library.

ABOVE
William J. Hammond and Margaret F. Hammond. *La Réunion, a French Settlement in Texas*.(Dallas: Royal Publishing Co., 1958).

ABOVE
"William Jackson Hammond," n.d. TCU Photograph Collection, RU 53. Photo Number: 321. https://repository.tcu.edu:443/handle/116099117/2592. Courtesy of TCU Special Collections. Mary Couts Burnett Library. Texas Christian University.

TCU and Music

Various musical organizations and clubs decorate TCU's history. As early as 1908, the university had ten different musical societies. By 1930, the number of clubs expanded further to include organizations such as the Horned Frog Band, TCU Music Club, Radio Players, Choral Club, Glee Club, Quartettes, and the TCU Orchestra. These clubs formed a robust part of TCU's continued growth as an artistic and intellectual community.

The Men's and Women's Glee Clubs performed at campus events beginning in 1898, but their membership remained limited until the 1930s, when an enlarged music faculty provided greater expertise and opportunities. The famed Professor William J. Marsh, who composed the Texas state song "Texas, Our Texas" in 1924, oversaw the Glee Club's expansion and orchestrated national and regional tours. Each year students earned places in the clubs via competitive tryouts. The clubs then practiced at least once a week in preparation for an annual Christmas Program and Spring tour that visited cities such as Abilene, Amarillo, Dallas, El Paso, Houston, Lubbock, Midland, Kansas City, Oklahoma City, Texarkana, and Tulsa. The glee club even performed at the 1939 World's Fair in New York City. In 1941, Melvin Dacus, a TCU freshman, kept a scrapbook of the Glee Club's West Texas tour, and the photos illustrate the community forged between faculty and students through musical performance.

Charles V. Kirkpatrick formed the Horned Frog Band in 1904 as the university's military band. The band maintained a small presence on campus until 1925, when Claude Sammis organized regular practice sessions and performances. By 1926, the Horned Frog Band played a series of concerts and served in the opening festivities for the annual Southwestern Exposition and Fat Stock Show. Amon Carter and TCU soon sponsored travel arrangements for the band to perform at away football games. The Horned Frog Band performed at games in Austin, Dallas, Houston, Los Angeles, New Orleans, New York City, and Shreveport during the 1930s. James Jacobsen directed the band beginning in 1955 and introduced the "moving diamond" drill move that has since become a staple of marching band repertoires. Today, the band continues to offer exhilarating pregame and halftime performances that enhance and strengthen TCU's atmosphere and traditions.

ABOVE
Portrait of William J. Marsh, music professor at TCU.
"William J. Marsh," c1930. Lyons Photography Collection, Box 2. Courtesy of the Genealogy, History and Archives Unit, Fort Worth Public Library.

ABOVE
TCU Women's Quartette. TCU Scrapbook Collection, RU 8, Box 35, Folder 9. "Student Life, 1920-1947." Courtesy of TCU Archives and Special Collections. Mary Couts Burnett Library. Texas Christian University.

LEFT
"Men's Glee Club," 1932. TCU Photograph Collection, RU 53. https://repository.tcu.edu/handle/116099117/11791. Courtesy of TCU Special Collections. Mary Couts Burnett Library. Texas Christian University.

LEFT
The Froggie Flag Twirlers were added to the band in 1946. From left to right: Betty Lou Hitson, Marion Graham, Billie Louise Rippeton, Betty Benton, and Jean Hill. Photo taken on November 22, 1946. AR406-6-1884. Courtesy, *Fort Worth Star-Telegram Collection*, Special Collections, The University of Texas at Arlington Libraries.

LEFT
Amon G. Carter with TCU band in California before Frogs played at the Rose Bowl Stadium. Photo taken in September 1939. File AR 406-6 Carter Files. Courtesy, *Fort Worth Star-Telegram Collection*, Special Collections, The University of Texas at Arlington Libraries.

RIGHT
TCU Men's Quartette.
TCU Scrapbook Collection, RU 8, Box 35, Folder 9. "Student Life, 1920-1947." Courtesy of TCU Archives and Special Collections. Mary Couts Burnett Library. Texas Christian University.

ABOVE
The 1934 TCU Marching Band. "TCU Marching Band." *The Horned Frog*, vol. 30. (Fort Worth: Stafford-Lowdon Co., 1934), 204. https://repository.tcu.edu/handle/116099117/11060. Courtesy of TCU Archives and Special Collections. Mary Couts Burnett Library. Texas Christian University.

ABOVE
"Women's Glee Club," 1925. TCU Photograph Collection, RU 53. Photo Number: 1231. https://repository.tcu.edu:443/handle/116099117/2378. Courtesy of TCU Special Collections. Mary Couts Burnett Library. Texas Christian University.

LEFT
TCU students and glee club members at Palo Duro Canyon. TCU Scrapbook Collection, RU 8, Box 6, Folder 35. "TCU Glee Club, 1940-1947." Courtesy of TCU Archives and Special Collections. Mary Couts Burnett Library. Texas Christian University.

LEFT
"Crowds watch the Texas Christian University Horned Frog Band march in Fort Worth's All America City Parade, May 17, 1965." Courtesy, *Fort Worth Star-Telegram Collection*, Special Collections, The University of Texas at Arlington Libraries.

RIGHT
This is TCU Magazine "Strike up the Band." TCU Special Collections. TCU Scrapbook Collection, Record Unit 8, Box 39, Folder 50; "President Sadler & New Buildings, 1958-1962." Courtesy of TCU Archives and Special Collections. Mary Couts Burnett Library. Texas Christian University.

TCU BAND Director Jim Jacobsen

Strike Up the Band!

PHOTOGRAPHY BY BOB BULLOCK '60

THE FIRST YEAR the TCU Horned Frog Band was formed, its only bass drummer nonchalantly withdrew in mid-season to become star of the baseball team! That was 1905 when the band consisted primarily of those boys who had a little extra time and wanted to blow a horn or beat a drum. Director of this first band was Arnold Kirkpatrick

Now, 54 years later, the polished 120-member Horned Frog Band is truly the "Show Window of TCU" as its slogan states.

Current members have come to the university from 13 states, including Texas, Florida, Arkansas, California, Oklahoma, Pennsylvania, Mississippi, Ohio, Missouri, Louisiana, Kansas, Colorado and North Carolina.

UNDER THE DIRECTION of Jim Jacobsen, the band plays upwards of 70 performances a year. It was featured on national television in the half-time show of the Cotton Bowl last New Year's Day in Dallas, when the TCU football team met with the fledgling Air Force Academy Falcons.

An exponent of the cadence-must-match-the-music school of marching, Director Jacobsen sets a varied pattern for the band, anywhere from 90 to 210 steps per minute, depending on the character of the music.

Actually, there are four distinctive units in the TCU department of bands: the marching band, the concert band, the symphonic band and the stage band.

When the football season is past, the marching band takes a back seat and the other groups take over. An

ABOVE
The TCU Horned Frog Marching Band in 1956. "Untitled," 1956. TCU Photograph Collection, RU 53. Photo Number: 2338. https://repository.tcu.edu:443/handle/116099117/3592. Courtesy of TCU Special Collections. Mary Couts Burnett Library. Texas Christian University.

Amon Carter Stadium

The development of the TCU campus began to take shape after 1911. In 1916 TCU acquired land east of University Drive to Lubbock Street, and between Lowden and Bowie Streets, and began using this space for athletic fields. The newly christened Clark Field would become the new home of TCU football, and by 1924 wooden bleachers of twenty-five tiers had been erected.

The 1920 TCU team surprisingly earned a 9-0 record; L. R. (Dutch) Meyer played on that team. Because of the success of those early 1920s teams, TCU received an invitation and joined the Southwest Conference in 1923. Increased attendance necessitated additional seating, including the use of movable stands in the end zone. On October 22, 1927, the Clark Field stands spilled over with twenty thousand-plus fans as TCU hosted and tied Texas A&M in the "biggest sports event in Fort Worth's history." This convinced the TCU board that the stadium needed to be enlarged.

TCU earned an 8-2 record in 1928. The following year, the Horned Frogs beat the University of Texas 15-12 for the first time ever, won the SWC title with a 7-7 tie against SMU at Clark Field's last game, and finished with a 9-0-1 record. The football success and throngs of fans convinced Fort Worth newspaperman and advocate Amon G. Carter that TCU football and Fort Worth's fortunes were interconnected. He agreed to spearhead the building of a new stadium and threw his money and personality into promoting the football team.

On October 11, 1930, TCU defeated the University of Arkansas Razorbacks 40-0 in the newly opened $350,000 Amon G. Carter Stadium. Homecoming that year against the University of Texas resulted in twenty thousand-plus fans, even though TCU lost 7-0. But TCU and Fort Worth fans were satisfied with the new stadium, and within ten years the university had won three SWC championships (1929, 1932, 1938), won games in the Sugar Bowl (1936) and Cotton Bowl (1937), and won the 1938 national championship with the fourth Heisman Trophy winner David (Davey) O'Brien.

OPPOSITE
Aerial photograph of Amon G. Carter Stadium in 1957. "TCU Campus," 1957. TCU Photograph Collection, RU 53. Photo Number: 62. https://repository.tcu.edu/handle/116099117/6663. Courtesy of TCU Special Collections. Mary Couts Burnett Library. Texas Christian University.

RIGHT
Newspaper Clipping, "Artist Sees Athletic Amphitheater." TCU Scrapbook Collection, Record Unit 8, Box 10, Folder 29; "Society and Athletics, 1937." Courtesy of TCU Archives and Special Collections. Mary Couts Burnett Library. Texas Christian University.

BELOW
Architectural sketch of the west stands' addition by Wyatt C. Hendrick. "West Stands Additions Amon Carter Stadium," Artist's Rendition by Wyatt C. Hendrick. https://repository.tcu.edu/handle/116099117/14078. Courtesy of TCU Archives and Special Collections. Mary Couts Burnett Library. Texas Christian University.

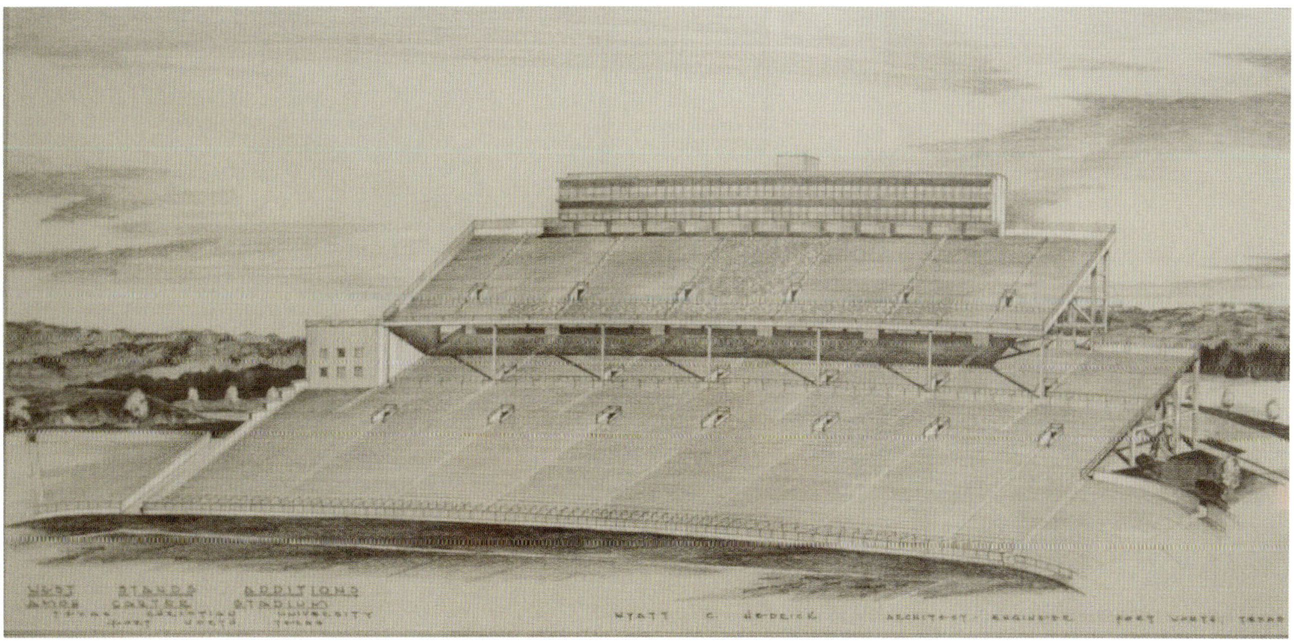

RIGHT
Aerial photograph of Clark Field during a 1930 TCU football game. "Clark Field Stadium," 1930. TCU Photograph Collection, RU 53. Photo Number: 2208. https://repository.tcu.edu:443/handle/116099117/3315. Courtesy of TCU Special Collections. Mary Couts Burnett Library. Texas Christian University.

OPPOSITE
"Leo R. 'Dutch' Meyer," n.d. TCU Photograph Collection, RU 53. Photo Number: 2488. https://repository.tcu.edu:443/handle/116099117/2557. Courtesy of TCU Special Collections. Mary Couts Burnett Library. Texas Christian University.

Football Puts TCU on the Map

Surprisingly, TCU has never named an athletic facility for Paul O. Williamson. A statue of national championship-winning coach L. R. "Dutch" Meyer and his star quarterback Sam Baugh greet fans as they enter Amon G. Carter Stadium. Meyer and Baugh certainly did their part to put Horned Frog Football on the map, but it was Williamson whose rating system was the standard of the day, and his calculations resulted in a No. 1 ranking for TCU in 1935.

The TCU Frogs were vaulted into national recognition thanks to Williamson. The following season, however, the Associated Press poll became the ranking system of record that determined the final No. 1 team. It has been either the deciding authority, or part of it, ever since.

The '35 TCU team featured Baugh, a future College and Pro Football Hall of Fame charter member, at quarterback, punter, and defensive back. The University of Chicago's Jay Berwanger won the Heisman Trophy for his efforts during the 1935 season, which was the first year that award was given. But Baugh has long been regarded as the most revolutionary quarterback of his generation for his ability to pass the ball. TCU went 12-1 in 1935, as did SMU, who beat TCU 20-14 on November 30 to claim the Southwest Conference title. The Frogs rebounded in the Sugar Bowl, beating LSU 3-2, while SMU lost to Stanford 7-0 in the Rose Bowl. Baugh threw eighteen touchdowns in '35, and passed for 1,241 yards.

The Frogs remained on the radar of college football pundits, and unanimously earned the national championship in 1938 behind an undefeated record (11-0) and wily quarterback Davey O'Brien. O'Brien was awarded the Heisman Trophy in 1938, and threw for 1,457 yards and nineteen touchdowns. The Frogs beat Carnegie Tech 15-7 in the Sugar Bowl.

SAM 'PASSES' IN CLASSROOM, TOO!

Sammy Baugh, T. C. U.'s sensational grid star gives those classroom chores quite a beating, too. Sam will have you know that he's a B student—and hopes to remain that way. Here he's seen poring over one of his books. (Star-Telegram Photo.)

RIGHT
Newspaper Article, "Sam 'Passes' in Classroom Too!" TCU Special Collections. TCU Scrapbook Collection, RU 8, Box 20, Folder 25. Scrapbook no. 9. "TCU Athletics, 1936 vol. 2." Courtesy of TCU Archives and Special Collections. Mary Couts Burnett Library. Texas Christian University.

FAR RIGHT
"Davey O'Brien," 1939. TCU Photograph Collection, RU 53. Photo Number: 2484. https://repository.tcu.edu:443/handle/116099117/2908. Courtesy of TCU Special Collections. Mary Couts Burnett Library. Texas Christian University.

ABOVE
"Davey O'Brien receiving Heisman Trophy," 1938. Courtesy of TCU Athletics.

RIGHT
Newspaper Cartoon, "Little Goldilocks TCU vs. Baylor Bears." TCU Scrapbook Collection, RU 8, Box 16, Folder 32. Scrapbook no. 15. "TCU Sports Scrapbook, Vol. 1 1938." Courtesy of TCU Archives and Special Collections. Mary Couts Burnett Library. Texas Christian University.

ABOVE

Texas Christian University football players gnawing on bones from a steer. Left to right are Glynn (Bull) Rogers, Ki Aldrich, Henry Swain, and I. B. Hale. Photo taken on October 5, 1937. AR406-6-525. Courtesy, *Fort Worth Star-Telegram Collection*, Special Collections, The University of Texas at Arlington Libraries.

LEFT

"Amon G. Carter Stadium," 1940s. TCU Photograph Collection, RU 53. Photo Number: 4. https://repository.tcu.edu:443/handle/116099117/3420. Courtesy of TCU Special Collections. Mary Couts Burnett Library. Texas Christian University.

Golden Gloves and Fencing

In February 1933, the TCU Ex-Students Association sponsored a performance of *Romeo and Juliet* on campus. William Gonder, who directed the play, enlisted the aid of Hermann Beckmann to make the dueling scenes as choreographed as possible. Beckmann instructed members of the cast in the art of fencing. He inadvertently started a new sport on campus. By September 1933, students formed men's and women's fencing clubs with Milli Faeris chosen as president of the women's club. The Women's Athletic Association frequently sponsored public fencing exhibitions on campus. In September 1935, TCU's intramural sports program appointed Travis Griffin, a TCU freshman and Southwest Fencing Champion, to teach fencing classes six days a week on campus. Beginning in December 1935, TCU's fencing teams competed against local YMCA, YWCA, and SMU teams. Richard Oliver won the inaugural TCU fencing tournament in March 1936 at the price of his pants. During the semifinal and final, his opponents poked off the buttons on his trousers and made a series of slices in the back of his pants that when combined were a yard long. In 1939, Florence Beheler, a TCU freshman, won the state fencing title as an individual and inspired the squad to the overall team title.

Simultaneously, TCU students added campus boxing tournaments to the intramural sports calendar. In 1934, students founded the annual Intramural Open House as a championship night for all spring intramural sports. By 1936, students in boxing squared off in six different weight classes. Organizers structured the tournament to hold semifinal bouts on Wednesday evenings before holding the championships at 9:00 p.m. on Saturday in the TCU gymnasium. Several fights, such as the 1937 scrap between Bobby Bass and O. A. Ritchie, almost brought the gymnasium down with bell-to-bell action and nearly five hundred screaming spectators. During this period, several TCU student champions entered the Fort Worth Golden Gloves tournament and emerged victorious. Glynn "Bull" Rogers won the 1936 and 1937 heavyweight crowns. Buster Nicks won the 1940 light-heavyweight title. The 1946 and 1947 TCU Boxing Teams even won the Fort Worth District Team Trophies. Paul Peebles (1959 and 1960), Brooks Hill (1962), Bud Deerinwater (1967), and Dan Burns (1971) later won regional Golden Gloves titles as TCU students.

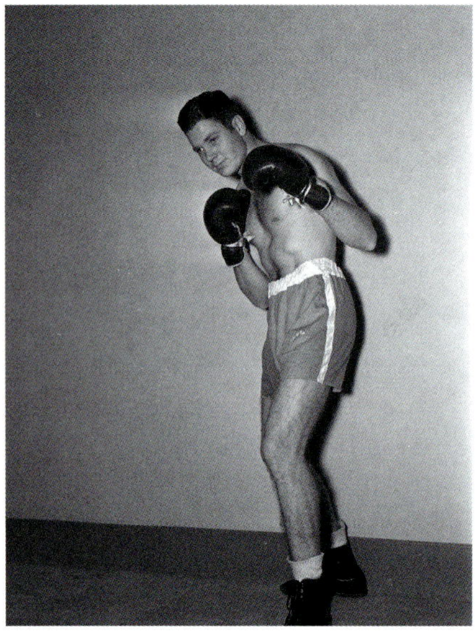

LEFT
Travis Griffin, an athlete from TCU, who competed in Fort Worth's Golden Gloves light-heavyweight division at Panther City Arena. Photo taken on January 4, 1938. AR406-6-989. Courtesy, *Fort Worth Star-Telegram Collection*, Special Collections, The University of Texas at Arlington Libraries.

Win Southwest Fencing Title Fourth Time in Six Years

April 1940

Frogs Will Play Longhorn Nine Here on Saturday

S.T. April 29, 1940

The T. C. U. baseballers, victors over Rice in two games last week-end to climb out of the Southwest Conference cellar, will face the mighty Texas Longhorns here Saturday.

Six games are on the docket for

The Frogs have now won four games and lost six and are only two games behind A. & M. in second place. Interest in the race seems likely to center on this battle for second position, with all teams but Rice having a chance.

In the opinion of Jack Wilson, the brawny Baylor athlete, shot putting is the most "comfortable" of sports. Besides throwing the shot, Jack heaves the javelin and plays a rough-house game at halfback in football. "I guess I get more bruises than

BELOW
Photo of 1940 TCU Women Fencing Champions. "Win Southwest Fencing Title Fourth Time in Six Years." Newspaper Article. TCU Scrapbook Collection, RU 8. Box 6, Folder 34. Scrapbook no. 17. "Athletics, Faculty, and Memorials, 1939-1940." Courtesy of TCU Archives and Special Collections. Mary Couts Burnett Library. Texas Christian University.

SHE'S TOPS IN SOUTHWEST

The Southwest's leading feminine fencer is Paula Murchison, above, T. C. U. freshman, who won the Southwestern foils title at the Mardi Gras meet in New Orleans recently. Miss Murchison is due to appear on the Intramural Open House program at T. C. U. Friday night.—Star-Telegram Photo.

ABOVE
The original gymnasium on the TCU campus. "Gymnasium," 1922. TCU Special Collections. TCU Photograph Collection, RU 53, Photo Number: 123. https://repository.tcu.edu:443/handle/116099117/3683. Courtesy of TCU Special Collections. Mary Couts Burnett Library. Texas Christian University.

RIGHT
"She's Tops in Southwest" newspaper article about Paula Murchison, TCU student who won the Southwest Fencing Championship in 1940. TCU Scrapbook Collection, RU 8, Box 6, Folder 34. Scrapbook no. 17. "Athletics, Faculty, and Memorials, 1939-1940." Courtesy of TCU Archives and Special Collections. Mary Couts Burnett Library. Texas Christian University.

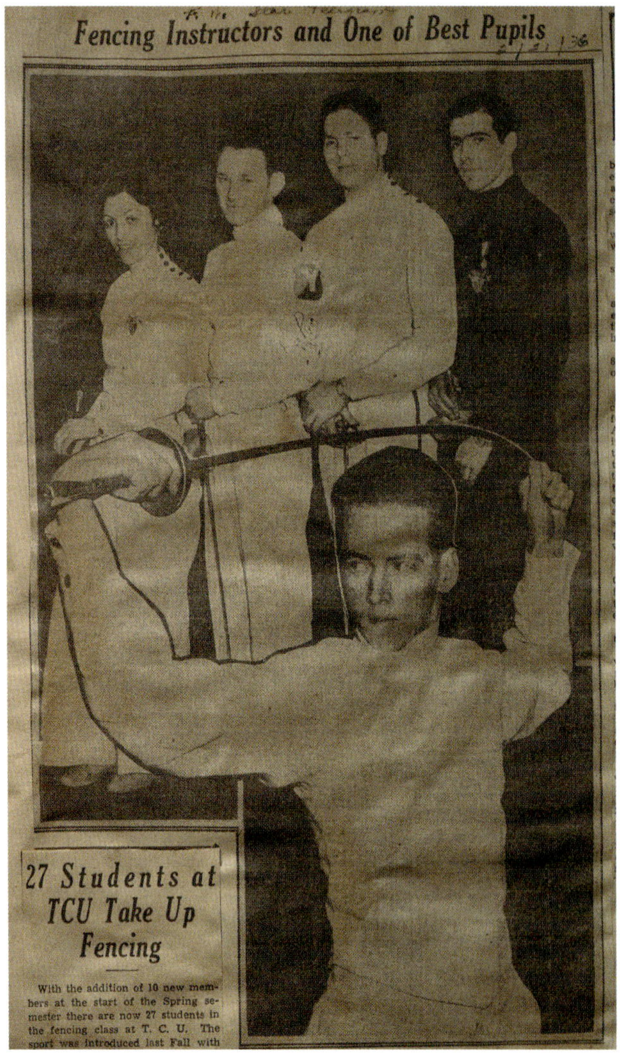

Fencing Instructors and One of Best Pupils

27 Students at TCU Take Up Fencing

With the addition of 10 new members at the start of the Spring semester there are now 27 students in the fencing class at T. C. U. The sport was introduced last Fall with

ABOVE
Bull Rogers and Travis Griffin, athletes from TCU, warming up before competing in Fort Worth's Golden Gloves at Panther City Arena. Photo taken on January 4, 1938. AR406-6-989. Courtesy, *Fort Worth Star-Telegram Collection*, Special Collections, The University of Texas at Arlington Libraries.

ABOVE (RIGHT)
Heavyweight bout at Golden Gloves Tournament at Panther City Arena; Bull Rogers, TCU football player, lands a punch on Dan Loos, also of TCU. Photo taken on January 17, 1938. AR406-6-989. Courtesy, *Fort Worth Star-Telegram Collection*, Special Collections, The University of Texas at Arlington Libraries.

RIGHT
Newspaper Article "27 Students at TCU take up Fencing" and Photo of "Fencing Instructors and One of Best Pupils." TCU Scrapbook Collection, RU 8, Box 19, Folder 24. Scrapbook no. 8. "TCU Athletics 1936, vol. 1. Courtesy of TCU Archives and Special Collections. Mary Couts Burnett Library. Texas Christian University.

ABOVE
1951 TCU Evening College Council. "Evening College Council." *The Horned Frog*, vol. 47. (Fort Worth: Stafford-Lowdon Co., 1951), 275. https://repository.tcu.edu/handle/116099117/11077. Courtesy of TCU Archives and Special Collections. Mary Couts Burnett Library. Texas Christian University.

ABOVE
TCU management seminar held in the Neeley School of Businessin 1964. "Neeley School of Business," 1964. TCU Photograph Collection, RU 53. Raw Files, TCU Management Seminar. https://repository.tcu.edu/handle/116099117/6742. Courtesy of TCU Special Collections. Mary Couts Burnett Library. Texas Christian University.

ABOVE
"Administration Building," 1930s. TCU Photograph Collection, RU 53. https://repository.tcu.edu/handle/116099117/12235. Courtesy of TCU Special Collections. Mary Couts Burnett Library. Texas Christian University.

ABOVE
Former TCU President Edward McShane Waits. "Edward McShane Waits," 1946. TCU Photograph Collection, RU 53. Photo Number: 256. https://repository.tcu.edu:443/handle/116099117/2420. Courtesy of TCU Special Collections. Mary Couts Burnett Library. Texas Christian University.

LEFT
"Alvord L. Boeck, Head of Business Administration." *The Horned Frog*, vol. 32. (Fort Worth: Stafford-Lowdon Co., 1936), 24. https://repository.tcu.edu/handle/116099117/11062. Courtesy of TCU Archives and Special Collections. Mary Couts Burnett Library. Texas Christian University.

CHAPTER 5

Construction and Expansion: 1941–1961

McGruder Ellis Sadler and Development of TCU

Born on November 5, 1896, in Hobucken, North Carolina, McGruder Ellis Sadler earned a BA degree from Atlantic Christian College, an MA from Vanderbilt University, and a PhD from Yale University. During his early career, Sadler held positions in religious education with several organizations, including the Rockefeller Foundation. In 1941, TCU selected him to be the sixth president of the university. He served until 1965.

Sadler brought the organizational energy TCU needed to gain national recognition. In 1943, he reorganized TCU into seven schools and colleges (Brite College of the Bible, School of Business, School of Education, Graduate School, School of Fine Arts, Evening College, and AddRan College of Arts and Sciences), and in 1946 added an eighth (Harris College of Nursing). He instituted a construction program to meet the space demands of increasing enrollment. He frequently spoke to groups across Texas and the country to encourage interest in TCU, to increase enrollment, and to raise funds to strengthen the academic mission and faculty compensation. Sadler also permitted the establishment of Greek societies (eight fraternities and eight sororities) and construction of new dorms to bolster enrollment. As a progressive-minded leader, Sadler announced in November 1951 that Black students had been attending the TCU Evening College since 1942.

LEFT
McGruder Ellis Sadler standing next to car with his family after arriving at TCU. "McGruder Ellis Sadler Family," 1941. TCU Photograph Collection, RU 53. Photo Number: 470. https://repository.tcu.edu:443/handle/116099117/3506. Courtesy of TCU Special Collections. Mary Couts Burnett Library. Texas Christian University.

ABOVE
Chancellor Sadler standing in front of Sadler Hall during its construction. "M. E. Sadler Hall," 1959–1960. TCU Photograph Collection, RU 53. Photo Number: 1921. https://repository.tcu.edu:443/handle/116099117/2191. Courtesy of TCU Special Collections. Mary Couts Burnett Library. Texas Christian University.

During his presidency, Sadler oversaw the creation of TCU's first six PhD programs in AddRan College of Arts and Sciences (psychology, physics, English, mathematics, chemistry, and history), expansion of the Evening College aimed at adult education, the Institute of Behavioral Research, and the Ranch Management Program, which offered classroom instruction combined with field study of ranching operations. In October 1956, with financial support from the Ford Foundation, Sadler's administration placed all full-time faculty on twelve months' salary, which guaranteed at least six weeks of summer work. He also increased faculty retirement contributions to 11.5 percent of their salary, believing faculty should have the same retirement as the Disciples of Christ ministers. During Sadler's tenure, his title changed from president to chancellor. He increased enrollment from 1,800 to more than 8,500, grew the endowment from about $5 million to an estimated $20 million, and saw the completion of nineteen major buildings, completely renovating and modernizing the TCU campus. He was the most successful leader in TCU's history.

ABOVE

"Sadler Hall," 1940s. TCU Photograph Collection, RU 53. Photo Number: 1884, PN Number: 601. https://repository.tcu.edu:443/handle/116099117/3304. Courtesy of TCU Special Collections. Mary Couts Burnett Library. Texas Christian University.

LEFT

President Sadler (left) next to TCU Coach "Dutch" Meyer. "Leo R. 'Dutch' Meyer and M. E. Sadler," 1950–1951. TCU Photograph Collection, RU 53. Photo Number: 421. https://repository.tcu.edu:443/handle/116099117/3325. Courtesy of TCU Special Collections. Mary Couts Burnett Library. Texas Christian University.

ABOVE
Chancellor Sadler (left) next to future Chancellor James Moudy after the 1965 Spring Commencement. "James M. Moudy and M. E. Sadler," 1965. TCU Photograph Collection, RU 53. Photo Number: 399. https://repository.tcu.edu:443/handle/116099117/3422. Courtesy of TCU Special Collections. Mary Couts Burnett Library. Texas Christian University.

RIGHT
"McGruder Ellis Sadler," 1959. TCU Photograph Collection, RU 53. Photo Number: 1967, PN Number: 507. https://repository.tcu.edu:443/handle/116099117/3379. Courtesy of TCU Special Collections. Mary Couts Burnett Library. Texas Christian University.

ABOVE
"McGruder Ellis Sadler," 1940s. TCU Photograph Collection, RU 53. Photo Number: 1993. https://repository.tcu.edu:443/handle/116099117/3498. Courtesy of TCU Special Collections. Mary Couts Burnett Library. Texas Christian University.

LEFT
President McGruder Ellis Sadler (right) shaking hands with Dean Colby Hall while former TCU President Edward McShane Waits looks on. "Colby Hall, E. M. Waits, & M. E. Sadler," 1941. TCU Photograph Collection, RU 53. Photo Number: 394. https://repository.tcu.edu:443/handle/116099117/2879. Courtesy of TCU Special Collections. Mary Couts Burnett Library. Texas Christian University.

TCU and World War II

The US entrance into World War II and the preceding Selective Service Act brought change to TCU. One policy change permitted degrees to be conferred to seniors who were drafted in their final semester. Other drafted students received full credit for the term they were drafted, if they had completed half the semester. The Registrar's Office kept a roster of the 1,324 students who served in the conflict, which included fifty-nine chaplains.

Lt. James Mecaskey, who had played as a reserve on the 1939–1940 TCU football team, reportedly was the first TCU student to die in the war. Leaving school, he had volunteered for the Army Air Force as a bomber pilot, and during the spring of 1942 while fighting Germans in North Africa, his plane went down in Egypt. The university ultimately held three memorial services, 1943–1946, honoring the fifty-nine students and alumni who died in the war.

TCU temporarily changed its academic schedule, dividing the year into trimesters, beginning July 1, November 1, and March 1, which accommodated the requirements of the US Navy's V-12 program. Summer school offerings were expanded with three-week terms and eight-week terms.

Even campus organizations continued operating, although restricted by shortages of paper and film. The *Horned Frog* yearbook appeared during the war because photographers Mr. and Mrs. Allen Orgain allocated their film rations during the war to the yearbook. The *Skiff* continued publication, often printing stories on the war and on the service of former students. The women of the TCU Orchestra and various glee clubs frequently presented concerts for servicemen. In 1943, because of the shortage of men on campus, females were admitted to band for the first time. Students also made generous contributions after 1942 to the Frog War Fund, which supported the Red Cross, the World Student Services Fund, and the Fort Worth War Chest. Campus drives for war bonds occurred annually, and President Sadler noted that TCU strongly supported the war. Even so, rationing and shortages affected all facets of life and travel, and many of these remained when the war ended.

RIGHT
Chaplain James Gary Jones, who graduated with a bachelor of divinity from TCU in 1939. The photo was taken in Cairo in 1943. "James Gary Jones," 1943. TCU Photograph Collection, RU 53. Photo Number: 1728. https://repository.tcu.edu:443/handle/116099117/3751. Courtesy of TCU Special Collections. Mary Couts Burnett Library. Texas Christian University.

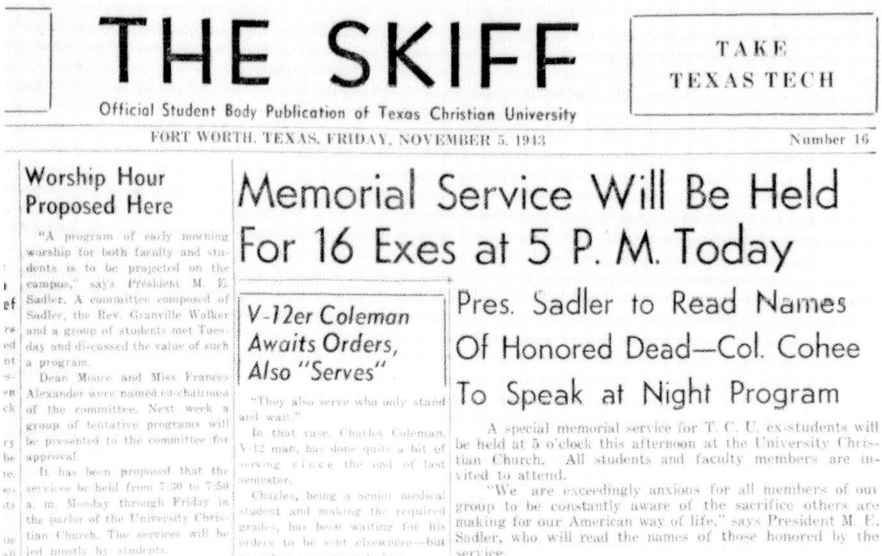

THE SKIFF

Official Student Body Publication of Texas Christian University

TAKE TEXAS TECH

FORT WORTH, TEXAS, FRIDAY, NOVEMBER 5, 1943 — Number 16

Memorial Service Will Be Held For 16 Exes at 5 P. M. Today

Worship Hour Proposed Here

"A program of early morning worship for both faculty and students is to be projected on the campus," says President M. E. Sadler. A committee composed of Sadler, the Rev. Granville Walker and a group of students met Tuesday and discussed the value of such a program.

Dean Moore and Miss Frances Alexander were named co-chairmen of the committee. Next week a group of tentative programs will be presented to the committee for approval.

It has been proposed that the services be held from 7:30 to 7:50 a. m. Monday through Friday in the parlor of the University Christian Church. The services will be led mostly by students.

"Definite announcements concerning the services will be an-

V-12er Coleman Awaits Orders, Also "Serves"

"They also serve who only stand and wait."

In that case, Charles Coleman, V-12 man, has done quite a bit of serving since the end of last semester.

Charles, being a senior medical student and making the required grades, has been waiting for his orders to be sent elsewhere—but no orders were given to him.

Going home for the few days' vacation Charles felt sure that

Pres. Sadler to Read Names Of Honored Dead—Col. Cohee To Speak at Night Program

A special memorial service for T. C. U. ex-students will be held at 5 o'clock this afternoon at the University Christian Church. All students and faculty members are invited to attend.

"We are exceedingly anxious for all members of our group to be constantly aware of the sacrifice others are making for our American way of life," says President M. E. Sadler, who will read the names of those honored by the service.

"These memorial services will be held from time to time as they are needed to honor those exes who have lost their

ABOVE

TCU Student Council officers, from left to right, James Moudy, M. C. Faris, and D. Sims. "Student Council," 1943. TCU Photograph Collection, RU 53. Photo Number: 986. https://repository.tcu.edu:443/handle/116099117/3702. Courtesy of TCU Special Collections. Mary Couts Burnett Library. Texas Christian University.

LEFT

Front page of the *Skiff* vol. 42, no. 16. (Fort Worth, TX), November 5, 1943. https://repository.tcu.edu/handle/116099117/13646. Courtesy of TCU Archives and Special Collections. Mary Couts Burnett Library. Texas Christian University.

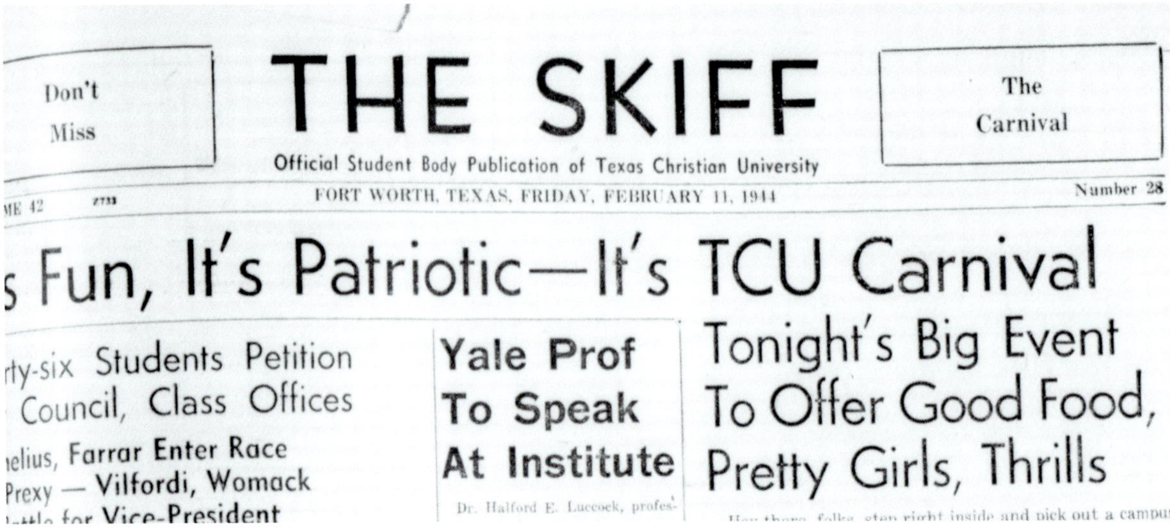

Don't Miss

THE SKIFF

Official Student Body Publication of Texas Christian University

The Carnival

FORT WORTH, TEXAS, FRIDAY, FEBRUARY 11, 1944

Number 28

s Fun, It's Patriotic—It's TCU Carnival

rty-six Students Petition Council, Class Offices

ielius, Farrar Enter Race Prexy — Vilfordi, Womack

Yale Prof To Speak At Institute

Dr. Halford E. Luccock, profes-

Tonight's Big Event To Offer Good Food, Pretty Girls, Thrills

ABOVE (TOP)
Front page of the *Skiff* vol. 42, no. 28. (Fort Worth, TX), February 11, 1944. https://repository.tcu.edu/handle/116099117/13658. Courtesy of TCU Archives and Special Collections. Mary Couts Burnett Library. Texas Christian University.

ABOVE
Image of Horned Frog in the 1945 yearbook. "Horned Frog." *The Horned Frog*, vol. 41. (Fort Worth: Stafford-Lowdon Co., 1945), 10. https://repository.tcu.edu/handle/116099117/11071. Courtesy of TCU Archives and Special Collections. Mary Couts Burnett Library. Texas Christian University.

ABOVE
Photo of the cover of *The Horned Frog*. Vol. 40. (Fort Worth: Stafford-Lowdon Co., 1944), outside cover. https://repository.tcu.edu/handle/116099117/11070. Courtesy of TCU Archives and Special Collections. Mary Couts Burnett Library. Texas Christian University.

ABOVE

Don and Dee Ezell, twin student-athletes at TCU, being sworn into the United States Marine Corps by Lt. Cleland E. Earl, a TCU graduate. Photo taken on March 3, 1942. AR406-6-1101. Courtesy, *Fort Worth Star-Telegram Collection*, Special Collections, The University of Texas at Arlington Libraries.

LEFT

Miss Betty Jo Gamble holding the new TCU Service Flag. Photo taken on December 8, 1944. AR406-6-325. Courtesy, *Fort Worth Star-Telegram Collection*, Special Collections, The University of Texas at Arlington Libraries.

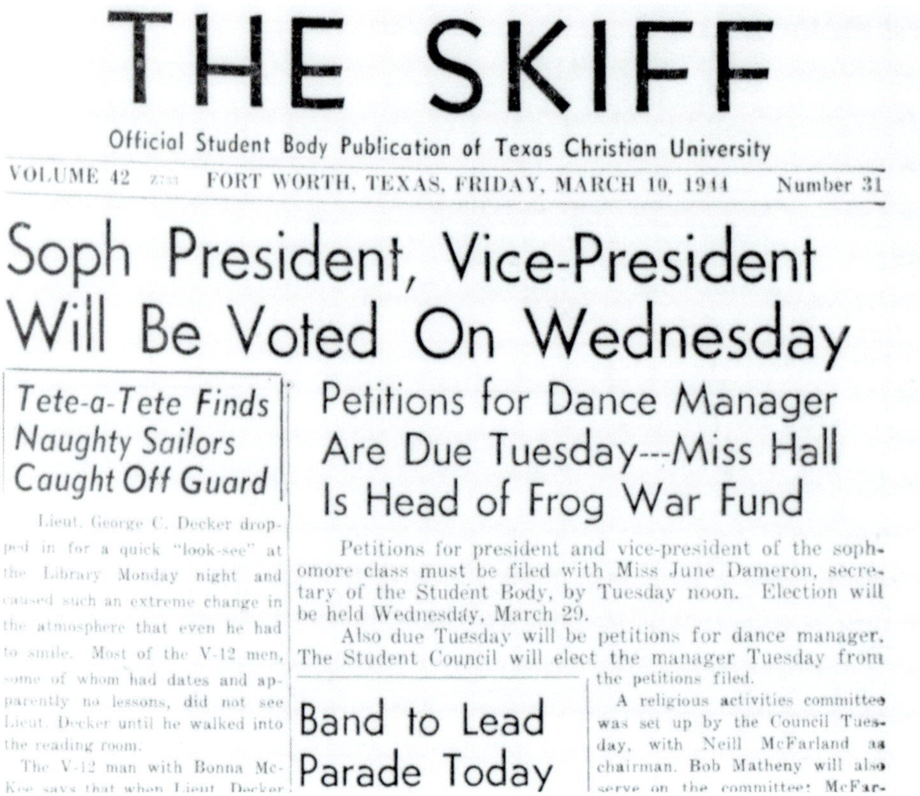

THE SKIFF

Official Student Body Publication of Texas Christian University

VOLUME 42 FORT WORTH, TEXAS, FRIDAY, MARCH 10, 1944 Number 31

Soph President, Vice-President Will Be Voted On Wednesday

Tete-a-Tete Finds Naughty Sailors Caught Off Guard

Lieut. George C. Decker dropped in for a quick "look-see" at the Library Monday night and caused such an extreme change in the atmosphere that even he had to smile. Most of the V-12 men, some of whom had dates and apparently no lessons, did not see Lieut. Decker until he walked into the reading room.

The V-12 man with Bonna McKee says that when Lieut. Decker

Petitions for Dance Manager Are Due Tuesday---Miss Hall Is Head of Frog War Fund

Petitions for president and vice-president of the sophomore class must be filed with Miss June Dameron, secretary of the Student Body, by Tuesday noon. Election will be held Wednesday, March 29.

Also due Tuesday will be petitions for dance manager. The Student Council will elect the manager Tuesday from the petitions filed.

A religious activities committee was set up by the Council Tuesday, with Neill McFarland as chairman. Bob Matheny will also serve on the committee; McFar-

Band to Lead Parade Today

LEFT
Front Page of the *Skiff* vol. 42, no. 31. (Fort Worth, TX), March 10, 1944. https://repository.tcu.edu/handle/116099117/13661. Courtesy of TCU Archives and Special Collections. Mary Couts Burnett Library. Texas Christian University.

LEFT
Image of TCU Seal in the 1945 *The Horned Frog* yearbook. "TCU Seal." *The Horned Frog*, vol. 41. (Fort Worth: Stafford-Lowdon Co., 1945), 5. https://repository.tcu.edu/handle/116099117/11071. Courtesy of TCU Archives and Special Collections. Mary Couts Burnett Library. Texas Christian University.

LEFT
Former TCU student A. L. Crouch in US Army uniform. "A. L. Crouch," 1943. TCU PhotographCollection, RU 53. Photo Number: 1478. https://repository.tcu.edu:443/handle/116099117/3865. Courtesy of TCU Special Collections. MaryCouts Burnett Library. Texas Christian University.

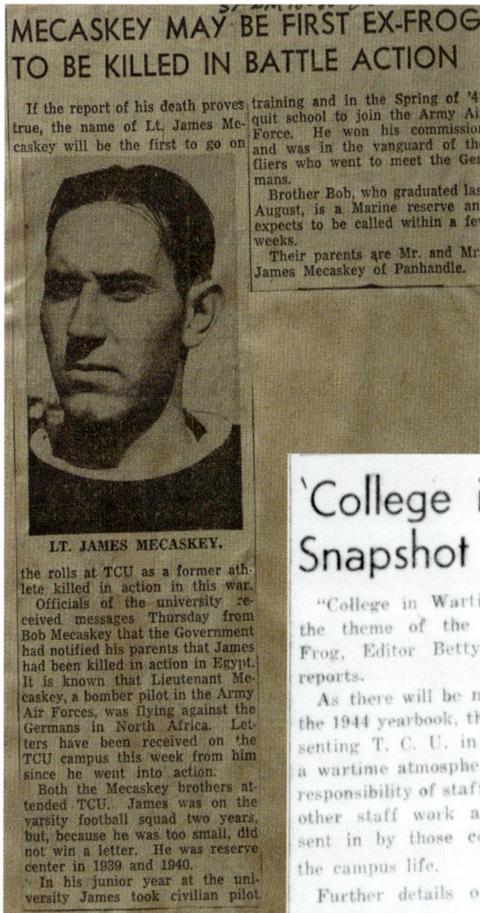

MECASKEY MAY BE FIRST EX-FROG TO BE KILLED IN BATTLE ACTION

If the report of his death proves true, the name of Lt. James Mecaskey will be the first to go on the rolls at TCU as a former athlete killed in action in this war.

LT. JAMES MECASKEY.

Officials of the university received messages Thursday from Bob Mecaskey that the Government had notified his parents that James had been killed in action in Egypt. It is known that Lieutenant Mecaskey, a bomber pilot in the Army Air Forces, was flying against the Germans in North Africa. Letters have been received on the TCU campus this week from him since he went into action.

Both the Mecaskey brothers attended TCU. James was on the varsity football squad two years, but, because he was too small, did not win a letter. He was reserve center in 1939 and 1940.

In his junior year at the university James took civilian pilot training and in the Spring of '4[illegible] quit school to join the Army Ai[r] Force. He won his commissio[n] and was in the vanguard of th[e] fliers who went to meet the Ger[-]mans.

Brother Bob, who graduated las[t] August, is a Marine reserve an[d] expects to be called within a fe[w] weeks.

Their parents are Mr. and Mr[s.] James Mecaskey of Panhandle.

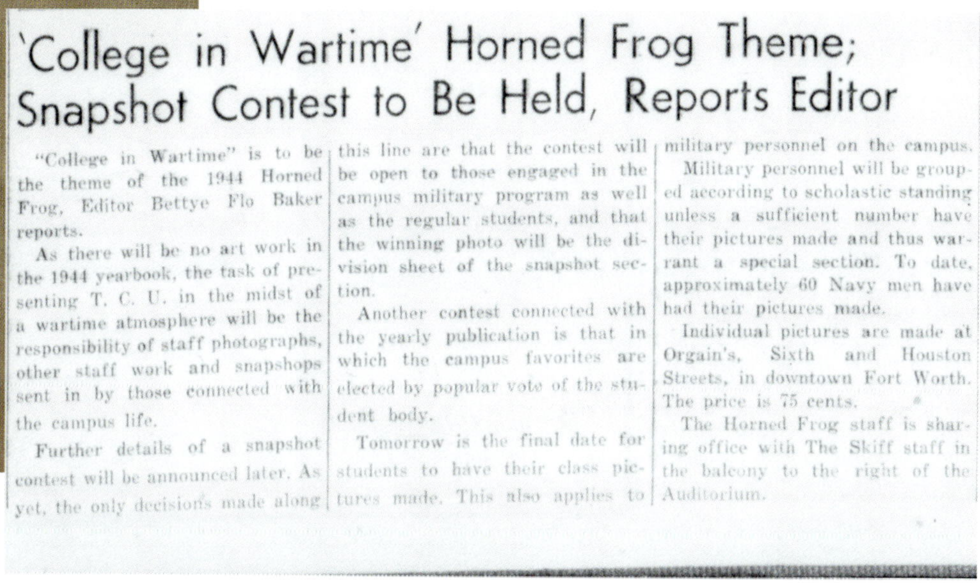

'College in Wartime' Horned Frog Theme; Snapshot Contest to Be Held, Reports Editor

"College in Wartime" is to be the theme of the 1944 Horned Frog, Editor Bettye Flo Baker reports.

As there will be no art work in the 1944 yearbook, the task of presenting T. C. U. in the midst of a wartime atmosphere will be the responsibility of staff photographs, other staff work and snapshops sent in by those connected with the campus life.

Further details of a snapshot contest will be announced later. As yet, the only decisions made along this line are that the contest will be open to those engaged in the campus military program as well as the regular students, and that the winning photo will be the division sheet of the snapshot section.

Another contest connected with the yearly publication is that in which the campus favorites are elected by popular vote of the student body.

Tomorrow is the final date for students to have their class pictures made. This also applies to military personnel on the campus.

Military personnel will be grouped according to scholastic standing unless a sufficient number have their pictures made and thus warrant a special section. To date, approximately 60 Navy men have had their pictures made.

Individual pictures are made at Orgain's, Sixth and Houston Streets, in downtown Fort Worth. The price is 75 cents.

The Horned Frog staff is sharing office with The Skiff staff in the balcony to the right of the Auditorium.

LEFT
Newspaper clipping detailing the death of former TCU student James Mecaskey in 1942. "Mecaskey May be First Ex-Frog to be Killed in Battle Action." *Fort Worth Star-Telegram* (Fort Worth, TX), Oct. 30, 1942. TCU Scrapbook Collection, RU 8, Box 11, Folder 36; "Society, 1941-1942." Courtesy of TCU Archives and Special Collections. Mary Couts Burnett Library. Texas Christian University.

ABOVE
Front page of the *Skiff* vol. 42, no. 16. (Fort Worth, TX), November 5, 1943. https://repository.tcu.edu/handle/116099117/13646. Courtesy of TCU Archives and Special Collections. Mary Couts Burnett Library. Texas Christian University.

LEFT
TCU English Professor Rebecca W. Smith in US Navy uniform. Smith was a lieutenant in the United States Naval Reserves during World War II. "Rebecca W. Smith," 1940s. TCU Photograph Collection, RU 53. Photo Number: 2017. https://repository.tcu.edu:443/handle/116099117/2850. Courtesy of TCU Special Collections. Mary Couts Burnett Library. Texas Christian University.

Clay Tile Roofs and Foster Hall

TCU's iconic architectural branding and visual identity is buff-colored bricks and red clay tile roofs. This has been the standard almost since the beginning of the campus in Fort Worth. When TCU returned to the city in 1910, construction began on the new campus in its current location. After the disastrous fire that drove TCU from Waco, the current campus was built with reinforced concrete and brick because they would not burn. Buff-colored brick apparently was the cheapest that could be secured at the time.

Red clay-tiled roofs arrived at TCU a generation later, in the early 1940s. By 1941 TCU desperately needed another women's dorm. New president M. E. Sadler agreed with the building and grounds committee recommendation that a dorm was the highest priority, and construction began in the late summer of 1941. The United States entered World War II in the midst of construction, however, and immediate mobilization for war put a strain on most basic supplies—petroleum and petroleum-based products in particular. Necessity dictated that the dorm would have a gabled roof with red clay tile because of the shortage of asphalt used in ordinary roofing.

Ultimately named for R. H. Foster, who had served as a Brite trustee, university trustee, and president of the board, the dorm was completed by June 1, 1942. Foster Hall established a pattern that would be used thereafter for TCU buildings—buff-colored brick and gabled roofs with red clay tile—still seen across campus.

LEFT
"Jarvis Hall," 1955. TCU Photograph Collection, RU 53. Photo Number: 77. https://repository.tcu.edu/handle/116099117/6797. Courtesy of TCU Special Collections. Mary Couts Burnett Library. Texas Christian University.

ABOVE (TOP)
"R. H. Foster Hall," 1948. TCU Photograph Collection, RU 53. Photo Number: 1895. https://repository.tcu.edu:443/handle/116099117/2116. Courtesy of TCU Special Collections. Mary Couts Burnett Library. Texas Christian University.

ABOVE
Architect's drawing of R. H. Foster Hall completed in 1942. "R. H. Foster Hall," 1942. TCU Photograph Collection, RU 53. Photo Number. 1801. https://repository.tcu.edu:443/handle/116099117/3692. Courtesy of TCU Special Collections. Mary Couts Burnett Library. Texas Christian University.

ABOVE
Winton-Scott Hall before its opening in 1952. "Winton-Scott Hall Construction," 1952. TCU Photograph Collection, RU 53. Photo Number: 2433. https://repository.tcu.edu:443/handle/116099117/2470. Courtesy of TCU Special Collections. Mary Couts Burnett Library. Texas Christian University.

ABOVE
Tom Brown Residence Hall before its completion in 1947. "Tom Brown Residence Hall," 1947. TCU Photograph Collection, RU 53. Photo Number: 680. https://repository.tcu.edu:443/handle/116099117/3678. Courtesy of TCU Special Collections. Mary Couts Burnett Library. Texas Christian University.

Navy V-12 Program at TCU

Under the stewardship of President Sadler, TCU received several government contracts to educate and train military personnel during World War II. The first of these contracts enrolled military personnel in the TCU Evening College beginning in 1942. Another contract authorized TCU to educate prospective pilots in physics courses from 1942 to 1944. The Navy V-12 program represented the largest federal program obtained and offered at TCU. From July 1, 1943, until October 25, 1945, TCU trained future naval officers through a general bachelor's degree program supplemented with technical coursework specified by the US Navy.

V-12 students attended classes at TCU's main campus with their fellow TCU classmates. They completed rhetoric, biology, and statistics courses just as any other TCU student would. But they also completed courses in naval history, engineering drawing, and celestial navigation, among other subjects required by the navy. V-12 cadets lived in Jarvis Hall during their stay in the program, with 750 cadets completing the program at TCU. Most of these cadets studied to become deck officers, although TCU also trained supply officers. Brite College of the Bible even trained naval chaplains as part of the program. TCU also offered courses for cadets interested in pre-medical, pre-dental, and business training so they could enroll in naval professional schools after completing the V-12 program at TCU.

The V-12 and other training programs played a vital role in stabilizing enrollment at TCU in the 1940s. These programs boosted TCU enrollment from 1,625 students in 1942 to 2,340 students in 1943. TCU's enrollment never dipped below 2,000 students after this period. These programs also helped TCU earn a place on the national stage as a reputable university fit to compete with any school in the country.

LEFT
President Sadler meeting with military personnel in his office during the 1940s. "McGruder Ellis Sadler," 1940s. TCU Photograph Collection, RU 53. Photograph Number: 1980. https://repository.tcu.edu:443/handle/116099117/3371. Courtesy of TCU Special Collections. Mary Couts Burnett Library. Texas Christian University.

LEFT

Navy V-12 unit at TCU standing in front of Jarvis Hall. "Navy V-12 Unit," 1945. TCU Photograph Collection, RU 53. Box 9, Photo Number: 1910. https://repository.tcu.edu/handle/116099117/7021. Courtesy of TCU Special Collections. Mary Couts Burnett Library. Texas Christian University.

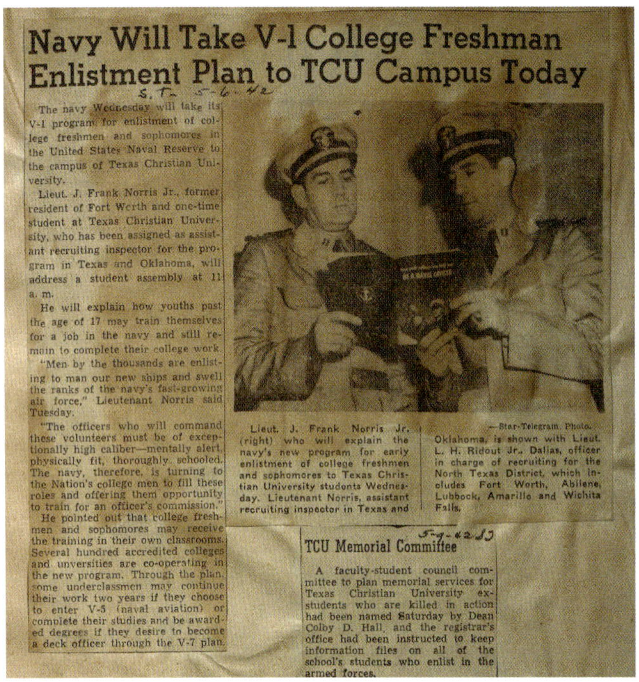

Navy Will Take V-1 College Freshman Enlistment Plan to TCU Campus Today

The navy Wednesday will take its V-1 program for enlistment of college freshmen and sophomores in the United States Naval Reserve to the campus of Texas Christian University.

Lieut. J. Frank Norris Jr., former resident of Fort Worth and one-time student at Texas Christian University, who has been assigned as assistant recruiting inspector for the program in Texas and Oklahoma, will address a student assembly at 11 a. m.

He will explain how youths past the age of 17 may train themselves for a job in the navy and still remain to complete their college work.

"Men by the thousands are enlisting to man our new ships and swell the ranks of the navy's fast-growing air force," Lieutenant Norris said Tuesday.

"The officers who will command these volunteers must be of exceptionally high caliber—mentally alert, physically fit, thoroughly schooled. The navy, therefore, is turning to the Nation's college men to fill these roles and offering them opportunity to train for an officer's commission."

He pointed out that college freshmen and sophomores may receive the training in their own classrooms. Several hundred accredited colleges and unversities are co-operating in the new program. Through the plan, some underclassmen may continue their work two years if they choose to enter V-5 (naval aviation) or complete their studies and be awarded degrees if they desire to become a deck officer through the V-7 plan.

—Star-Telegram Photo.

Lieut. J. Frank Norris Jr. (right) who will explain the navy's new program for early enlistment of college freshmen and sophomores to Texas Christian University students Wednesday. Lieutenant Norris, assistant recruiting inspector in Texas and Oklahoma, is shown with Lieut. L. H. Ridout Jr., Dallas, officer in charge of recruiting for the North Texas District, which includes Fort Worth, Abilene, Lubbock, Amarillo and Wichita Falls.

TCU Memorial Committee

A faculty-student council committee to plan memorial services for Texas Christian University ex-students who are killed in action had been named Saturday by Dean Colby D. Hall, and the registrar's office had been instructed to keep information files on all of the school's students who enlist in the armed forces.

ABOVE

Newspaper clipping detailing the navy training program at TCU. "Navy Will Take V-1 College Freshman Enlistment Plan to TCU Campus Today," *Fort Worth Star-Telegram* (Fort Worth, TX), May 6, 1942. Found in TCU Special Collections. TCU Scrapbook Collection, RU 8, Box 11, Folder 36: "Society, 194-1942." Courtesy of TCU Archives and Special Collections. Mary Couts Burnett Library. Texas Christian University.

ABOVE

Navy V-12 unit at TCU. Lieutenant George Decker, front, commanding officer, and Lieutenant B. C. Watts, his assistant, inspecting the unit. Photo taken on July 10, 1943. AR406-6-1763. Courtesy, *Fort Worth Star-Telegram Collection*, Special Collections, The University of Texas at Arlington Libraries.

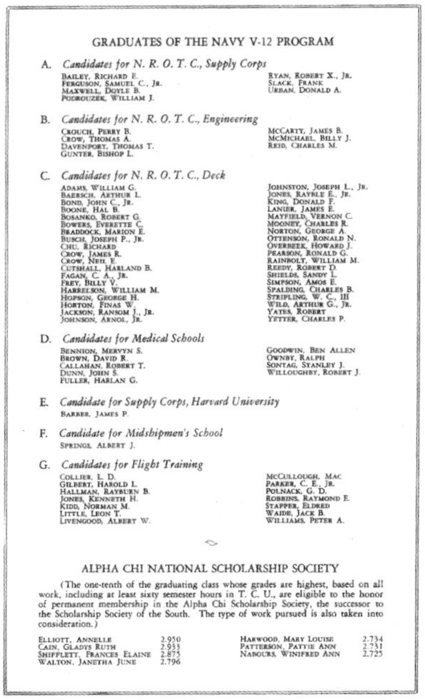

GRADUATES OF THE NAVY V-12 PROGRAM

A. *Candidates for N. R. O. T. C., Supply Corps*

BAILEY, RICHARD E.
FERGUSON, SAMUEL C., JR.
MAXWELL, DOYLE B.
PODROUZEK, WILLIAM J.
RYAN, ROBERT X., JR.
SLACK, FRANK
URBAN, DONALD A.

B. *Candidates for N. R. O. T. C., Engineering*

CROUCH, PERRY B.
CROW, THOMAS A.
DAVENPORT, THOMAS T.
GUNTER, BISHOP L.
MCCARTY, JAMES B.
MCMICHAEL, BILLY J.
REID, CHARLES M.

C. *Candidates for N. R. O. T. C., Deck*

ADAMS, WILLIAM G.
BAERSCH, ARTHUR L.
BOND, JOHN C., JR.
BOONE, HAL B.
BOSANKO, ROBERT G.
BOWERS, EVERETTE C.
BRADDOCK, MARION E.
BUSCH, JOSEPH P., JR.
CHU, RICHARD
CROW, JAMES R.
CROW, NEIL E.
CUTSHALL, HARLAND B.
FAGAN, C. A., JR.
FREY, BILLY V.
HARRELSON, WILLIAM M.
HOPSON, GEORGE H.
HORTON, FINAS W.
JACKSON, RANSOM J., JR.
JOHNSON, ARNOL, JR.
JOHNSTON, JOSEPH L., JR.
JONES, RAYBLE E., JR.
KING, DONALD F.
LANIER, JAMES E.
MAYFIELD, VERNON C.
MOONEY, CHARLES R.
NORTON, GEORGE A.
OTTENSON, RONALD N.
OVERBEEK, HOWARD J.
PEARSON, RONALD G.
RAINBOLT, WILLIAM M.
REEDY, ROBERT D.
SHIELDS, SANDY L.
SIMPSON, AMOS E.
SPALDING, CHARLES B.
STRIPLING, W. C., III
WILD, ARTHUR G., JR.
YATES, ROBERT
YETTER, CHARLES P.

D. *Candidates for Medical Schools*

BENNION, MERVYN S.
BROWN, DAVID R.
CALLAHAN, ROBERT T.
DUNN, JOHN S.
FULLER, HARLAN G.
GOODWIN, BEN ALLEN
OWNBY, RALPH
SONTAG, STANLEY J.
WILLOUGHBY, ROBERT J.

E. *Candidate for Supply Corps, Harvard University*

BARBER, JAMES P.

F. *Candidate for Midshipmen's School*

SPRINGS, ALBERT J.

G. *Candidates for Flight Training*

COLLIER, L. D.
GILBERT, HAROLD L.
HALLMAN, RAYBURN B.
JONES, KENNETH H.
KIDD, NORMAN M.
LITTLE, LEON T.
LIVENGOOD, ALBERT W.
MCCULLOUGH, MAC
PARKER, C. E., JR.
POLNACK, G. D.
ROBBINS, RAYMOND E.
STAPPER, ELDRED
WAIDE, JACK B.
WILLIAMS, PETER A.

ALPHA CHI NATIONAL SCHOLARSHIP SOCIETY

(The one-tenth of the graduating class whose grades are highest, based on all work, including at least sixty semester hours in T. C. U., are eligible to the honor of permanent membership in the Alpha Chi Scholarship Society, the successor to the Scholarship Society of the South. The type of work pursued is also taken into consideration.)

ELLIOTT, ANNELLE	2.950	HARWOOD, MARY LOUISE	2.734
CAIN, GLADYS RUTH	2.933	PATTERSON, PATTIE ANN	2.731
SHIFFLETT, FRANCES ELAINE	2.875	NABOURS, WINIFRED ANN	2.725
WALTON, JANETHA JUNE	2.796		

ABOVE
List of graduates from the TCU Navy V-12 Program. "Commencement Program 1945- Spring" (Fort Worth: TCU, 1945). https://repository.tcu.edu/handle/116099117/7891. Courtesy of TCU Archives and Special Collections. Mary Couts Burnett Library. Texas Christian University.

ABOVE RIGHT
Carl Schmidt receiving degree from Jerome A. Moore during 1945 Commencement at TCU. "Carl Schmidt," 1945. TCU Photograph Collection, RU 53. Photograph Number: 1735. https://repository.tcu.edu:443/handle/116099117/3169. Courtesy of TCU Special Collections. Mary Couts Burnett Library. Texas Christian University.

RIGHT
Photo of sailor being pinned during Navy V-12 completion of training ceremony at TCU. "Navy V-12 Training Program," 1944. TCU Photograph Collection, RU 53. https://repository.tcu.edu/handle/116099117/12233. Courtesy of TCU Special Collections. Mary Couts Burnett Library. Texas Christian University.

THE SKIFF

HAPPY NEW YEAR

Official Student Body Publication of Texas Christian University

FORT WORTH, TEXAS, FRIDAY, DECEMBER 17, 1943 — Number 22

...tionally Offense

...19 passes out of 40 at...—both figures representing ...al season's records for a game.

...passing record, plus 13 car... and six punts, also gives him ...o. 1 spot in the nation for offense plays in a single...

Frogs had 65 plays on of... that day—running, passing, ...g—and Lucas handled 59 of ... Runner-up for a day's work ...eon Pense, workhorse of the ...sas Razorbacks, who han... 9 plays against Oklahoma A...

Navy V-12 Men Will Serve Up "Hornpipe" for Tomorrow Night

"Merry Christmas," Says Pres. M. E. Sadler

Christmas greetings to the students. As we approach the Christmas season, let me express heartiest good wishes to every student in the University. You have shown a marvelous spirit of co-operation during this session. Because of this fine attitude, the work of the school has moved along smoothly in spite of many unusual circumstances.

Service Band of 11 Pieces To Be Intermission Feature Of Pre-Christmas Dance

Ach, the hornpipe! Yessirree, the Christmas dance will be a lively hornpipe. The Navy V-12 men are hosts tomorrow night in the Basketball Gymnasium.

"The dance will start at 9 p. m. and last until 12 midnight, with lots of surprises and fun," says Maestro Ray Wood.

Ray is the leader of a Navy...

ABOVE
Front page of the *Skiff* vol. 42, no. 22. (Fort Worth, TX), Dec. 12, 1943. https://repository.tcu.edu/handle/116099117/13652. Courtesy of TCU Archives and Special Collections. Mary Couts Burnett Library. Texas Christian University.

ABOVE
Navy V-12 Unit at TCU in front of Jarvis Hall. "Navy V-12 Training Program," 1945. Taken by W. D. Smith Photography, TCU Photograph Collection, RU 53. https://repository.tcu.edu/handle/116099117/12237. Courtesy of TCU Special Collections. Mary Couts Burnett Library. Texas Christian University.

RIGHT
Richard Chu, a native of Los Angeles, attended TCU as part of the Navy V-12 program. Photo taken on December 6, 1944. AR406-6-324. Courtesy, *Fort Worth Star-Telegram Collection*, Special Collections, The University of Texas at Arlington Libraries.

ABOVE
Dr. Harrison Miller Moseley while in US Navy in the 1940s. Courtesy of Stella Brooks, author of *Unbelievable: The Unmasking of Dr. Harrison Miller Moseley* (Self-published by Stella Brooks, 2014).

ABOVE (RIGHT)
Physics Professor Newton Gaines singing old-time cowboy songs. Photo taken on January 31, 1947. AR4 06-6-1924. Courtesy, *Fort Worth Star-Telegram Collection*, Special Collections, The University of Texas at Arlington Libraries.

Folk Ballads and Atomic Bombs: Newton Gaines and Harrison Moseley

Born in 1890 in Fort Worth, Newton Gaines developed passions for both science and folk music. Graduating from UT-Austin with a degree in electrical engineering in 1912, Gaines later earned his PhD from UT-Austin in 1931. He arrived at TCU in 1924 as the university's only physics professor, and he chaired the Physics Department from 1927 until his 1958 retirement. During his tenure, Gaines published an array of articles that investigated the use of ultrasound waves to sterilize milk. In addition to his educational and scientific accomplishments, Gaines possessed an alternate persona, Jim New. Since his youth, he possessed an affinity for Texas folk ballads and hoped to preserve them through recordings beginning in the 1920s. In 1928 and 1929, he recorded a series of songs in Dallas including "Wreck of the Six-wheeler" and "For Work I'm Too Lazy." In 1940, Gaines recorded thirty ballads for John A. Lomax and the American Folk Music Project sponsored by the Library of Congress. His recordings included "Frog Went a-Courtin," "Whoop-ti-yo, Get Along Little Dogies," and "O Bury Me Not on the Lone Prairie." Gaines also served as president of the Texas Folklore Society from 1928 to 1929. The TCU Music Department even enlisted Gaines to teach a course on the physics of music, which he did beginning in 1936. In the fall of 1954, Gaines, Jim Potter of Texas A&M, and Herbert Schwetman of Baylor University formed the Texas section of the American Association of Physics Teachers, which became the Texas section of the American Physical Society in 1981. Today, TCU honors Gaines through an annual scholarship to a female physics student.

Harrison Miller Moseley was born in 1922 in Dundee, Texas. After his father died during the early 1930s, Moseley and his siblings arrived at the steps of the Fort Worth Masonic Home. He attended the Masonic Home and School, where he became a gridiron star with the "Mighty Mites," despite only weighing 126 pounds. Upon graduation, Moseley received a scholarship from TCU and studied physics under Newton Gaines. Gaines recommended that Moseley further hone his gift for physics under the tutelage of Nathan Rosen at UNC-Chapel Hill. By 1943, Rosen and Moseley earned an invitation to work on the Manhattan Project, where they served on the S-1 Uranium Committee. Their work directly contributed to the successful creation of atomic weapons. After the bombing of Hiroshima and Nagasaki in August 1945, Moseley completed his PhD at UNC-Chapel Hill. He returned to TCU in 1950 as a physics professor and worked in the department until his retirement in 1990.

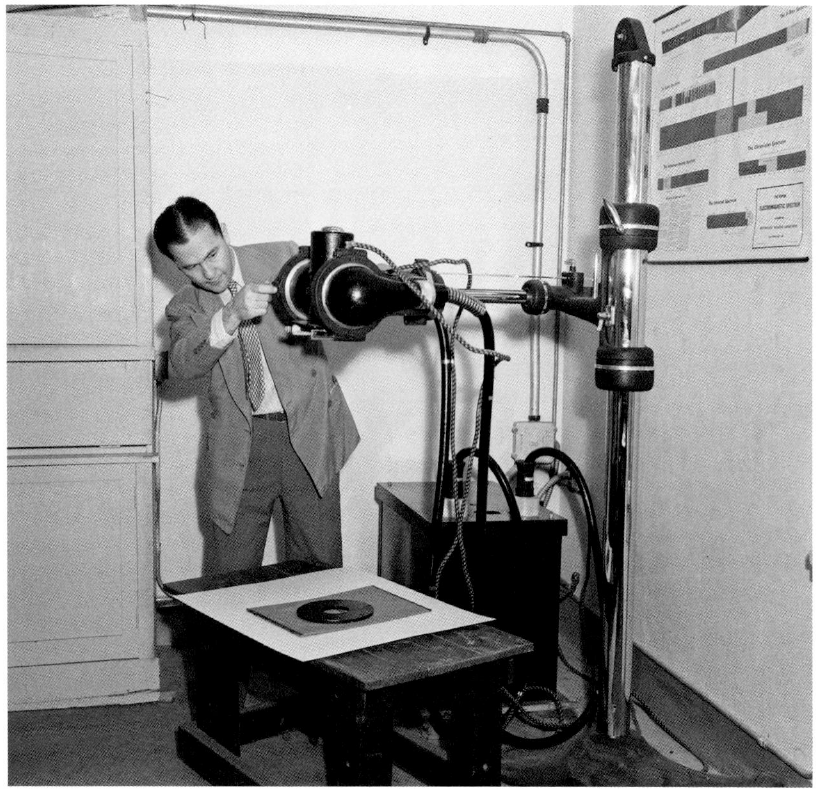

ABOVE
Dr. Joseph Morgan examines a new industrial X-ray machine acquired by the TCU physics department. Photo taken on April 19, 1946. AR406-6-413. Courtesy, *Fort Worth Star-Telegram Collection*, Special Collections, The University of Texas at Arlington Libraries.

ABOVE
Portrait of Dr. Newton Gaines. "Newton Gaines," n.d. TCU Photograph Collection, RU 53. Photo Number: 904. https://repository.tcu.edu:443/handle/116099117/2271. Courtesy of TCU Special Collections. Mary Couts Burnett Library. Texas Christian University.

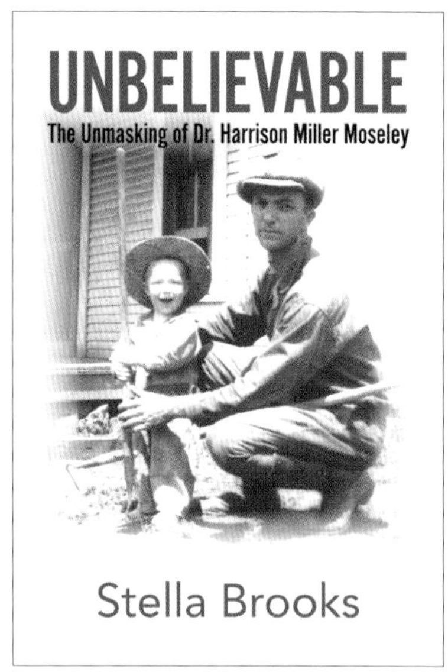

ABOVE
Book cover of *Unbelievable: The Unmasking of Dr. Harrison Miller Moseley* by Stella Brooks. Courtesy of Stella Brooks, author of *Unbelievable: The Unmasking of Dr. Harrison Miller Moseley* (Self-published by Stella Brooks, 2014).

ABOVE
Dr. Newton Gaines and Dr. Joseph Morgan working in the physics lab at TCU. "Newton Gaines," 1940s. Taken by W. D. Smith Photography. TCU Photograph Collection, RU 53. Photo Number: 806. https://repository.tcu.edu:443/handle/116099117/2330. Courtesy of TCU Special Collections. Mary Couts Burnett Library. Texas Christian University.

ABOVE
Image of Harrison Miller Moseley from the 1943 *The Horned Frog* yearbook. "Harrison Miller Moseley." *The Horned Frog*, vol. 39. (Fort Worth: Stafford-Lowdon Co., 1943), 105. https://repository.tcu.edu/handle/116099117/11069. Courtesy of TCU Archives and Special Collections. Mary Couts Burnett Library. Texas Christian University.

ABOVE (TOP)
Coach H. N. "Rusty" Russell of the Masonic Home Football Team diagrams a play for an unidentified player. Photo taken in 1939. AR406-6-995. Courtesy, *Fort Worth Star-Telegram Collection*, Special Collections, The University of Texas at Arlington Libraries.

ABOVE
Postcard with the Masonic Orphans' Home in Fort Worth, Texas. Undated postcard. AR416, Box 9. Courtesy, Jenkins Garrett Texas Postcard Collection, Special Collections, The University of Texas at Arlington Libraries.

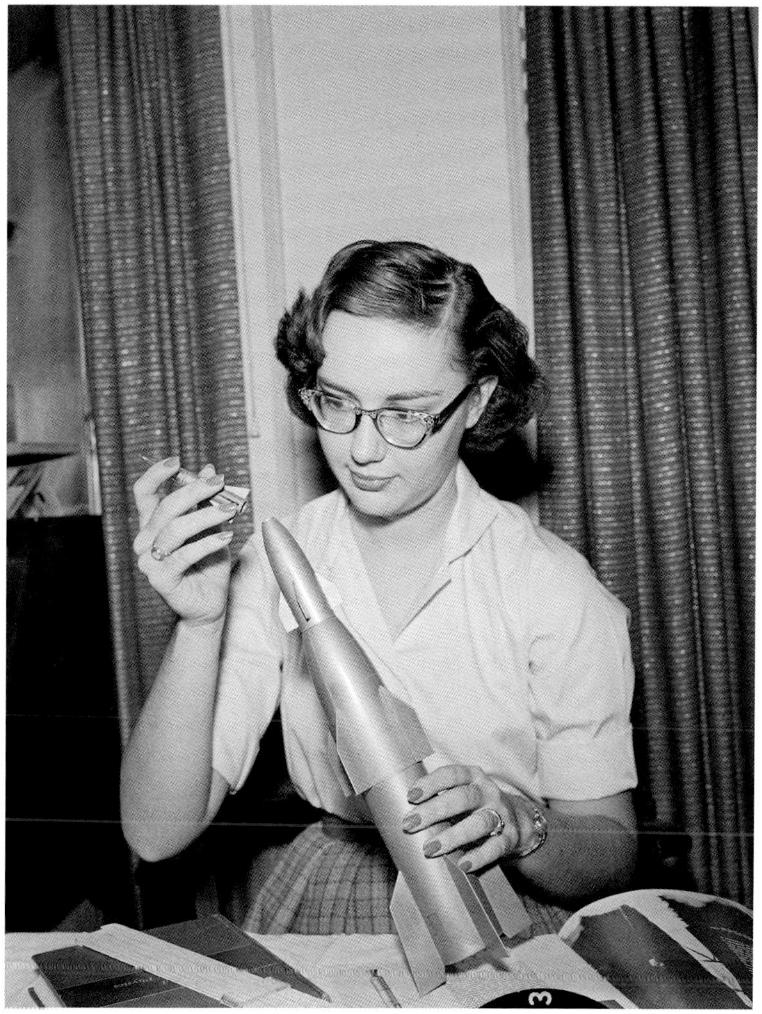

ABOVE
Newton Gaines strumming a guitar and singing old-time cowboy songs on his porch. Photo taken on January 31, 1947. AR406-6-1924. Courtesy, *Fort Worth Star-Telegram Collection*, Special Collections, The University of Texas at Arlington Libraries.

RIGHT
Image of Dr. Harrison Miller Moseley from the 1960 *The Horned Frog* yearbook. "Dr. Harrison Miller Moseley." *The Horned Frog*, vol. 56. (Fort Worth: University Supply and Equipment Co., 1960), 40. https://repository.tcu.edu/handle/116099117/11086. Courtesy of TCU Archives and Special Collections. Mary Couts Burnett Library. Texas Christian University.

ABOVE
Miss Mary Jo Smith, a junior at TCU and a physics and mathematics major, spent the summer of 1958 working in the US Army ballistic missile program at Redstone, Alabama. She was one of only eighteen women chosen for the summer program. Photo taken on October 3, 1958. AR406-6-131. Courtesy, *Fort Worth Star-Telegram Collection*, Special Collections, The University of Texas at Arlington.

Ranch Week

Fort Worth's history as a "Cowtown" dates back to the 1870s and the annual cattle drives that meandered through the region. With the arrival of the railroad in the late 1870s, the city witnessed the development of a large meatpacking industry and stockyards district. Fort Worth began the annual Fat Stock Show and Exposition beginning in the 1890s to celebrate its industry. TCU students and faculty eagerly attended and participated in the annual event beginning in 1910.

To honor this unique heritage, TCU students and staff organized a university-wide Ranch Week to coincide with the annual Stock Show in 1940. All student organizations aided the annual festivities by either sponsoring or supporting events. These events ranged from a downtown parade to a square-dancing competition in the gym to Roy Bean trials. One of the trials even ensnared President Sadler! The *Skiff* included a suggested dress code for the week for students: For boys, writers recommended "10-gallon hats, blue jeans, chaps, cowboy boots, and spurs"; for girls, it called for "calico and gingham creations and old-fashioned bonnets." It reminded students to forsake manufactured cigarettes and roll their own!

For the next nineteen years, students eagerly anticipated the annual festivities that encompassed Ranch Week. The TCU Chamber of Commerce promoted the event until 1959. Today, the Annual Fort Worth Stock Show still sponsors TCU week in which students receive discounted tickets to attend the carnival and rodeo.

RIGHT
TCU Ranch Program Car in West Texas. "Ranch Training Program Car," 1966. TCU Photograph Collection, RU 53. Photo Number: 2301. https://repository.tcu.edu:443/handle/116099117/3722. Courtesy of TCU Special Collections. Mary Couts Burnett Library. Texas Christian University.

RANCH TRAINING PROGRAM
TEXAS CHRISTIAN UNIVERSITY

LEFT
"Louis 'Cowboy' Monroe," 1950s. Photo-graph by Whelan Patrick. TCU Photograph Collection, RU 53. https://repository.tcu.edu/handle/116099117/11754. Courtesy of TCU Special Collections. Mary Couts Burnett Library. Texas Christian University.

LEFT
Front Cover of the 1951 *Frog Horn* Booklet. *Frog Horn*: September 1951. (Fort Worth: Student Association Congress, 1951). https://repository.tcu.edu/handle/116099117/7112. Courtesy of TCU Archives and Special Collections. Mary Couts Burnett Library. Texas Christian University.

LEFT
Ed Farrens, left, Bob Buschman, right, and Jerita Foley, Ranch Week Queen, being thrown into jail following a Roy Bean Trial during Ranch Week. Photo taken on February 7, 1942. AR406-6-391. Courtesy, *Fort Worth Star-Telegram Collection*, Special Collections, The University of Texas at Arlington Libraries.

RIGHT
TCU students, Cy Rickel, Maxine Shaw, and Jack Tunstill, playing cards during Ranch Week festivities. Photo taken on February 6, 1942. AR406-6-1312. Courtesy, *Fort Worth Star-Telegram Collection*, Special Collections, The University of Texas at Arlington Libraries.

RIGHT
Three TCU students riding on a mule; from left to right: Bubba Schmid, Lee Gallagher, and Henry Mullins. Photo taken on February 7, 1946. AR406-6-391. Courtesy, *Fort Worth Star-Telegram Collection*, Special Collections, The University of Texas at Arlington Libraries.

LEFT
From left to right: Alice Ann Ward, Carolyn McCartney, Ruth Rawlls, Patricia Ward, Jean Carol McCullough, Frances Leak, Margaret Ann Lowrey, and Elizabeth Davis smoking pipes as they sit on a rail during Ranch Week. Photo taken on February 16, 1945. AR406-6-338. Courtesy, *Fort Worth Star-Telegram Collection*, Special Collections, The University of Texas at Arlington.

LEFT
TCU students dressed as cowboys and cowgirls roll their own cigarettes in a cigarette-rolling contest during 1942 Ranch Week. From left to right: Edwin Dowell, winner of boy's division; Betty Bowman, winner of girl's division; F. S. Radcliff, second place in boy's; Elna Jean Higginbotham, second place in girl's; and Bill Hall, third place in boy's. Photo taken on February 6, 1942. AR406-6-1487. Courtesy, *Fort Worth Star-Telegram Collection*, Special Collections, The University of Texas at Arlington Libraries.

ABOVE
President Sadler being thrown into jail. "Dr. Sadler being thrown into jail in Roy Bean Trial during TCU Ranch Week." TCU Special Collections. TCU Scrapbook Collection, RU 8, Box 5, Folder 37. "President Sadler, 1942-1951." Courtesy of TCU Archives and Special Collections. Mary Couts Burnett Library. Texas Christian University.

RIGHT
TCU students Tom Barber and Doreen Reuther, walk in front of storefronts during Ranch Week. Photo taken on February 6, 1942. AR406-6-1312. Courtesy, *Fort Worth Star-Telegram Collection*, Special Collections, The University of Texas at Arlington Libraries.

Air-Conditioning Finally Comes to Campus

Texas generally has mild winters, very pleasant springs, and then brutally hot summers. By the mid-twentieth century, air-conditioning became a modern necessity for those living in the Lone Star State. Generally unknown, in 1945 the twenty-one story Milam Building in San Antonio became the first high-rise, air-conditioned office building in the United States. It became the model for air-conditioned buildings in Texas.

TCU's growth to more than two thousand students during the early 1940s and more than five thousand students in the mid-1940s meant that the university needed additional classroom space. President Sadler acknowledged in September 1945 that the university should have a new building with a suitable auditorium for campus use. While the board of trustees approved the plans to build the first new structure for instructional purposes in early March 1946, postwar economic development delayed the signing of contracts until April 1948.

The new building consisted of a basement and three floors and included soundproofing and air-conditioning. It was designed with an auditorium, a little theater, and teaching laboratories for instructional work in the fine arts. The eighty-two rooms in the building included classrooms, radio studios and control rooms, painting and sculpture studios, music studios, and even a speech-correction laboratory. Named for trustee E. A. Landreth and opened on December 4, 1949, the facility represented the first completely air-conditioned building on the TCU campus, and it started a trend for future construction and building renovation. To this day, Ed Landreth auditorium remains in use for a variety of university functions.

ABOVE
"Ed Landreth Hall with Auditorium," 1947. TCU Photograph Collection, RU 53. Photo Number: 1894. https://repository.tcu.edu:443/handle/116099117/2327. Courtesy of TCU Special Collections. Mary Couts Burnett Library. Texas Christian University.

OPPOSITE
Architect's drawing of Ed Landreth Hall completed in 1947. "Ed Landreth Hall," 1947–1948. TCU Photograph Collection, RU 53. Photo Number 53. https://repository.tcu.edu/handle/116099117/6789. Courtesy of TCU Special Collections. Mary Couts Burnett Library. Texas Christian University.

ABOVE

TCU A Cappella Choir standing on steps in front of Ed Landreth Hall. "Choir," 1966. TCU Photograph Collection, RU 53. Photo Number: 2381. https://repository.tcu.edu:443/handle/116099117/3181.Courtesy of TCU Special Collections. Mary Couts Burnett Library. Texas Christian University.

LEFT

Chancellor Sadler speaking at TCU convocation in Fall 1965. "McGruder Ellis Sadler," 1965. TCU Photograph Collection, RU 53. Photo Number: 404. https://repository.tcu.edu:443/handle/116099117/3268. Courtesy of TCU Special Collections. Mary Couts Burnett Library. Texas Christian University.

ABOVE
The auditorium seating in Ed Landreth Hall. "Ed Landreth Hall," 1949. TCU Photograph Collection, RU 53. Photo Number: 54. https://repository.tcu.edu/handle/116099117/6788. Courtesy of TCU Special Collections. Mary Couts Burnett Library. Texas Christian University.

RIGHT
Professor Tom Noel playing Mark Twain during Parents' Weekend entertainment in Ed Landreth Auditorium. "Tom Noel," 1973-1974. TCU Photograph Collection, RU 53. Photo Number: 2430. https://repository.tcu.edu:443/handle/116099117/3882. Courtesy of TCU Special Collections. Mary Couts Burnett Library, Texas Christian University.

Evening College, Professional Programs, and TCU Integration

Integration at TCU occurred in a piecemeal fashion beginning in 1942. Four colleges at TCU integrated before Chancellor Sadler and the board of trustees ordered the integration of TCU's main campus in 1963. The Evening College represented the first program to provide instruction in an integrated classroom. The advent of World War II led TCU to bid for and subsequently obtain government contracts to provide educational instruction to naval and marine officers and airplane pilots, and the subsequent partnership between the US military and TCU required the university to include Black servicemen in its classrooms. In 1942, TCU offered its first evening classes to an integrated student body of military personnel. The program helped pave a route for the desegregation of other colleges at TCU.

The College of Education was the next college to offer integrated courses. In 1951, Professor Sandy A. Wall offered evening courses for Black public school teachers at Gay Street Elementary School. Principal Lottie Mae Hamilton and Bertice Bates enrolled as the program's first students. Numerous teachers earned graduate degrees from TCU during the 1950s and 1960s via the program, including: Lottie Mae Hamilton, 1955; Bertice Bates, 1960; Reva Bell, 1965; and Juanita Cash, 1965.

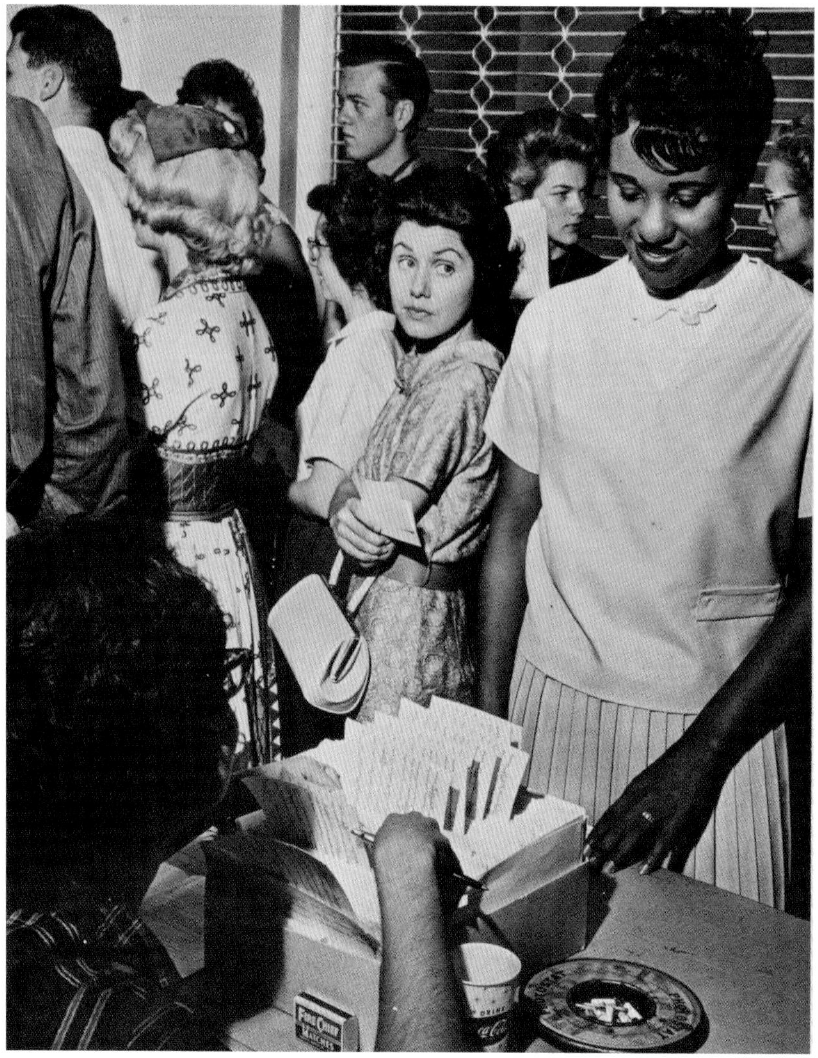

ABOVE
Image of Allene Jones registering for classes at TCU for the 1962 fall semester. *The Horned Frog*, vol. 59. (Fort Worth: Taylor Publishing Co., 1963), 55. https://repository.tcu.edu/handle/116099117/11089. Courtesy of TCU Archives and Special Collections. Mary Couts Burnett Library. Texas Christian University.

RIGHT
Senior portrait of Vada Felder. *The Horned Frog*, vol. 50. (Fort Worth: University Supply and Equipment Co., 1954), 305. https://repository.tcu.edu/handle/116099117/11080. Courtesy of TCU Archives and Special Collections. Mary Couts Burnett Library. Texas Christian University.

ABOVE
Two nursing students talking. *The Horned Frog*, vol. 60. (Fort Worth: Taylor Publishing Co., 1964), 371. https://repository.tcu.edu/hadle/116099117/11090. Courtesy of TCU Archives and Special Collections. Mary Couts Burnett Library. Texas Christian University.

RIGHT
Brite students Vada Felder, Daniel Goodspeed, and James Claiborne. Page 5 of the *Skiff* 51, no. 12 (Fort Worth, TX). Dec. 12, 1951. https://repository.tcu.edu/hadle/116099117/14487. Courtesy of TCU Archives and Special Collections. Mary Couts Burnett Library. Texas Christian University.

It's a Great Feeling . . .

. . . to stand in this pulpit, Mrs. Vada Felder, left, is explaining to Daniel Goodspeed, center, and James Claiborne. Goodspeed will speak in Morro Chapel next Tuesday. Mrs. Felder had her first opportunity to address the chapel audience Dec. 4. The three students are juniors in Brite College.

In 1952, Brite College became the first school on TCU's main campus to desegregate its program. James Lee Claiborne, Daniel Goodspeed, and Vada Phillips Felder enrolled as the first black students in Brite's seminary program. Felder graduated in 1954 with a master's in religious education. She also served as a senior class officer in Brite College. Claiborne earned the bachelor of divinity in 1955. In 1959, Felder hosted Martin Luther King Jr. in Fort Worth. King spoke multiple times across the city and even met with Brite faculty, though TCU prohibited King from speaking on campus.

Harris College of Nursing represented the final professional program to integrate before TCU's main campus. In 1962, the Harris College Board of Directors and Dean Lucy Harris voted unequivocally to integrate the nursing program. Patsy Brown, Allene Jones, and Doris McBride enrolled as the first Black students for the fall semester. Allene Jones graduated in 1965 and later became the first Black faculty member at TCU in 1968, when Harris College hired her.

ABOVE RIGHT
"Robert Carr Chapel," n.d. TCU Photograph Collection, RU 53. Photo Number: 980. https://repository.tcu.edu:443/handle/116099117/3217. Courtesy of TCU Special Collections. Mary Couts Burnett Library. Texas Christian University.

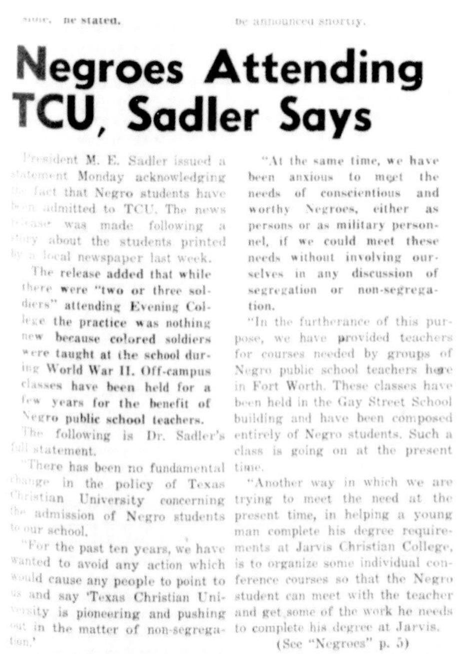

Negroes Attending TCU, Sadler Says

President M. E. Sadler issued a statement Monday acknowledging the fact that Negro students have been admitted to TCU. The news release was made following a story about the students printed by a local newspaper last week.

The release added that while there were "two or three soldiers" attending Evening College the practice was nothing new because colored soldiers were taught at the school during World War II. Off-campus classes have been held for a few years for the benefit of Negro public school teachers.

The following is Dr. Sadler's full statement.

"There has been no fundamental change in the policy of Texas Christian University concerning the admission of Negro students to our school.

"For the past ten years, we have wanted to avoid any action which would cause any people to point to us and say 'Texas Christian University is pioneering and pushing out in the matter of non-segregation.'

"At the same time, we have been anxious to meet the needs of conscientious and worthy Negroes, either as persons or as military personnel, if we could meet these needs without involving ourselves in any discussion of segregation or non-segregation.

"In the furtherance of this purpose, we have provided teachers for courses needed by groups of Negro public school teachers here in Fort Worth. These classes have been held in the Gay Street School building and have been composed entirely of Negro students. Such a class is going on at the present time.

"Another way in which we are trying to meet the need at the present time, in helping a young man complete his degree requirements at Jarvis Christian College, is to organize some individual conference courses so that the Negro student can meet with the teacher and get some of the work he needs to complete his degree at Jarvis.

(See "Negroes" p. 5)

RIGHT
Front page of the *Skiff* 50, no. 7. (Fort Worth, TX), Nov. 2, 1951. https://repository.tcu.edu/handle/116099117/14454. Courtesy of TCU Archives and Special Collections. Mary Couts Burnett Library. Texas Christian University.

ABOVE
Gay Street School in Fort Worth. "Gay Street School," c. 1956. Courtesy of the Billy W. Sills Center for Archives of the Fort Worth Independent School District.

RIGHT
Brite College Senior Class Officers, from left to right: James F. Smith, treasurer; Mrs. Vada Felder, secretary; Roy Rutherford, vice president; and Warren Newman, president. *The Horned Frog*, vol. 50. (Fort Worth: University Supply and Equipment Co., 1954), 304. https://repository.tcu.edu/handle/116099117/11080. Courtesy of TCU Archives and Special Collections. Mary Couts Burnett Library. Texas Christian University.

ABOVE
Yearbook portrait of James Lee Claiborne. *The Horned Frog*, vol. 50. (Fort Worth: University Supply and Equipment Co., 1954), 306. https://repository.tcu.edu/handle/116099117/11080. Courtesy of TCU Archives and Special Collections. Mary Couts Burnett Library. Texas Christian University.

ABOVE
Senior portrait of Patsy Brown. *The Horned Frog*, vol. 602. (Fort Worth: Taylor Publishing Co., 1964), 380. https://repository.tcu.edu/handle/116099117/11090. Courtesy of TCU Archives and Special Collections. Mary Couts Burnett Library. Texas Christian University.

ABOVE
Senior Portrait of Doris Ann McBride. *The Horned Frog*, vol. 59. (Fort Worth: Taylor Publishing Co., 1963), 387. https://repository.tcu.edu/handle/116099117/11089. Courtesy of TCU Archives and Special Collections. Mary Couts Burnett Library. Texas Christian University.

ABOVE
Image of Allene Jones as faculty member of Harris College of Nursing. *The Horned Frog*, vol. 65. (Fort Worth: Taylor Publishing Co., 1969), 400. https://repository.tcu.edu/handle/116099117/11095. Courtesy of TCU Archives and Special Collections. Mary Couts Burnett Library. Texas Christian University.

ABOVE
Martin Luther King Jr. with Vada Felder and others after Dr. King's speech in Fort Worth in October 1959. Negative #111. Calvin Littlejohn Photographic Archive Collection. Box 3L30a-d, Folder 3L30a. Courtesy of the Dolph Briscoe Center of American History. University of Texas Libraries. University of Texas at Austin.

Dean Lucy Harris and the Harris College of Nursing

Dating back to the early 1900s, TCU's Harris College of Nursing is deeply connected to the medical history of Fort Worth. Dr. Charles Houston Harris moved to Fort Worth from Moran, Texas, in 1904, and opened the Harris Hospital at the corner of Rosedale and Fifth Avenue. In 1912, he opened the Harris School of Nursing as means to train more highly qualified nurses for both his own hospital and the larger Fort Worth area. In 1935, Dr. Harris hired Lucy Harris (no familial relation) as the hospital's director of Nursing and Nursing Services. While it may have seemed inconsequential at the time, the partnership between Dr. Harris and Lucy Harris would have profound implications for TCU and Fort Worth.

Dean Lucy Harris was born in Dickson County, Tennessee, on June 18, 1899. She graduated from the John Sealy School of Nursing in Galveston, Texas, before earning her bachelor of science in nursing education from Columbia University in 1942. While she earned her degrees Dean Harris also served as the director of Nursing and Nursing Service at Harris Methodist Hospital (1935–1937) and Georgia Baptist Hospital (1937–1942). In 1942, she returned to Harris Methodist Hospital to serve as the director of the Harris School of Nursing until 1947.

In 1946, Dr. Charles H. Harris, Lucy Harris, and President Sadler founded the Harris College of Nursing as a partnership between Harris Methodist Hospital and TCU. Dr. Harris established a $750,000 trust to underwrite the newly formed Harris College of Nursing and selected a board of trustees to administer the nursing college. The partnership promoted Lucy Harris to serve as the first dean of the college. In 1947, the college received national accreditation and became the first accredited baccalaureate program for nursing in the state of Texas. Nursing students lived in a dorm two blocks from the hospital and attended classes on the hospital's campus.

Beginning in 1965, Dean Harris served a six-year term on the Texas Board of Nurse Examiners that underscored her immense impact on the field of nursing in Texas. She also pushed the College of Nursing to integrate its program in 1962. Retiring from TCU in June 1967, Dean Harris published a memoir in 1973 entitled *The Harris College of Nursing: Five Decades of Struggle for a Cause*. Her memoir provided a firsthand account of how the field of nursing evolved from a trained apprenticeship to a professional program in the state of Texas. Dean Harris truly played a remarkable role in transforming healthcare in Texas. In 1984, the Harris College disbanded its association with Harris Methodist and officially merged with TCU.

ABOVE
Dean Lucy Harris holding brochure on the TCU nursing program. "Lucy Harris," 1950s. TCU Photograph Collection, RU 53. Photo Number: 2791. https://repository.tcu.edu/handle/116099117/6513. Courtesy of TCU Special Collections. Mary Couts Burnett Library. Texas Christian University.

OPPOSITE
Title Page in Lucy Harris, *The Harris College of Nursing: Five Decades of Struggle for a Cause* (Published by TCU Press, 1973).

The Harris College of Nursing

FIVE DECADES OF STRUGGLE FOR A CAUSE

BY LUCY HARRIS

TEXAS CHRISTIAN UNIVERSITY PRESS
Fort Worth, Texas 76129

ABOVE
Portrait of Dean Lucy Harris taken in the 1960s. "Lucy Harris," n.d. TCU Photograph Collection, RU 53. Photo Number: 927. https://repository.tcu.edu:443/handle/116099117/2759. Courtesy of TCU Special Collections. Mary Couts Burnett Library. Texas Christian University.

ABOVE (LEFT)
Portrait of Charles H. Harris. "Charles H. Harris," n.d. TCU Photograph Collection, RU 53. Photo Number: 892. https://repository.tcu.edu:443/handle/116099117/2391. Courtesy of TCU Special Collections. Mary Couts Burnett Library. Texas Christian University.

Brown-Lupton: Finally, a Student Center

Increased student enrollment provided the motivation for facilities expansion at TCU from the 1940s onward. President Sadler admitted that the increase in enrollment during the early 1940s stimulated the need for a university student center, even though the first allocation of space did not occur until 1948, when a section of the basement of the Administration Building (Reed Hall) was remodeled into a student lounge. The board of trustees voted to approve an expenditure in 1950 to remodel the auditorium of the Administration Building into a student lounge, but student enrollment grew so quickly that the space was deemed inadequate.

The student government, the *Skiff*, and other student organizations lobbied aggressively for a space. By the summer of 1953, plans had been drafted for a student center that would cost more than $1,000,000, a portion of which the Fort Worth-based Brown-Lupton Foundation agreed to provide. By late 1953 construction had begun, and by the fall term (September) 1954 the cafeteria and kitchen on the first floor were in use. In January 1955 the remainder of the building was opened to student use, and thereafter known as the Brown-Lupton Student Center.

This facility greatly met student needs. The first floor of the building had eating areas, a game room, the university store, an information center, and student organizational offices. The second floor, with its ballroom, also had lounges, offices, and meeting rooms. The unused third floor space eventually encompassed additional meeting space and was eventually assigned to the School of Education's Instructional Media Center. The horseshoe quad to the west, surrounded by live-oak trees planted immediately after World War II, provided parking and a grassy area that eventually included a fountain. It was a majestic approach to the Student Center.

During the mid-1960s, as enrollment approached ten thousand, the Student Center was remodeled and expanded. Two-story additions were added in 1963 at the north and south end of the building, as was a large basement that housed the university store. Finally, a new building was added in the rear (east side) of the Student Center, which accommodated an enlarged kitchen and connected the Student Center to the Administration Building (Reed Hall). This enlarged complex served as the Student Center until the summer of 2008, when it was demolished and Scharbauer Hall (College of Liberal Arts) was built on the site. A new Brown-Lupton University Union and a series of university dorms surrounding the quad were constructed and opened in 2010.

RIGHT
Brown-Lupton Student Center just prior to its completion. "Brown-Lupton Student Center Construction," 1955. TCU Photograph Collection, RU 53. Photo Number: 2449. https://repository.tcu.edu:443/handle/116099117/2337. Courtesy of TCU Special Collections. Mary Couts Burnett Library. Texas Christian University.

ABOVE
The Brown-Lupton Student Center Bookstore. "Student Center," 1967. TCU Photograph Collection, RU 53. Student Center Folder 2. https://repository.tcu.edu/handle/116099117/6218. Courtesy of TCU Special Collections. Mary Couts Burnett Library. Texas Christian University.

LEFT
The Student Center interior. "Student Center," 1967. TCU Photograph Collection, RU 53. Student Center Folder. https://repository.tcu.edu/handle/116099117/6225. Courtesy of TCU Special Collections. Mary Couts Burnett Library. Texas Christian University.

OPPOSITE
Scaffolding on side of Brown-Lupton Student Center during its construction. "Student Center," 1967. TCU Photograph Collection, RU 53. Student Center Folder 2. https://repository.tcu.edu/handle/116099117/6217. Courtesy of TCU Special Collections. Mary Couts Burnett Library. Texas Christian University.

ABOVE
"Brown-Lupton Student Center Second Floor," 1967. TCU Photograph Collection, RU 53. Photo Number: 2450. https://repository.tcu.edu:443/handle/116099117/3504. Courtesy of TCU Special Collections. Mary Couts Burnett Library. Texas Christian University.

RIGHT
Looking up the side of Brown-Lupton Student Center during its construction. "Brown-Lupton Student Center Construction," 1967. TCU Photograph Collection, RU 53. Photo Number: 2455. https://repository.tcu.edu:443/handle/116099117/3131. Courtesy of TCU Special Collections. Mary Couts Burnett Library. Texas Christian University.

TCU Airport

In 1951 TCU created army and air force training units of the Reserve Officers' Training Corps, and ROTC graduates could be commissioned as second lieutenants in the United States Army or Air Force, depending on which branch they selected during their first two years of college. Though both programs thrived, neither program ever enrolled more than three hundred (army) participants before 1973. Women were not enrolled in ROTC until 1971 (air force) and 1973 (army).

Since TCU had air force ROTC, many believe the emergence of a TCU airfield or airport was associated with this development. A TCU student club—Flying Frogs—existed from 1947 to 1963, and another, the New Flyers Club, existed from 1971 to 1972. TCU also had an affiliated airfield at some time between 1944 and 1947; a March 1947 Dallas Sectional aeronautical chart depiction shows the TCU Airfield facility, which at the time had two perpendicular grass runways, with a few small buildings northeast of the runway intersection.

ABOVE LEFT
President Sadler and Sergeant Julius Slaughter preparing a Texas Flag and TCU pennant to send to Corporal George Dortch in French Morocco. "McGruder Ellis Sadler," 1952. TCU Photograph Collection, RU 53. Photo Number: 1928. https://repository.tcu.edu:443/handle/116099117/2586. Courtesy of TCU Special Collections. Mary Couts Burnett Library. Texas Christian University.

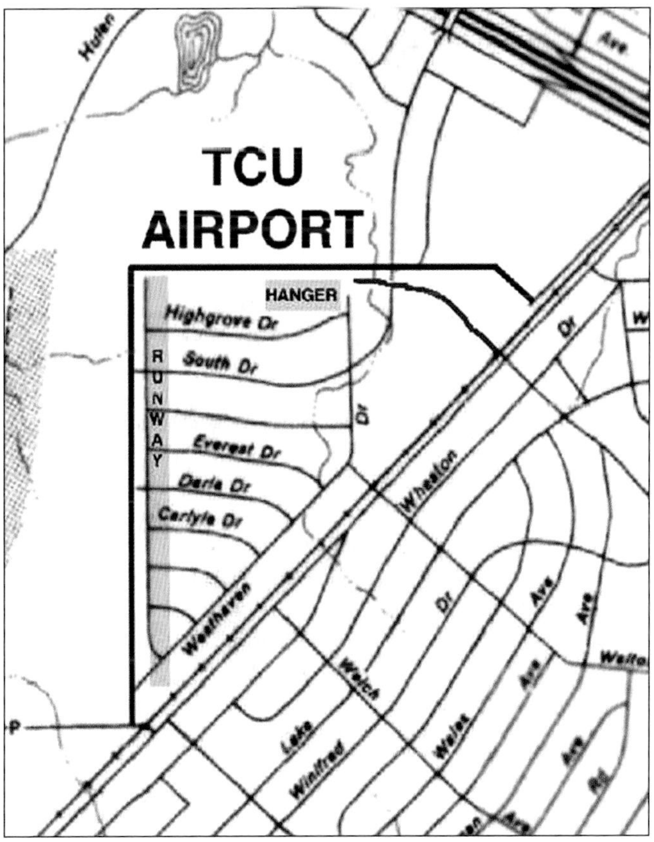

ABOVE
Map of Southwest Fort Worth showing TCU Airport.

Located southeast of Granbury Road, just south of present-day I-20, the entrance to the irregularly shaped facility crossed the railroad tracks at the present-day Wedgmont Circle North. By the early 1950s Air Force ROTC reportedly conducted flight training at the airport. Additionally, the facility offered government-approved private and commercial flight training, fuel and tie-down spaces for private planes, as well as repair and maintenance for planes. By the mid-1950s the facility had grown to three runways, multiple taxiways, a ramp, and two small buildings.

But by 1955 the TCU Airport closed, as the 1955 USGS topographical map depicted the area as "Airport (Abandoned)," and a 1957 DFW Sectional Chart does not show the TCU Air Field at all. By 1959, a housing development had emerged to cover much of the site.

ABOVE RIGHT
TCU Flying Frogs officers, from left to right: James Haynes, president, and Elaine Ellzey, secretary-treasurer. *The Horned Frog*, vol. 50. (Fort Worth: University Supply and Equipment Co., 1954), 202. https://repository.tcu.edu/handle/116099117/11080. Courtesy of TCU Archives and Special Collections. Mary Couts Burnett Library. Texas Christian University.

RIGHT
TCU Flying Frogs club, from left to right: Mr. Troy Stimson, faculty sponsor; Dick Sanders, vice president; La Rue Jaudon, secretary; and, "Boogie" Robinson, president. Image of the TCU Flying Frogs in *The Horned Frog*, vol. 49. (Fort Worth: Stafford-Lowdon Co., 1953), 213. https://repository.tcu.edu/handle/116099117/11079. Courtesy of TCU Archives and Special Collections. Mary Couts Burnett Library. Texas Christian University.

ABOVE
Advertisement for TCU Airport, Inc.

:lying Frogs Take 4 Firsts
At Intercollegiate Air Meet

;peech-Drama
;eries to Open

Thursday Night Program
Features Fallis Players,
T. C. U. Theatre Group

ABOVE
Chancellor Sadler, Dean Cortell Holsapple, and others standing in front of SAC aircraft. "SAC Airport," 1955. TCU Photograph Collection, RU 53. Photo Number: 443. https://repository.tcu.edu:443/handle/116099117/3242. Courtesy of TCU Special Collections. Mary Couts Burnett Library. Texas Christian University.

LEFT
Flying Frogs Club on front page of the *Skiff*. Front page of the *Skiff* 46, no. 8 (Fort Worth, TX), November 7, 1947. https://repository.tcu.edu/handle/116099117/14292. Courtesy of TCU Archives and Special Collections. Mary Couts Burnett Library. Texas Christian University.

TIME TO PL
MIN.
T. C. U.
VISITORS
YE
EEDD
DD CC

Evolution of TCU's Mascot: Addy the Frog

In 1897, "Little Addie" coined the term "Horned Frogs" as the nickname for the AddRan University football team, believing the nickname packed a better punch than the previously used moniker "Fightin' Preacher Boys." Five years later, TCU officially adopted the nickname "the Horned Frogs," and during the university's first hundred years a variety of animals and people served as both official and unofficial mascots.

Beginning in 1921, a young boy served as the official "Horned Frog" mascot, though he did not wear a costume. He wore a purple uniform and stood on the sidelines with the team for each home game. In 1954 and 1955, seven-year-old Victor "Little Vic" McDonald wore the jersey number ½ on the sideline for every TCU football game. The TCU football team continued this tradition of having a young "Horned Frog" on the field until the 1960s.

Other sports teams adopted a variety of animals as team mascots. In the early 1920s, the TCU baseball team adopted a dog as the team mascot. The dog wore a purple cover and white hat on game day. In 1930, the TCU band adopted a goat named Samuel as its mascot. The band received "Samuel" from an amazed spectator who donated the goat to band director Claude Sammis after watching the band perform at the annual Southwestern Exposition and Fat Stock Show. In 1941, the TCU football team also adopted a dog, Blackie, as its team mascot. The dog purportedly showed up early to watch practice each day and offered pointers to the team.

In 1949 Jimmy Paschal developed the idea for a costumed "Horned Frog" mascot. The Student Government Council earmarked fifty dollars for a costume. On September 24, 1949, Paschal appeared as the "Addy the Frog" mascot on TCU's sidelines for the first time. "Addy the Frog" lasted until the 1960s, when student leaders changed the spelling to "Addie the Frog" and then "Addie the Fightin' Frog." Annual elections determined the student who served as the mascot until the mid-1960s. The TCU cheerleaders and Student Government Council then took the lead in nominating and choosing the next mascot via a preliminary screening and nomination process. Today, SuperFrog serves as the current iteration of the TCU mascot with up to six students wearing the costume each year to complete the numerous required appearances and duties.

OPPOSITE
Addie the Fighting Frog standing in front of Amon G. Carter Stadium scoreboard. "Addie the Fighting Frog Mascot," 1966. TCU Photograph Collection, RU 53. Photo Number: 2377. https://repository.tcu.edu:443/handle/116099117/3789. Courtesy of TCU Special Collections. Mary Couts Burnett Library. Texas Christian University.

LEFT
Addy the Frog holding a steer's skull labeled Bevo during a TCU football game. *The Horned Frog*, vol. 49. (Fort Worth: Stafford-Lowdon Co., 1953), 105. https://repository.tcu.edu/handle/116099117/11079. Courtesy of TCU Archives and Special Collections. Mary Couts Burnett Library. Texas Christian University.

ABOVE
Addie the Fighting Frog stands on top of a bulldozer at groundbreaking ceremony for Brown-Lupton Student Center. "Addie the Fighting Frog Mascot," 1967. TCU Photograph Collection, RU 53. Photo Number: 2373. https://repository.tcu.edu:443/handle/116099117/3040. Courtesy of TCU Special Collections. Mary Couts Burnett Library. Texas Christian University.

ABOVE
Addie the Fighting Frog greets new students during Howdy Week in 1968. "Howdy Week," 1968. TCU Photograph Collection, RU 53. Photo Number: 2395. https://repository.tcu.edu:443/handle/116099117/3001. Courtesy of TCU Special Collections. Mary Couts Burnett Library. Texas Christian University.

ABOVE
Photo of Addie the Fighting Frog in an empty Amon G. Carter Stadium. "Addie the Fighting Frog Mascot," 1966. TCU Photograph Collection, RU 53. Photo Number: 2312. https://repository.tcu.edu:443/handle/116099117/2418. Courtesy of TCU Special Collections. Mary Couts Burnett Library. Texas Christian University.

RIGHT
Paul O. Riddings next to Addie the Fighting Frog. "Paul O. Ridings," 1971. TCU Photograph Collection, RU 53. Photo Number: 923. https://repository.tcu.edu:443/handle/116099117/2645. Courtesy of TCU Special Collections. Mary Couts Burnett Library. Texas Christian University.

ABOVE
"Cheerleaders and Addie the Fighting Frog Mascot," 1960s. TCU Photograph Collection, RU 53. Photo Number: 2376. https://repository.tcu.edu:443/handle/116099117/3411. Courtesy of TCU Special Collections. Mary Couts Burnett Library. Texas Christian University.

LEFT
Addie the Fighting Frog petting Baylor's black bear mascot. "Addie the Fighting Frog Mascot," 1965. TCU Photograph Collection, RU 53. Photo Number: 2309. https://repository.tcu.edu:443/handle/116099117/2707. Courtesy of TCU Special Collections. Mary Couts Burnett Library. Texas Christian University.

ABOVE
Addie the Fighting Frog and cheerleaders with TCU Centennial sign. "Cheerleaders and Addie the Fighting Frog Mascot," 1973. TCU Photograph Collection, RU 53. Photo Number: 2374. https://repository.tcu.edu:443/handle/116099117/3808. Courtesy of TCU Special Collections. Mary Couts Burnett Library. Texas Christian University.

Dan Jenkins

Fort Worth native Dan Jenkins wrote "The Glory Game at Goat Hills," published in *Sports Illustrated* in August of 1965. It could easily have been mistaken for fiction, but was as true as any well-read putt. The article showcased the growing popularity of amateur sports, told through a singular tale of municipal golf and its inner game of gambling. "Goat Hills" single-handedly gave a voice to novice athletes everywhere.

"Glory Game" was set on a public, 18-hole track called Worth Hills Golf Course. It was known as "Goat Hills" because the terrain was reportedly so unkept that only a mountain goat could clamber across its fairways. TCU campus progress acquired and consumed Worth Hills in 1963. But readers found in "Glory Game" a dialogue surprisingly similar to the script they recited with friends on local golf courses and at country clubs across America. As *Sports Illustrated* and other magazines enjoyed a rise in popularity during the 1960s, so did golf. Thus "Glory Game" appeared at the confluence of accessibility and awareness.

Jenkins graduated from Paschal High School and TCU, and he joined SI in 1962 after writing for Fort Worth and Dallas newspapers throughout the 1950s. He gained a massive infusion of fans following the article's publication, as did Fort Worth and the golf played here.

Jenkins covered Fort Worth's Ben Hogan and Byron Nelson and other golf celebrities for over sixty years. And while "Glory Game" teed up his national career, his subsequent best-selling novels sank the proverbial birdie putt on his legacy. He provided weekly and monthly insight into the lives of Jack Nicklaus and Tiger Woods through his magazine columns, just as he had brought "Glory Game" characters Magoo and Cecil the Parachute to life.

The World Golf Hall of Fame inducted Jenkins in 2012 for his many international accolades. Only the third writer to be inducted, he was the first living author to be given the honor. His last two books were published by TCU Press, and his final novel, *The Reunion at Herb's Café,* was still in production when he passed away on March 7, 2019.

RIGHT
Golfer Dan Jenkins looking at a trophy. Photo taken on August 19, 1946. AR406-6-1875. Courtesy, *Fort Worth Star-Telegram Collection*, Special Collections, The University of Texas at Arlington Libraries.

ABOVE
Image of TCU Varsity Golf Team, from left to right: Dan Jenkins, Bill Tatum, Jimmy Hickey, and Grover Swift. *The Horned Frog* vol. 47 (Fort Worth: Stafford-Lowdon Co., 1951), 263. https://repository.tcu.edu/handle/116099117/11077. Courtesy of TCU Archives and Special Collections. Mary Couts Burnett Library. Texas Christian University.

LEFT
Paschal High School golfers, from left to right: Carroll Baird, Ernie Vossler, Dan Jenkins, and Johnny Ray at Worth Hills Municipal Golf Course. Photo taken on May 11, 1946. AR406-6-429. Courtesy, *Fort Worth Star-Telegram Collection,* Special Collections, The University of Texas at Arlington Libraries.

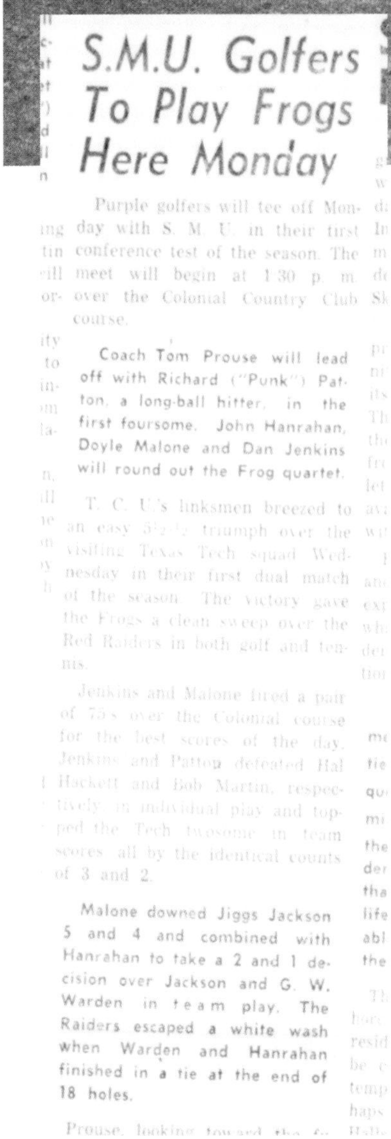

S.M.U. Golfers To Play Frogs Here Monday

Purple golfers will tee off Monday with S. M. U. in their first conference test of the season. The meet will begin at 1:30 p. m. over the Colonial Country Club course.

Coach Tom Prouse will lead off with Richard ("Punk") Patton, a long-ball hitter, in the first foursome. John Hanrahan, Doyle Malone and Dan Jenkins will round out the Frog quartet.

T. C. U.'s linksmen breezed to an easy 5½-½ triumph over the visiting Texas Tech squad Wednesday in their first dual match of the season. The victory gave the Frogs a clean sweep over the Red Raiders in both golf and tennis.

Jenkins and Malone fired a pair of 75's over the Colonial course for the best scores of the day. Jenkins and Patton defeated Hal Hackett and Bob Martin, respectively, in individual play and topped the Tech twosome in team scores, all by the identical counts of 3 and 2.

Malone downed Jiggs Jackson 5 and 4 and combined with Hanrahan to take a 2 and 1 decision over Jackson and G. W. Warden in team play. The Raiders escaped a white wash when Warden and Hanrahan finished in a tie at the end of 18 holes.

Prouse, looking toward the ...

ABOVE
TCU Varsity Golf Team, from left to right: Gene Shields, Dan "Double Bogie" Jenkins, Bill Tatum, Coach Tom Prouse, Dick Jetton, and Grover Swift. *The Horned Frog*, vol. 48. (Fort Worth: Stafford-Lowdon Co., 1952), 270. https://repository.tcu.edu/handle/116099117/11078. Courtesy of TCU Archives and Special Collections. Mary Couts Burnett Library. Texas Christian University.

LEFT
Dan Jenkins preparing to hit golf ball. *The Horned Frog*, vol. 48. (Fort Worth: Stafford-Lowdon Co., 1952), 271. https://repository.tcu.edu/handle/116099117/11078. Courtesy of TCU Archives and Special Collections. Mary Couts Burnett Library. Texas Christian University.

FAR LEFT
The *Skiff* Newspaper Clipping, "SMU Golfers to Play Frogs here on Monday." Page 10. The *Skiff* 48, no. 25 (Fort Worth, TX), March 31, 1950. https://repository.tcu.edu/handle/116099117/14398. Courtesy of TCU Archives and Special Collections. Mary Couts Burnett Library. Texas Christian University.

RIGHT
"Dan Jenkins Speaking at Inaugural Awards Given in his Honor in October 2017." Photo by Mark Graham. Lisa Martin and Mark Graham, "Dan Jenkins is a TCU Treasure." *TCU Magazine* (Winter, 2018). Courtesy of *TCU Magazine*.

RIGHT
Dan Jenkins, *His Ownself: A Semi-Memoir* (Published by Anchor Books Inc., 2014). Photo by the authors.

RIGHT
Dan Jenkins, *Semi-Tough* (Published by Antheneum, 1972).

ABOVE
"TCU Ring given to Dan Jenkins after Rose Bowl." Photo by Mark Graham. Lisa Martin and Mark Graham, "Dan Jenkins is a TCU Treasure." *TCU Magazine* (Winter, 2018). Courtesy of *TCU Magazine*.

OPPOSITE
Bob Lilly making a tackle during a game. Image courtesy of TCU Athletics.

Robert Lewis (Bob) Lilly

Standing 6'5" and wearing number 72 during his three playing years at TCU, the Throckmorton-raised Bob (nicknamed Tiger) Lilly ultimately became a two-time All-Southwest Conference defensive tackle (1959, 1960) and a 1960 Kodak All-American. As a part of his award, Lilly also received a 35 mm camera and some two hundred rolls of film; for a kid who had never taken a picture, photography quickly became his off-field passion and it remains so today. In 1983 Lilly co-authored *Reflections* with sportswriter Sam Blair, which featured his black-and-white photographs of teammates in candid poses.

The former high school basketball, track, and football star had furious pass-rushing skills and the agility and instincts to disrupt offensive plays. His strength became legendary at TCU; as a freshman he had lifted a friend's car that had a flat tire because there was no jack. Lilly had shown up at TCU unannounced after playing his high school senior football season in Pendleton, Oregon. Athletic director Abe Martin called Lilly TCU's "greatest bargain" and "the finest tackle [he] ever coached."

Drafted as the first player ever by the Dallas Cowboys in 1961, Lilly became a seven-time All-Pro selection and played in eleven Pro Bowl games during his fourteen-year career. He scored four defensive touchdowns during his career and altogether returned eighteen fumbles for 109 yards. Bob Lilly was the "gentle giant," and the "unblockable, unstoppable, force" of the Cowboys' vaunted "Doomsday Defense." His size, speed, and agility, combined with his natural understanding of the game, made him one of the greatest defensive players ever to play the game. Throughout his career opponents regularly double- and triple-teamed him, to no avail. In fact, his twenty-nine-yard sack of Miami Dolphins quarterback Bob Griese during the Cowboys' 1972 Super Bowl victory remains one of the game's most memorable plays.

Lilly spent his entire career as a Dallas Cowboy and played in 196 consecutive regular-season games, missing only the NFC Championship Game on December 30, 1973. Lilly became affectionately known as "Mr. Cowboy," and on November 23, 1975, the Cowboys made him the first inductee into the famed Ring of Honor. The team also unofficially retired his number 74 jersey. A member of Sigma Phi Epsilon in college, Lilly has also been named to the College Football Hall of Fame (1980) and the East-West Shrine Game Hall of Fame (2006).

LEFT
Bob Lilly. Courtesy of TCU Athletics

LEFT
Bob Lilly with Coach Abe Martin in *The Horned Frog*, vol. 57. (Fort Worth: University Supply and Equipment Co., 1961), 275. https://repository.tcu.edu/handle/116099117/11087. Courtesy of TCU Archives and Special Collections. Mary Couts Burnett Library. Texas Christian University.

ABOVE
Bob Lilly in *The Horned Frog*, vol. 57. (Fort Worth: University Supply and Equipment Co., 1961), 156. https://repository.tcu.edu/handle/116099117/11087. Courtesy of TCU Archives and Special Collections. Mary Couts Burnett Library. Texas Christian University.

LEFT
Portrait of Bob Lilly after being drafted by the Dallas Cowboys football team. Courtesy of Bob Lilly.

LEFT
Current-day photograph of Bob Lilly holding the camera he received when becoming an All-American in 1960. Courtesy of Bob Lilly.

ABOVE
Donald Floyd, Robert Lilly, and Coach Allie White in *The Horned Frog*, vol. 56. (Fort Worth: University Supply andEquipment Co., 1960), 282. https://repository.tcu.edu/handle/116099117/11086. Courtesy of TCU Archives and Special Collections. Mary Couts Burnett Library. Texas Christian University.

LEFT
The camera Bob Lilly received in 1960 after being named a Kodak All-American. Courtesy of Bob Lilly.

CHAPTER 6

Concluding the First Hundred Years: 1961–1973

Phi Beta Kappa Comes to TCU

Cementing a spot for TCU in the prestigious national honor society Phi Beta Kappa was a longtime dream of TCU President and Chancellor M. E. Sadler. He spearheaded the 1949 submission of the university's first formal application to the elite organization.

J. M. Moudy, a 1943 TCU graduate, returned to TCU in 1957 as dean of the graduate school. Having been a Phi Beta Kappa initiate during his doctoral studies at Duke, Moudy joined Sadler in beating the drums for joining its ranks.

TCU leaders applied every three years but were rebuffed by Phi Beta Kappa's gatekeepers, who were intent on keeping membership selective and limited to the upper 10 percent echelon of American universities.

Two Phi Beta Kappa representatives finally visited campus in 1966. Speaking with students and administrators, they assessed TCU's methods for conducting academic business. According to a *Skiff* report on the visit, the representatives were "deeply impressed" by athletic director and football coach Abe Martin, who told them, "Athletes should be treated like all other students in the area of admissions, class attendance and standards."

Voting on TCU's charter would wait four more years, until members of the 184 Phi Beta Kappa universities assembled in Indiana in September 1970. At that time, Phi Beta Kappa approved the admission request. On February 4, 1971, TCU's Delta of Texas chapter was born, meaning the university had joined the University of Texas at Austin, Rice, and SMU as the only Phi Beta Kappa-approved institutions in the Lone Star State.

Moudy told *TCU Magazine* in 1973 that he was "prouder of the Phi Beta Kappa charter we were extended in 1970 than I would be of a 30-game streak. But don't tell [football coach Billy] Tohill I said so."

LEFT
Chancellor James M. Moudy talking with TCU students Bill Barlow and Richard Hays, Texas Interscholastic League Scholars. "Student Awards," 1972. TCU Photograph Collection, RU 53. Raw files, Who's Who. https://repository.tcu.edu/handle/116099117/6291. Courtesy of TCU Special Collections. Mary Couts Burnett Library. Texas Christian University.

ABOVE
Dr. Gentry Shelton with students and faculty at Brite Divinity School. "Brite Divinity School Class," 1965. TCU Photograph Collection, RU 53. Photo Number: 2162. https://repository.tcu.edu:443/handle/116099117/2977. Courtesy of TCU Special Collections. Mary Couts Burnett Library. Texas Christian University.

ABOVE
"Professor Donald Worcester receiving his Phi Betta Kappa key" in *The Horned Frog*, Vol. 68, Book II. (Taylor Publishing Co., 1972), 224. https://repository.tcu.edu/handle/116099117/11100. Courtesy of TCU Archives and Special Collections. Mary Couts Burnett Library. Texas Christian University.

ABOVE
Valerie Neal winner of the 1971 Phi Beta Kappa Award. *The Horned Frog*, vol. 67. (Fort Worth: Taylor Publishing Co., 1971), 389. https://repository.tcu.edu/handle/116099117/11097. Courtesy of TCU Archives and Special Collections. Mary Couts Burnett Library. Texas Christian University.

ABOVE
Students in physics class in 1970. "Physics Class," 1970. TCU Photograph Collection, RU 53. Raw Files, Physics 1966–1975. https://repository.tcu.edu/handle/116099117/6274. Courtesy of TCU Special Collections. Mary Couts Burnett Library. Texas Christian University.

ABOVE
1973 Phi Betta Kappa Honor Society initiates. *The Horned Frog*, vol. 69. (Fort Worth: Taylor Publishing Co., 1973), 425. https://repository.tcu.edu/handle/116099117/11101. Courtesy of TCU Archives and Special Collections. Mary Couts Burnett Library. Texas Christian University.

RIGHT
"James M. Moudy," n.d. TCU Photograph Collection, RU 53. Photo Number: 1168. https://repository.tcu.edu:443/handle/116099117/2931. Courtesy of TCU Special Collections. Mary Couts Burnett Library. Texas Christian University.

Worth Hills Campus Evolution

Colonial Country Club has hosted its share of parties on the thirteenth hole. But nothing compared to the congregation that took place on the neighboring Worth Hills Golf Course underneath the roof of the snack shack during the mid-twentieth century.

Before the Bayard H. Friedman Tennis Center was built atop it, Vance Minter—then a young worker for the Worth Hills pro shop—was told to go do his best unprotected work to eradicate the bees that had built their hive under the eaves of the municipal golf course restroom near what is now the indoor tennis center at TCU.

The Worth Hills Golf Course, not quite Fort Worth's first public golf location, was among its most revered. And not for the scenery and lush landscaping that now covers the same topography. It was known as "Goat Hills" because of its rock-strewn terrain, but it was loved because many of Fort Worth's golfers spent countless hours abusing the sparsely watered fairways between 1921 and 1955.

In the mid-1950s, Texas Christian University started building lecture halls and dorm rooms all over the intersection of Berry Street and University Drive. Worth Hills Golf Course would not be spared, and a campaign to acquire it from the city was successful. In time, accompanying many of the structures today's TCU students learn in, Goat Hills became dorm rooms in the 1960s, the Friedman Tennis Center in the '70s, and various Horned Frog Athletics facilities in the '80s and '90s.

In the twenty-first century, much of the property was transformed into what stands today. TCU attempts—and often succeeds—in attracting the top baseball, track and field, soccer, and tennis student-athletes in the world. And, of course, thinkers. The original structures that took over the fairways and greens were dormitories, which have continually been rebuilt for student and Greek life today.

But somewhere underneath all of that progress lies some old balata from an errant shank that likely cost its golfer a couple of bucks on a Nassau press.

ABOVE
"Worth Hills Complex," 1964. TCU Photograph Collection, RU 53. Raw files, Worth Hills Cafeteria Folder 2. https://repository.tcu.edu/handle/116099117/6403. Courtesy of TCU Special Collections. Mary Couts Burnett Library. Texas Christian University.

LEFT
Painting of Worth Hills Municipal Golf Course that previously hung in the Worth Hills Clubhouse. Courtesy of Dan Jenkins Estate.

ABOVE
"Worth Hills Dormitories," 1967. TCU Photograph Collection, RU 53. Photo Number: 2473. https://repository.tcu.edu:443/handle/116099117/2578. Courtesy of TCU Special Collections. Mary Couts Burnett Library. Texas Christian University.

RIGHT
"Worth Hills Dormitories under Construction," 1964. TCU Photograph Collection, RU 53. Photo Number: 2475. https://repository.tcu.edu:443/handle/116099117/3533. Courtesy of TCU Special Collections. Mary Couts Burnett Library. Texas Christian University.

KTCU Radio

TCU Radio Studio began operations in 1938 under the direction of Claude Sammis. The station broadcast over 150 programs annually on the local KTAT and WBAP stations. Soon afterward, Professor Katherine Moore offered two courses in radio production and programming. In 1947, Moore expanded the curriculum to offer six courses in radio, which allowed TCU to offer a minor in the field. KTCU, the official TCU radio station, began operations in 1949 under the supervision of Fred Folk. Students Walter Jones, Charles Beseda, Dick Horst, Dick Harris, Howard Beckall, and Bill Shopshire operated a six-hour programming schedule, complete with campus news, informal discussions, debate, student musicians, and popular recordings. Perhaps the radio's only hiccup occurred in 1963, when Station Manager Bill Rohde played Kingston Trio's "Greenback Dollar." The song contained the expletive word "damn," which led Student Social Director Elizabeth Youngblood to immediately cut the record off. Rohde fired off an editorial criticizing Youngblood's censorial act. Ultimately, both parties expressed their dissenting opinions and let the matter rest. The incident did little to quell the station's continued growth. The FCC licensed KTCU-FM as an educational radio station in 1964. Today, KTCU still offers programming over the sound waves with musical programming, news coverage, and TCU athletics play-by-play.

ABOVE
Students working on set in 1966. "Radio, TV, Film," 1966. TCU Photograph Collection, RU 53. Raw files, Radio and TV Film. https://repository.tcu.edu/handle/116099117/6235. Courtesy of TCU Special Collections. Mary Couts Burnett Library. Texas Christian University.

OPPOSITE
Student working in the KTCU soundbooth. "Radio, TV, Film," 1967. TCU Photograph Collection, RU 53. Raw files, Radio and TV Film. https://repository.tcu.edu/handle/116099117/6237. Courtesy of TCU Special Collections. Mary Couts Burnett Library. Texas Christian University.

TCU
MARCH
13-18

ABOVE

Students presenting in front of camera for TCU TV. "Radio, TV, and Film," 1970. TCU Photograph Collection, RU 53. Photo Number: 2426. https://repository.tcu.edu:443/handle/116099117/3330. Courtesy of TCU Special Collections. Mary Couts Burnett Library. Texas Christian University.

LEFT

"Bill Rohde receiving an award during the Communications banquet." *The Horned Frog*, vol. 59. (Fort Worth: Taylor Publishing Co., 1963), 99. https://repository.tcu.edu/handle/116099117/11089. Courtesy of TCU Archives and Special Collections. Mary Couts Burnett Library. Texas Christian University.

ABOVE (TOP)
A group of students working in the KTCU sound-booth. “Radio, TV, Film,” 1972. TCU Photograph Collection, RU 53. Raw files, Radio and TV Film. https://repository.tcu.edu/handle/116099117/6239. Courtesy of TCU Special Collections. Mary Couts Burnett Library. Texas Christian University.

ABOVE
Student worker filming student speaker on TCU TV set. “Radio, TV, Film,” 1968. TCU Photograph Collection, RU 53. Raw files, Radio and TV Film. https://repository.tcu.edu/handle/116099117/6240. Courtesy of TCU Special Collections. Mary Couts Burnett Library. Texas Christian University.

ABOVE LEFT
Professor Katherine Moore, who taught radio and television courses at TCU. "Katherine Moore," n.d. TCU Photograph Collection, RU 53. Photo Number: 1885. https://repository.tcu.edu:443/handle/116099117/3783. Courtesy of TCU Special Collections. Mary Couts Burnett Library. Texas Christian University.

ABOVE
Claude Sammis, who oversaw TCU radio operations from 1938 until his death in 1941. "Claude Sammis," n.d. TCU Photograph Collection, RU 53. Photo Number: 919. https://repository.tcu.edu:443/handle/116099117/3753. Courtesy of TCU Special Collections. Mary Couts Burnett Library. Texas Christian University.

LEFT
Two students working a camera. *The Horned Frog*, vol. 64. (Fort Worth: Taylor Publishing Co., 1968), 263. https://repository.tcu.edu/handle/116099117/11094. Courtesy of TCU Special Collections. Mary Couts Burnett Library. Texas Christian University.

TCU TV

In 1949, TCU offered its first courses in television production and film. The course offerings coincided with the opening of Amon Carter's WBAP television station in September 1948. The partnership between Carter's station and TCU enabled the expansion of media and programming courses, and by 1955 students were able to earn a major in radio-television. In 1960, William K. Hawes offered the first courses in cinematography and film. Hawes and his students soon developed a telecast series in conjunction with local television stations. The programs appeared on the local WBAP, KFJZ, and KTVT stations. These programs sought to provide unique programming options and to engage broader community discussions. For example in 1964, TCU TV sponsored a debate between local parents and educators over the introduction of sex education in public schools. These programs aimed to provide educational material and multiple perspectives for viewers. Student programmers also filled programming hours with taped recordings of fine arts performances, athletic competitions, and a TCU-centric newscast for local audiences.

TCU Press

TCU Press's first publication was Colby Hall's *History of Texas Christian University: A College of the Cattle Frontier*, in 1947. In the decades since, TCU Press has published approximately twenty scholarly and general interest books a year. Its lists include novels, story collections, poetry collections by Texas poets laureate, and creative nonfiction by such writers as Dan Jenkins, Jan Reid, Beverly Lowry, Bob Ray Sanders, Thomas Zigal, Shelby Heron, Lonn Taylor, and James Ward Lee, among many others. Histories centering on the Southwest, Texas, and Fort Worth proper; biographies of important Texas historical figures; books on Texas art, architecture, and music; books for children and young adults; and books such as this one—about TCU itself—are among the hundreds of titles available from TCU Press, which is perched on the eastern frontier of the campus.

Marguerite Potter and the GE Scholar's Bowl

The College Quiz Bowl first aired on NBC Radio in 1953. The show paired teams of student scholars competing against scholars from another college or university. Beginning in 1959, the show aired on CBS television stations across the country. TCU received an invitation to participate on the show in fall of 1961.

University leaders nominated Professor Marguerite Potter to coach TCU's College Bowl Team. Born in Sedalia, Missouri, in 1907, Potter graduated from Southwest Baptist College in 1926 before earning a BA in education from Central Missouri State College and a master of arts in history from Columbia University. She joined TCU's faculty in 1945 before completing her PhD at the University of Texas in 1955, with a specialty in British history. From 1972 to 1975, she chaired the History Department at TCU.

Potter hosted tryouts for the College Bowl team during the Spring 1961 semester. After a taxing competition, four students and two alternates made the final cut. Randie Guenther, a sophomore from Fort Worth; Joseph E. Lake, a senior from Gainesville; Richard Bond, a sophomore from Denison; and James Dunkly, the team captain and a junior from Arlington formed the starting four. Pat Susan Potter and Fred Kemp, both of Fort Worth, served as the alternates who flew with the team to New York.

Each team member possessed unique expertise meant to provide team balance. Guenther specialized in music, art, and Shakespeare. Dunkly provided expertise in Greco-Roman classics, physics, chemistry, mathematics, and mythology. Bond specialized in English, American, and European literature, musical comedy, and semiclassical music. Lake provided knowledge in international affairs, current events, government, American history, and geography. After finalizing the team, Potter hosted practices twice a week in her office, where she peppered students with a variety of questions for two hours. By September, the team felt confident for its first show.

ABOVE
Front cover of red GE College Bowl pamphlet. TCU Scrapbook Collection, RU 8. Box 38, Folder 54. "Dr. Marguerite Potter, G.E. College Bowl (1961)." https://repository.tcu.edu/handle/116099117/4611. Courtesy of TCU Archives and Special Collections. Mary Couts Burnett Library. Texas Christian University.

TCU's team faced off against DePaul University on September 24, 1961. The Horned Frogs won the showdown decisively, by a score of 190-45. TCU then squared off against SUNY-Buffalo in week two. Again, the Horned Frogs won handily, 210-80. Week three proved more challenging, as TCU narrowly outscored Upsala College 145-140. TCU's winning streak made them the first representative west of the Mississippi to win three times in the College Bowl. Unfortunately, the streak ended against Pomona College, who defeated the Horned Frogs, 200-105. Although they'd been defeated on their fourth outing, TCU hosted a public ceremony in honor of their exploits, celebrating their scholastic performance with trophies and certificates.

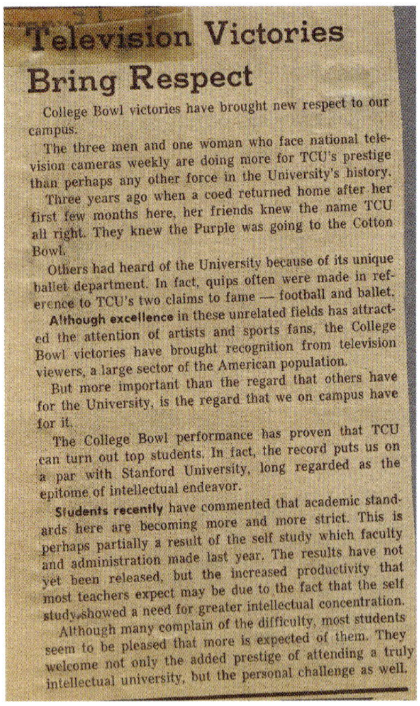

Television Victories Bring Respect

College Bowl victories have brought new respect to our campus.

The three men and one woman who face national television cameras weekly are doing more for TCU's prestige than perhaps any other force in the University's history.

Three years ago when a coed returned home after her first few months here, her friends knew the name TCU all right. They knew the Purple was going to the Cotton Bowl.

Others had heard of the University because of its unique ballet department. In fact, quips often were made in reference to TCU's two claims to fame — football and ballet.

Although excellence in these unrelated fields has attracted the attention of artists and sports fans, the College Bowl victories have brought recognition from television viewers, a large sector of the American population.

But more important than the regard that others have for the University, is the regard that we on campus have for it.

The College Bowl performance has proven that TCU can turn out top students. In fact, the record puts us on a par with Stanford University, long regarded as the epitome of intellectual endeavor.

Students recently have commented that academic standards here are becoming more and more strict. This is perhaps partially a result of the self study which faculty and administration made last year. The results have not yet been released, but the increased productivity that most teachers expect may be due to the fact that the self study showed a need for greater intellectual concentration.

Although many complain of the difficulty, most students seem to be pleased that more is expected of them. They welcome not only the added prestige of attending a truly intellectual university, but the personal challenge as well.

ABOVE
Front cover of "Dr. Marguerite Potter and GE College Bowl Scrapbook." TCU Scrapbook Collection, RU 8. Box 38, Folder 54. "Dr. Marguerite Potter, G.E. College Bowl (1961)." https://repository.tcu.edu/handle/116099117/4611. Courtesy of TCU Archives and Special Collections. Mary Couts Burnett Library. Texas Christian University.

LEFT
Newspaper clipping with story "Television Victories Bring Respect." Pdf image 13. TCU Scrapbook Collection, RU 8. Box 38, Folder 54. "Dr. Marguerite Potter, G.E. College Bowl (1961)." https://repository.tcu.edu/handle/116099117/4611. Courtesy of TCU Archives and Special Collections. Mary Couts Burnett Library. Texas Christian University.

ABOVE
Dr. Marguerite Potter.
TCU Scrapbook Collection, RU 8. Box 38, Folder 54. "Dr. Marguerite Potter, G.E. College Bowl (1961)." https://repository.tcu.edu/handle/116099117/4611. Courtesy of TCU Archives and Special Collections. Mary Couts Burnett Library. Texas Christian University.

RIGHT
Richard Bond, Jim Dunkly, Randie Guenther, and Joe Lake behind desk during College Bowl competition. TCU Scrapbook Collection, RU 8. Box 38, Folder 54. "Dr. Marguerite Potter, G.E. College Bowl (1961)." https://repository.tcu.edu/handle/116099117/4611. Courtesy of TCU Archives and Special Collections. Mary Couts Burnett Library. Texas Christian University.

RIGHT
Dr. Marguerite Potter with Jim Dunkly, Randie Guenther, Richard Bond, and Joseph Lake standing outside of CBS Studios in New York City. TCU Special Collections. Scrapbook Collection, RU 8. Box 38, Folder 54. "Dr. Marguerite Potter, G.E. College Bowl (1961)." https://repository.tcu.edu/handle/116099117/4611. Courtesy of TCU Archives and Special Collections. Mary Couts Burnett Library. Texas Christian University.

Ben Procter— Historian and leader

Almost larger than life, 6'3" Ben Procter, a native of Temple, Texas, towered over most students. Known as a teacher who offered rigorous courses and animated lectures, his enthusiasm for political involvement urged many students to get involved with local politics. He would often tell his class "I'm a democrat with a big 'D' and a little 'd.'" Whether students agreed with him or not, Procter caused people to think.

The Procter family had moved to Austin in 1939, where Ben graduated from Stephen F. Austin High School in the spring of 1945. After graduation, he enlisted in the US Navy, serving during the last months of World War II. Enrolling in 1946 at the University of Texas, he played football as a receiver and secured All Southwest Conference and All American honors his senior year. He also earned Phi Beta Kappa membership when he graduated in 1951 with a BA and MA in history. He played two years of pro ball: one year with the Los Angeles Rams and a second with the Washington Redskins, but a back injury ended his brief career as a professional football player. Taking the money he had earned in football, Procter pursued an MA and PhD in history at Harvard University.

Procter started teaching at TCU in 1957, even though he had not finished his degree. The move was welcomed by his father, Leslie Chambers Procter, who had lettered in baseball from 1905–1908 while attending TCU in Waco. Despite a heavy teaching load of five classes, the younger Procter completed his PhD by 1960. During his forty-three-year career, Procter helped form chapters of Phi Beta Kappa and Phi Alpha Theta (an honorary history fraternity) at TCU and also helped create the PhD program in history. He taught nearly ten thousand students in seminars and classes on US history, Texas history, and the American West. He wrote or cowrote several books and articles that brought him awards and recognition. He won the Summerfield G. Roberts Award (best book on Texas history), was a Minnie Piper Fellow (one of ten professors chosen each year in Texas for outstanding teaching and scholarship), and was voted a "Favorite Teacher" at TCU. When he retired in 2000, TCU named him an "honorary alumnus."

Procter never distanced himself from family life and his wife Phoebe. According to his son Ben Jr., a 1981 TCU graduate, people always dropped by the house to discuss academic issues. While Procter had a larger-than-life presence, those around him never felt in the shadows. His passion for education and interaction with students led him to embody TCU's academic goals.

BELOW
Dr. Ben Procter standing in front of Amon G. Carter Stadium. Courtesy of Ben Procter Family. Texas Christian University.

ABOVE
Portrait of Dr. Ben Procter. Courtesy of Ben Procter Family.

ABOVE
1971 TCU Ex-Lettermen's Hall of Fame induction with H. H. "Slim" Kinzey, Johnny Vaught, Walter Roach, Bryon "Buster" Brannon, and L. C. Procter (seated). "Lettermen's Hall of Fame," 1971. TCU Photograph Collection, RU 53.Photo Number: 896. https://repository.tcu.edu:443/handle/116099117/3527. Courtesy of TCU Special Collections. Mary Couts Burnett Library. Texas Christian University.

LEFT
Dr. Ben Procter speaking at Mary Couts Burnett Library. Courtesy of Ben Procter Family.

ABOVE
TCU and Jarvis Trustees meeting to discuss partnership in 1963. "Jarvis Christian College of Board of Trustees," c. 1960-1964. TCU Photograph Collection, RU 53. Photo Number: 2064. https://repository.tcu.edu:443/handle/116099117/3032. Courtesy of TCU Special Collections. Mary Couts Burnett Library. Texas Christian University.

OPPOSITE
"Members of Omega Psi Phi Performing during the 1972 NAACP Super Show Fundraiser" in *The Horned Frog*, vol. 68, book II. (Taylor Publishing Co., 1972), 75. https://repository.tcu.edu/handle/116099117/11100. Courtesy of TCU Archives and Special Collections. Mary Couts Burnett Library. Texas Christian University.

Civil Rights and Integration—Just the Beginning

While TCU's charter and bylaws never precluded the admission of Black students, progressive-minded Chancellor Sadler understood the need for integration of the TCU campus.

As the civil rights movement expanded in January 1964, the TCU board announced that several of our peer and aspirant institutions were in the midst of litigation to enroll Black students. Since TCU faculty and the student government association had voted overwhelmingly to admit Black students, TCU Trustees agreed to remove the last racial restrictions on student enrollment. By a five-to-one vote, the board agreed: "That from this day henceforth students be enrolled at T.C.U. without any reference to race, creed, or nationality, and that the Board of Trustees trust the administration to carry out this responsibility."

Simply voting to permit Black students to enroll did not change TCU overnight. In November 1963, TCU Trustees had met with leaders of Jarvis Christian College, a historically Black school in Hawkins, Texas, about establishing a relationship between the two Disciples institutions. In 1964, the year TCU fully integrated, the board approved a five-year formal affiliation between TCU and Jarvis. Under this agreement, TCU assisted Jarvis with its finances and its academic responsibilities, and within one year, Jarvis's enrollment increased by more than 20 percent.

By January 1967, new Chancellor James M. Moody authorized a faculty exchange in which twenty-two TCU faculty (history, English, and sociology professors) taught classes twice a week on the Jarvis campus. Staff consulted with Jarvis representatives, and Jarvis faculty attended workshops on the TCU campus for additional educational training. In 1968 seventeen Jarvis students came to TCU for one week to attend class and live in dorms; meanwhile fourteen TCU students made a day trip to the Jarvis campus.

The partnership created new opportunities in TCU classrooms. In 1968, the TCU Experimental College (Extended Education) offered an evening course called "The Negro in American Life"; the noncredit, tuition-free course was designed to enlighten students, faculty, and the community, and included six lectures given by TCU and Jarvis speakers, followed by Q&A sessions. The following year the *Skiff* announced the university's first Black history course, which covered "the Negro in America up to the present day, but also will include African civilizations." TCU was progressing!

SAAC

TCU's history as an integrated institution is not a long one. It was somewhat of a novelty, then, for an organization for blacks to be established on campus.

SAAC, the Students for the Advancement of Afro-American Culture, held its most successful activity when it presented the SAAC style and fashion show in the fall. The show not only raised money for the organization, but it also acquainted many members of the TCU community with Afro-American styles such as the dashiki.

ABOVE
SAAC (Students for Advancement of Afro-American Culture) student organization at TCU in 1970. *The Horned Frog*, vol. 66. (Fort Worth: Taylor Publishing Co., 1970), 137. https://repository.tcu.edu/handle/116099117/11096. Courtesy of TCU Archives and Special Collections. Mary Couts Burnett Library. Texas Christian University.

Communications Retreat Termed Successful (See Page 3)

The Skiff

TEXAS CHRISTIAN UNIVERSITY ★ ★ ★ ★ FORT WORTH, TEXAS

Starpoint School Stresses Three 'I'S' (See Page 5)

House Faces Up to Fund Woes

Members Recognize Financial Problems

Jarvis College Students Differ In Views of Visit, McKissick

Chancellor To Host 'Who's Who' Event

ABOVE
Front page of the *Skiff*. The *Skiff* vol. 67, no. 11 (Fort Worth, TX). October 25, 1968. https://repository.tcu.edu/handle/116099117/15221. Courtesy of TCU Archives and Special Collections. Mary Couts Burnett Library. Texas Christian University.

ABOVE
Professor from Jarvis Christian College who taught the inaugural African American literature course at TCU. *The Horned Frog*, vol. 65. (Fort Worth: Taylor Publishing Co., 1969), 70. https://repository.tcu.edu/handle/116099117/11095. Courtesy of TCU Archives and Special Collections. Mary Couts Burnett Library. Texas Christian University.

ABOVE (TOP)
African American literature course at TCU. Image of "Unnamed professor from Jarvis College teaching six-part course on Negro Literature at TCU." *The Horned Frog*, vol. 65. (Fort Worth: Taylor Publishing Co., 1969), 70. https://repository.tcu.edu/handle/116099117/11095. Courtesy of TCU Archives and Special Collections. Mary Couts Burnett Library. Texas Christian University.

ABOVE
1970 SAAC style and fashion show with an unnamed TCU student modeling African-American style dress. *The Horned Frog*, vol. 66. (Fort Worth: Taylor Publishing Co., 1970), 137. Courtesy of TCU Archives and Special Collections. Mary Couts Burnett Library. Texas Christian University.

Dr. James Cash

Dr. James Cash knew how to finish first. He and his teammates at Texas Christian University won the Southwest Conference basketball title in 1967–68. Those Horned Frogs advanced to the NCAA Tournament's Elite Eight, which still stands as the deepest run into the tournament that a TCU team has experienced.

Perhaps a greater legacy of the Fort Worth native and I.M. Terrell High School graduate is how he broke barriers. Long before racial turmoil and Black Lives Matter walked through our streets in 2020, they permeated America in 1966 when Cash enrolled at TCU.

He was the first African American to enroll as a student athlete at TCU and was also the first to do so in the Southwest Conference. After graduating as an Academic All-American in 1969 (he also achieved that mark in 1968), he continued his education, completing his master's and doctoral degrees at Purdue. He then became the first African American to earn tenure at Harvard University, which set the stage for the opening of the Cash House, the first Harvard building to be named for an African American.

Soon he'll be the first African American to have a statue at TCU. In February 2021, the university announced that Cash's statue will join others at Ed and Rae Schollmaier Arena, the site where he poured in 1,026 points and grabbed 856 rebounds over three years of play.

Two years after Cash enrolled at TCU, Linzy Cole enrolled, too, becoming TCU's first African American football player. In 1977, Minnie Vernell Armstrong became the first African American woman basketball player to take the court at TCU. After scoring 1,102 points in her career, she would quietly go on to help coach the men's basketball team.

Perhaps the greatest contribution Cash made was not in starting or finishing first, but in helping other African Americans do the same—in Fort Worth, at TCU, and beyond.

BELOW
James Cash sitting on the bench during a TCU basketball game. "TCU Men's Basketball," 1969. TCU Photograph Collection, RU 53. Photo Number: 2333. https://repository.tcu.edu:443/handle/116099117/3128. Courtesy of TCU Special Collections. Mary Couts Burnett Library. Texas Christian University.

ABOVE
James Cash wearing graduation regalia after TCU graduation. Courtesy of TCU Athletics.

ABOVE
TCU Men's Basketball Team in 1968. "TCU Men's Basketball," 1968. TCU Photograph Collection, RU 53. Photo Number: 2324. https://repository.tcu.edu:443/handle/116099117/3559. Courtesy of TCU Special Collections. Mary Couts Burnett Library. Texas Christian University.

RIGHT
I. M. Terrell Basketball team from left to right: Wayne Lewis, Edward Sanders, Sherman Evans, Charles Jefferson, Nathaniel Carroll, Ollie Ledbetter, and James Cash. They led I. M. Terrell to the 1965 Texas Class 4A African American High School Basketball Championship. Photo taken on March 2, 1965. AR406-6-5014A. Courtesy, *Fort Worth Star-Telegram Collection*, Special Collections, The University of Texas at Arlington Libraries.

ABOVE
Dr. James Cash and his family during his jersey retirement ceremony on Saturday, January 29, 2011. Courtesy of TCU Athletics.

LEFT
James Cash blocking a shot against Oklahoma City University. Courtesy of TCU Athletics.

LEFT
Dr. James Cash speaking. "James Cash," n.d. TCU Photograph Collection, RU 53. Photo Number: 2127. https://repository.tcu.edu:443/handle/116099117/3623. Courtesy of TCU Special Collections. Mary Couts Burnett Library. Texas Christian University.

ABOVE
James Cash shooting a basketball during a game. Courtesy of TCU Athletics.

LEFT
James Cash slamming a reverse dunk. Courtesy of TCU Athletics.

RIGHT
Illustration advertising Parents' Weekend at TCU. TCU Scrapbook Collection, RU 8. Box 38, Folder 54. "Dr. Marguerite Potter, G.E. College Bowl (1961)" scrapbook. https://repository.tcu.edu/handle/116099117/4611. Courtesy of TCU Archives and Special Collections. Mary Couts Burnett Library. Texas Christian University.

TCU/Fort Worth Week

OPPOSITE
Fort Worth Leaders Jerry Brownlee and Charles Hetrick meeting with TCU student Emilee Fossler. "TCU/Fort Worth Week," 1972. TCU Photograph Collection, RU 53. Raw files, TCU Fort Worth Week, Folder 2. https://repository.tcu.edu/handle/116099117/6754. Courtesy of TCU Special Collections. Mary Couts Burnett Library. Texas Christian University.

During the 1960s and 1970s, Dr. W. Earl Waldrop served in a variety of roles at TCU, including Chief Development Officer, Director of Development, Vice Chancellor for External Affairs, and Senior Vice Chancellor. During his tenure, Waldrop developed numerous programs aimed at expanding TCU's educational and communal outreach. Together with civic leader Bayard Friedman, Waldrop developed a celebration of the partnership between TCU and the city of Fort Worth.

The first annual TCU/Fort Worth Week was held April 21–April 27, 1968. The week emphasized the many connections between the city and university through a variety of events held across the city and on campus. The first year developed fine arts as a connecting theme. Activities opened with a performance by New Orleans jazz musician Pete Fountain at the Daniel-Meyer Coliseum on April 20. Madame Lili Kraus then performed with the TCU Symphony Orchestra on April 21. The TCU Opera performed Mozart's "Cosi Fan Tutte" throughout the week. The celebration concluded with the annual Purple and White intra-squad spring football game, followed by folk duo Simon and Garfunkel performing in the Daniel-Meyer Coliseum.

In 1969, TCU/Fort Worth Week highlighted religious connections, as TCU faculty and administrative officials preached sermons in twenty-eight churches across Fort Worth. The 1970 celebration centered on the theme "Future Seekers," as city and university leaders collaborated to promote the intertwined futures of both entities. During 1972 the theme focused on the charitable service of Fort Worth citizens and TCU students in serving the larger community. In 1973, Fort Worth Mayor R. M. Stovall issued a proclamation that named April 1 through April 7, 1973, "TCU/Fort Worth Centennial Week," in honor of the hundredth anniversary of both entities.

TCU/Fort Worth Week sought to bridge potential divides between city and university. The week forged academic, artistic, cultural, religious, and service connections between Fort Worth citizens and TCU students. The success of TCU/Fort Worth Week provides a blueprint for helping to strengthen bonds between city and university—bonds that could enhance the potential of both.

RIGHT
TCU cheerleader Susan Beard and Spirit Committee Chairman David Holmes planting a sign in the Michero family yard. "TCU/Fort Worth Week," 1969. TCU Photograph Collection, RU 53. Raw files, TCU Fort Worth Week, Folder 2. https://repository.tcu.edu/handle/116099117/675. Courtesy of TCU Special Collections. Mary Couts Burnett Library. Texas Christian University.

ABOVE
TCU students on Main Street in downtown Fort Worth; from left to right: Wayne Massey, Jerry Cox, Steve Holder, Carolyn Thompson, John Harris, Bill Heaberg, Feagin Wing, Cheryl Pickens, Dan Carter, Kathy Saunders, Cherry Jones, Jim Heaberg, and Michele Seras. TCU Photograph Collection, RU 53. Raw files, TCU Fort Worth Week. https://repository.tcu.edu/handle/116099117/6851. Courtesy of TCU Special Collections. Mary Couts Burnett Library. Texas Christian University.

ABOVE
Vice Chancellor W. Earl Waldrop and TCU student Beverly Fecil in front of TCU/Fort Worth Week sign. "TCU/Fort Worth Week," 1971. TCU Photograph Collection, RU 53. Raw files, TCU Fort Worth Week, Folder 4. https://repository.tcu.edu/handle116099117/6753. Courtesy of TCU Special Collections. Mary Couts BurnettLibrary. Texas Christian University.

ABOVE
TCU/Fort Worth Week banner in downtown Fort Worth. "TCU/Fort Worth Week," 1973. TCU Photograph Collection, RU 53. Raw files, TCU Fort Worth Week, Folder 5. https://repository.tcu.edu/handle/116099117/6738. Courtesy of TCU Special Collections. Mary Couts Burnett Library. Texas Christian University.

RIGHT
TCU and city leaders presenting TCU Today Program in downtown Fort Worth. "TCU/Fort Worth Week," 1968. TCU Photograph Collection, RU 53. Raw files, TCU Fort Worth Week, Folder 2. https://repository.tcu.edu/handle/116099117/6752. Courtesy of TCU Special Collections. Mary Couts Burnett Library. Texas Christian University.

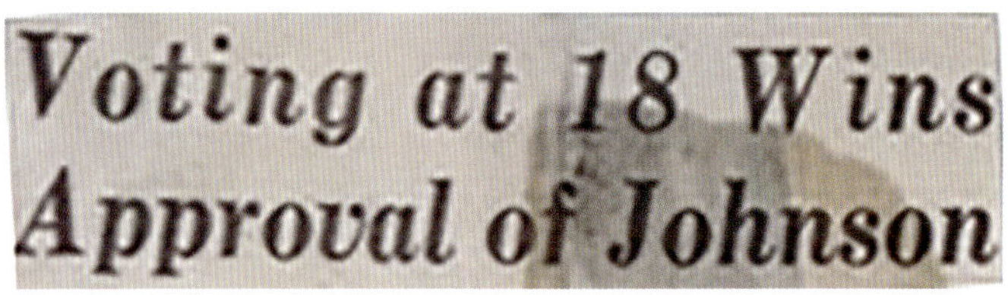

Voting at 18 Wins Approval of Johnson

LEFT
Image of President Lyndon B. Johnson speaking during 1968 TCU commencement address. TCU Scrapbook Collection, RU 8. Box 7, Folder 30. "Lyndon Baines Johnson Commencement Speech at TCU, 1968." Courtesy of TCU Archives and Special Collections. Mary Couts Burnett Library. Texas Christian University.

ABOVE
Newspaper clipping "Voting at 18 Wins Approval of Johnson" detailing President Johnson's plan to lower the federal voting age. TCU Scrapbook Collection, RU 8. Box 7, Folder 30. "Lyndon Baines Johnson Commencement Speech at TCU, 1968." Courtesy of TCU Archives and Special Collections. Mary Couts Burnett Library. Texas Christian University.

Lyndon B. Johnson Comes to Town

OPPOSITE
Lyndon B. Johnson standing next to a car and talking to a group of students and citizens. "Lyndon Johnson," 1971. TCU Photograph Collection, RU 53. Raw files, Richardson Building. https://repository.tcu.edu/handle/116099117/6374. Courtesy of TCU Special Collections. Mary Couts Burnett Library. Texas Christian University.

As the culture wars accelerated in the late 1960s, college students, including some at TCU, railed against war hawks and federal politicians. Complaints about the draft conscripting young men for the long-running war in Vietnam were especially voluminous. A 1968 column by *Skiff* writer James Gordon lambasted President Lyndon Baines Johnson after the Paris peace talks for the politician's "super-rigid" war policies.

But TCU administrators felt kindlier toward the president from Texas. They invited President Johnson to deliver the May 1968 commencement address and collect an honorary doctor of letters degree from the university. Surprisingly, in his commencement address, President Johnson simultaneously shocked and excited those in attendance when he publicly called to lower the federal voting age to eighteen—perhaps the first time Johnson had made such a public statement.

When Johnson's presidential term ended in January 1969, rumors swirled that he would return to TCU to give occasional lectures, but that possibility never materialized. Lyndon Johnson and his wife, Lady Bird Johnson, did make one more appearance on South University Drive. In April 1971, they arrived in a white limousine for the formal dedication of the Sid W. Richardson Physical Sciences Building. The former president defended his Vietnam choices to attendees at a pre-ribbon-cutting luncheon, saying, "We must fight today's wars in order that our children live in peace."

Though the formal ribbon-cutting for the Sid Richardson building was brief, the event did culminate in a memorable moment. Longtime TCU photographer Linda Kaye had positioned herself on the roof of the new building to memorialize the sight of the thirty-sixth US president sitting next to Chancellor Moudy. Fearing she was a sniper, Secret Service agents scrambled to the roof with guns drawn. Realizing their mistake, they calmly escorted Kaye back to ground level. Johnson departed the campus soon after.

BELOW
Lyndon Johnson after Sid Richardson Building dedication. "Lyndon Johnson," 1971. TCU Photograph Collection, RU 53. Raw files, Richardson Building. https://repository.tcu.edu/handle/116099117/6379. Courtesy of TCU Special Collections. Mary Couts Burnett Library. Texas Christian University.

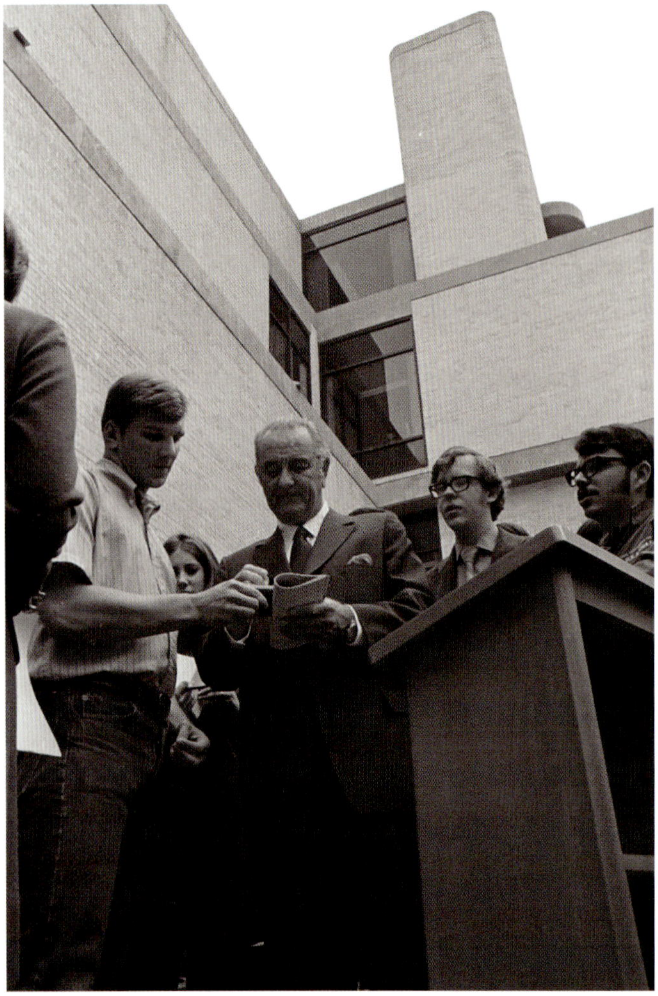

LEFT
President Lyndon B. Johnson signing a pamphlet in front of Sid Richardson Building. "Lyndon Johnson," 1971. TCU Photograph Collection, RU 53. Raw Files, Richardson Building. https://repository.tcu.edu/handle/116099117/6370. Courtesy of TCU Special Collections. Mary Couts Burnett Library. Texas Christian University.

ABOVE
Chancellor James Moudy conferring an honorary doctorate to President Lyndon B. Johnson during May 1968 Commencement. TCU Scrapbook Collection, RU 8. Box 7, Folder 30. "Lyndon Baines Johnson Commencement Speech at TCU, 1968." Courtesy of TCU Archives and Special Collections. Mary Couts Burnett Library. Texas Christian University.

LEFT
Lyndon Johnson, Jim Wright (at left), and Olin Teague upon arrival in Fort Worth. TCU Scrapbook Collection, RU 8. Box 7, Folder 30. "Lyndon Baines Johnson Commencement Speech at TCU, 1968." Courtesy of TCU Archives and Special Collections. Mary Couts Burnett Library. Texas Christian University.

OPPOSITE
Lyndon B. Johnson at Sid Richardson Building dedication. "Lyndon Johnson," 1971. TCU Photograph Collection, RU 53. Raw files, Richardson Building. https://repository.tcu.edu/handle/116099117/6376. Courtesy of TCU Special Collections. Mary Couts Burnett Library. Texas Christian University.

TEXAS CHRISTIAN UNIVERSITY
FORT WORTH

Queen Jennifer Giddings

When Jennifer Giddings transferred to TCU from California's Chapman College in 1969, TCU was in its fifth year of admitting Black applicants into the general student population. Many of her TCU classmates welcomed her with open arms. Members of the Students for the Advancement of Afro American Culture joined residents of Tom Brown and Jarvis Halls in nominating Giddings to be Homecoming Queen in 1970.

That year, winners of the ritual honor were announced at a bonfire in advance of the big homecoming football game. Giddings won, and told the *Skiff* a few days later that the designation "shocked" her. Soon she realized that she was not just TCU's inaugural Black queen, but also the first in the Southwest Conference.

"Cheers immediately erupted from the crowd. It was a celebratory night of kindness that I will never forget," Jennifer Giddings Brooks told *TCU Magazine* in 2021. Her good feelings about the milestone soon evaporated.

ABOVE
Senior portrait of Jennifer Giddings in *The Horned Frog*, vol. 67 (Fort Worth: Taylor Publishing Co., 1971), 416. https://repository.tcu.edu/handle/116099117/11097. Courtesy of TCU Archives and Special Collections. Mary Couts Burnett Library. Texas Christian University.

Despite the honor, bearing the torch as a groundbreaking integrator in the South was not without challenges. Giddings was not invited to appear at the annual Cotton Bowl parade, as was traditional for TCU's queen representative.

She brought up the exclusion at a press conference in February 1971. Four Black football players had just quit the team, citing restrictive dress codes and inequitable treatment from football coach Jim Pittman. Giddings was among the students who chose to speak out publicly on the challenges of integrating TCU, drawing attention to "racist attitudes among general and athletic administrations," reported the *Skiff*.

ABOVE
Homecoming Queen Jennifer Giddings in the stands with crown and bouquet of flowers after receiving the 1970 Homecoming crown. *The Horned Frog*, vol. 67. (Fort Worth: Taylor Publishing Co., 1971), 16. https://repository.tcu.edu/handle/116099117/11097. Courtesy of TCU Archives and Special Collections. Mary Couts Burnett Library. Texas Christian University.

ABOVE
Portrait of Jennifer Giddings from the 1970 *The Horned Frog*, vol. 66. (Fort Worth: Taylor Publishing Co., 1970), 364. https://repository.tcu.edu/handle/116099117/11096. Courtesy of TCU Archives and Special Collections. Mary Couts Burnett Library. Texas Christian University.

ABOVE
Jennifer Giddings and the Mortar Board. Giddings served as secretary for the TCU chapter during her senior year. Image in *The Horned Frog*, vol. 67. (Fort Worth: Taylor Publishing Co., 1971), 345. https://repository.tcu.edu/handle/116099117/11097. Courtesy of TCU Archives and Special Collections. Mary Couts Burnett Library. Texas Christian University.

LEFT
Jennifer Giddings being crowned Homecoming Queen by Chancellor Moudy. *The Horned Frog*, vol. 67. (Fort Worth: Taylor Publishing Co., 1971), 38. https://repository.tcu.edu/handle/116099117/11097. Courtesy of TCU Archives and Special Collections. Mary Couts Burnett Library. Texas Christian University.

RIGHT
Homecoming Queen Jennifer Giddings working with a child at the Miller Speech Clinic. Pdf Image 279 in *The Horned Frog*, vol. 67. (Fort Worth: Taylor Publishing Co., 1971), 275. https://repository.tcu.edu/handle/116099117/11097. Courtesy of TCU Archives and Special Collections. Mary Couts Burnett Library. Texas Christian University.

A senior speech pathology major from Dallas, JENNIFER GIDDINGS had the honor of being TCU's first Black Homecoming Queen. Jennifer was vice president of Jarvis Dorm, recording secretary of Mortar Board, communications chairman of AWS, and a member of SAAC and Sigma Alpha Eta. "My stay here at TCU has given me the opportunity to meet some of the nicest people I've ever met," Jennifer said. "I hope the future will bring many advantages to the campus, especially for minority groups."

Sue Monk Kidd

Born in Sylvester, Georgia, in 1948, Sue Monk Kidd's childhood experiences generated a worldview that offered limited options for women. The list of acceptable careers was brief: librarian, teacher, or nurse. So Kidd enrolled in the nursing school at the Medical College of Georgia for the fall semester of 1966. Her life changed after she met Sandy Kidd, whom she married after her second year of college. The newlyweds soon relocated to Fort Worth so Sandy could attend Southwestern Baptist Theological Seminary.

Sue Monk Kidd enrolled at TCU for the Fall 1968 semester, intent on finishing her nursing degree. Yet TCU's liberal arts requirements forced Kidd also to complete several literature and writing courses, where she demonstrated an innate writing ability. During a 2020 interview, Kidd recalled one English professor telling her, "You're a born writer." After earning her nursing degree from TCU in 1970, Kidd worked as a nurse for several years before pursuing her interest in writing—a field that allowed her to combine her personal experiences with spirituality and feminism to explore the larger world.

Her writing career soon took off. Kidd has published numerous books, including *When the Heart Waits* (1990), *The Dance of a Dissident Daughter* (1996), *The Secret Life of Bees* (2002), *The Mermaid Chair* (2005), *The Invention of Wings* (2014), and *The Book of Longings* (2020). *The Secret Life of Bees* sold over eight million copies and spent over two years on the *New York Times* best-seller list. In 2008, FOX Searchlight produced a full-length feature film of the book starring Queen Latifah, Jennifer Hudson, Alicia Keys, Dakota Fanning, and Sophie Okonedo. In 2016, TCU conferred an honorary doctorate on Kidd for her achievements. Sue Monk Kidd's story unquestionably highlights the power of a liberal arts education to unlock the potential of each and every student.

RIGHT
Photograph of Sue Monk Kidd in nursing uniform. Courtesy of Sue Monk Kidd.

ABOVE
Sue Monk Kidd and the Sigma Theta Tau Honor Society at TCU. Seated from left to right: Sue Monk Kidd, president, and Cherry Jones, vice president. Standing from left to right, Ann Lane and Allene Jones, faculty sponsors, and unnamed persons. "Officers of Sigma Theta Tau," 1970-1971. TCU Photograph Collection, RU 53. Photo Number: 2416. https://repository.tcu.edu:443/handle/116099117/2755. Courtesy of TCU Special Collections. Mary Couts Burnett Library. Texas Christian University.

LEFT
Sue Monk Kidd being hooded when receiving her honorary doctorate from TCU in 2016. Courtesy of Sue Monk Kidd.

LEFT
Sue Monk Kidd in her office. Courtesy of Sue Monk Kidd.

ABOVE
The book cover of *The Secret Life of Bees* (Published by Penguin Books, 2001).

ABOVE
Sue Monk Kidd with her daughter after receiving an honorary doctorate from TCU in 2016. Courtesy of Sue Monk Kidd.

Demands for Change and Accountability

On February 4, 1971, Black TCU students including Larry Dibbles, Frank Callaway, Homecoming Queen Jennifer Giddings, and Eddie Miles held a press conference to announce ongoing issues on campus and to demand institutional accountability.

The previous day Larry Dibbles, Hodges Mitchell, Raymond Rhodes, and Ervin Garrett met with head football coach Jim Pittman to inform him that they were leaving the team. Pittman released a statement to the press indicating the players "expressed no dissatisfaction" with him. Yet the February 4 press conference exemplified the ongoing struggle many Black students faced at TCU.

Coach Pittman did not have a reputation for being overtly discriminatory toward the players, so at the press conference the students revealed that Pittman had devised and enforced a dress code policy that all TCU football players, regardless of race, be clean-shaven and well-groomed. The problem was that out of the sixty-two players who made up the Horned Frogs football team, only six athletes had facial hair and voluminous hairdos in need of "grooming." These six athletes happened to be the only Black players on the team. Pittman's policy specifically targeted Black players.

ABOVE LEFT
Image of Dr. James H. Cone, the first African American professor in the Brite Divinity School at TCU. "James H. Cone," n.d. TCU Photograph Collection, RU 53. Photo Number: 2367. https://repository.tcu.edu:443/handle/116099117/3367. Courtesy of TCU Special Collections. Mary Couts Burnett Library. Texas Christian University.

LEFT
Image of Alpha Phi Alpha members Kenneth Daniel, Herman Wright, Lonnie Woods, Charles Davis, and James Perry in *The Horned Frog*, vol. 68, Book 2. (Fort Worth: Taylor Publishing Co., 1972), 228. https://repository.tcu.edu/handle/116099117/11100. Courtesy of TCU Archives and Special Collections. Mary Couts Burnett Library. Texas Christian University.

The students also critiqued the confusing non-invitation to TCU's first Black Homecoming Queen, Jennifer Giddings, to the Cotton Bowl Parade—an invitation that had previously been tradition. The university instead sent the TCU Sweetheart, TCU cheerleaders, and the TCU student body president in her place. Dibbles and his cohort compiled a series of written complaints and demands that addressed these and other discriminatory practices affecting African American students on campus.

Several prescient demands included a call for an increase in Black faculty (there were only three total for the entire campus at the time); an administrative professional to address student-specific needs; a Black campus minister; a Black counselor; and the integration of "black-oriented courses" in the curriculum leading to a Black studies minor.

Not until forty-five years later would these goals become realized with the creation of a new faculty position: Chief Inclusion Officer, and an African American and Africana Studies minor program, both in 2016. Hopefully more substantive steps towards reconciliation will not take another forty-five years to accomplish. The press conference and the lethargic pace of institutional change underscore the importance of the modern-day Race and Reconciliation Initiative at TCU.

Where Is Rights Proposal? (See Page 6) / **The Skiff** / Volume 69, Number 32 Friday, February 5 1971

Texas Christian University • • • • Fort Worth, Texas 76129

Walkout Spurs Black Outcry

By JOHNNY LIVENGOOD
GREG BURDEN
and GEORGE STONE

Voluntary withdrawal of four black athletes from the University's grid squad Thursday triggered a chain of demands by black students generally.

The four players are Larry Dibbles, Hodges Mitchell, Raymond Rhodes, and Ervin Garnett. They officially removed themselves from the team Wednesday.

Underlying the statement released at a 9 a.m. press conference was the charge of racist attitudes among general and athletic administrations of the Univeristy.

In a meeting Wednesday night at Clark Dormitory blacks, led by Eddie Miles and SAAC president Franklin Callaway, determined now was the time for action in fighting institutionalized racism as well as writing the demands for the press conference the next morning. The students discussed inadequacies of the recruiting systems for blacks and a black studies program. After the decisions were made their previous nerveusness changed to a calm strength coming from their commitment. During the writing of the press release, they joked about Coach Jim Pittman, Dr. J.M. Moudy, and the possibilities of being thrown out of school for their actions.

General Denial

First, they denied that the black athletes left, as Pittman claimed, because of inadequate social life and that the reasons are based on the policy changes and dress codes.

Second, they charged discrimination against Jennifer Giddings, 1970 Homecoming Queen. The blacks charge she was purposely excluded from Cotton-Bowl activities in which she was entitled to participate. A formal public apology, to be printed in the 1971 edition of the Horned Frog on an entire page across from the Queen's picture, was demanded.

Because of the unique problems related to blackness the students also demanded that a black minister and black psychologist be hired to handle these problems and that more black professors be hired for more relevant teaching. They feel the exposure would also be educational for the white students as well.

A full investigation of the denial of the enrollment of Jimmie Leach was also demanded. Because they feel that Leach was denied under questionable circumstances they want to determine if discrimination has taken

(Continued on Page 8)

AT THURSDAY'S Press Conference Frank Callaway, Larry Dibbles, Jennifer Giddings, and Eddie Miles answered reporter's questions.

ABOVE (RIGHT)
Front page of the *Skiff* vol. 69, no. 32 (Fort Worth, TX), Feb. 5, 1971. https://repository.tcu.edu/handle/116099117/15353. Courtesy of TCU Archives and Special Collections. Mary Couts Burnett Library. Texas Christian University.

ABOVE
Larry Dibbles and Jennifer Giddings at press conference. "Images of February 4, 1971 press conference with Larry Dibbles, Jennifer Giddings, Frank Callaway, and Eddie Miles." *The Horned Frog*, vol. 67. (Fort Worth: Taylor Publishing Co., 1971), 102–103. https://repository.tcu.edu/handle/116099117/11097. Courtesy of TCU Archives and Special Collections. Mary Couts Burnett Library. Texas Christian University.

ABOVE
Ray Turner reading at the 1972 NAACP Super Show Fundraiser. *The Horned Frog*, vol. 68, book II. (Taylor Publishing Co., 1972), 74. https://repository.tcu.edu/handle/116099117/11100. Courtesy of TCU Archives and Special Collections. Mary Couts Burnett Library. Texas Christian University. Christian University.

ABOVE
NAACP student organization at TCU in 1973. Image of "National Association for the Advancement of Colored People Club at TCU." *The Horned Frog*, vol. 69. (Fort Worth: Taylor Publishing Co., 1973), 408. https://repository.tcu.edu/handle/116099117/11101. Courtesy of TCU Archives and Special Collections. Mary Couts Burnett Library. Texas Christian University.

ABOVE
Larry Dibbles, Jennifer Giddings, Frank Callaway, and Eddie Miles at February 4, 1971 Press Conference. *The Horned Frog*, vol. 67. (Fort Worth: Taylor Publishing Co., 1971), 102–103. https://repository.tcu.edu/handle/116099117/11097. Courtesy of TCU Archives and Special Collections. Mary Couts Burnett Library. Texas Christian University.

ABOVE
TCU students standing beside vehicles in front of university buildings. *The Horned Frog*, vol. 68. (Fort Worth: Taylor Publishing Co., 1973), 16. https://repository.tcu.edu/hadle/116099117/11101. Courtesy of TCU Archives and Special Collections. Mary Couts Burnett Library. Texas Christian University.

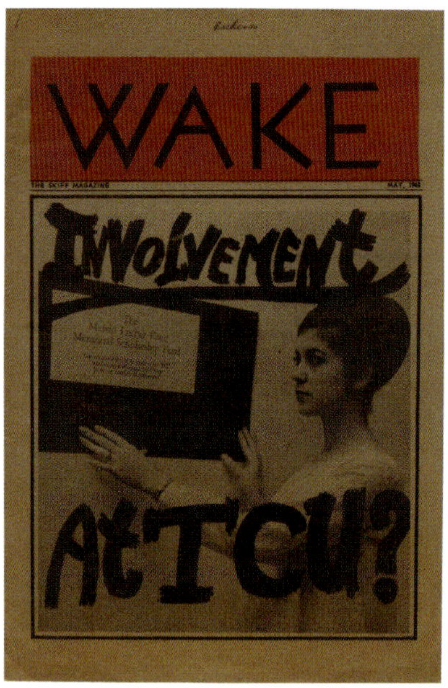

ABOVE
Front cover of *Wake: The Skiff Magazine* that detailed stories regarding the struggles of integration at TCU in 1968. Front cover of *Wake: The Skiff Magazine*, (Fort Worth, TX) May 1968. TCU Special Collections. Vertical Files, RU 32. https://repository.tcu.edu/handle/116099117/21235. Courtesy of TCU Archives and Special Collections. Mary Couts Burnett Library. Texas Christian University.

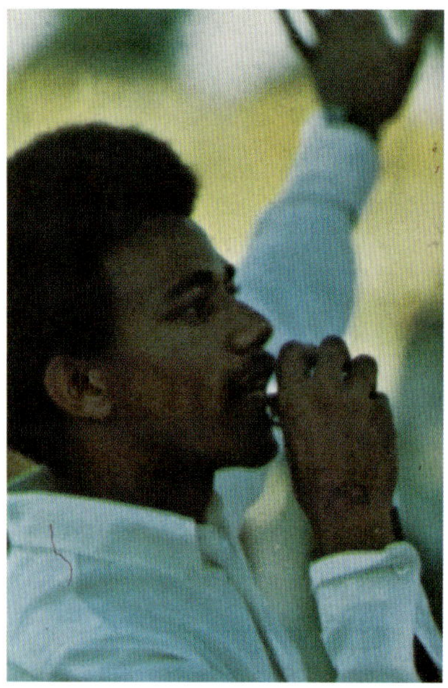

ABOVE
TCU Cheerleader Ronnie Hurdle speaking to a crowd in *The Horned Frog*, vol. 66 (Fort Worth: Taylor Publishing Co., 1970), 308. https://repository.tcu.edu/handle/116099117/11096. Courtesy of TCU Archives and Special Collections. Mary Couts Burnett Library. Texas Christian University.

The TCU Frog Fountain

The TCU Frog Fountain is one of the most iconic landmarks at TCU. Originally located in the quadrangle to the west of the original Brown-Lupton Student Center, the fountain, often running purple water, has remained a focal point of campus life for five-plus decades. Graduating students dressed in their caps and gowns frequently have their picture made by the fountain with their families.

Funded as a gift to TCU by Mr. and Mrs. Houghton H. Phillips of San Antonio, the Buck Winn-designed fountain features four stylized flutes topped with lotus petals. The lotus flower often is regarded as a symbol of purity, enlightenment, self-regeneration, and rebirth. Its characteristics are a perfect analogy for the human condition: even when its roots are in the dirtiest waters, the lotus produces the most beautiful flower. Given the traditional meaning of the lotus, the fountain's flutes represent the historic connection of the lotus with enlightenment or education. Each flute in the fountain symbolizes a different university class of students, with the shortest representing freshmen or incoming students and the tallest representing the senior class. The flowing water represents the transfer or sharing of knowledge between classes, or regeneration and rebirth.

While much beloved today, Frog Fountain has not always held a place in the hearts of TCU students. Since the university erected the fountain during the era of the Vietnam War, some students felt the lotus represented peace overtures, while other students supported the war. Some students criticized the erection of the fountain believing it a waste of money, while other students believed the fountain and its location occupied important space that could serve as additional parking. Despite the occasional prank where students put soap or washing powder in the fountain to create an overflow of multicolored bubbles, the fountain has survived and is today a much-loved piece of TCU's campus!

RIGHT
Artist's Rendition of Frog Fountain. "Frog Fountain," 1969. TCU Photograph Collection, RU 53. Photo Number: 2315. https://repository.tcu.edu:443/handle/116099117/3429. Courtesy of TCU Special Collections. Mary Couts Burnett Library. Texas Christian University.

ABOVE

Faculty and students releasing balloons at the Frog Fountain to announce Town and Gown Theatre. "Theater," 1970. TCU Photograph Collection, RU 53. Raw Files, Town and Gown. https://repository.tcu.edu/handle/116099117/6356. Courtesy of TCU Special Collections. Mary Couts Burnett Library. Texas Christian University.

LEFT

"Frog Fountain," 1973. TCU Photograph Collection, RU 53. Raw files, Picnic/Parties. https://repository.tcu.edu/handle/116099117/6821. Courtesy of TCU Special Collections. Mary Couts Burnett Library. Texas Christian University.

RIGHT
"Howdy Week," 1973. TCU Photograph Collection, RU 53. Raw files, Picnic/Parties. https://repository.tcu.edu/handle/116099117/6813. Courtesy of TCU Special Collections. Mary Couts Burnett Library. Texas Christian University.

RIGHT
"Frog Fountain and Amon G. Carter Stadium," 1972. TCU Photograph Collection, RU 53. Photo Number: 953. https://repository.tcu.edu:443/handle/116099117/3336. Courtesy of TCU Special Collections. Mary Couts Burnett Library. Texas Christian University.

TCU Centennial—the First Hundred Years

During 1963, TCU's leadership began planning for the momentous celebration of the university's first one hundred years, to be held ten years later. The official centennial celebrations began on January 25, 1973, with the Centennial Convocation in the Ed Landreth Auditorium. Chancellor James M. Moudy presided over the opening festivities, in which delegates from two hundred colleges and universities, forty learned and professional societies, thirty-seven professional and departmental societies, twelve sororities, and ten fraternities attended. With greetings from the chancellor, representatives from the board of trustees and Alumni Association, the Faculty Senate and Student House of Representatives, the university paid tribute to the founders of the University—Addison and Randolph Clark—a tribute acknowledged by Dr. Randolph Lee Clark, grandson of Randolph Clark. Then Duke University President Terry Sandford

ABOVE RIGHT
Students roasting marshmallows and hot dogs on centennial flame. "Student Life," 1973. TCU Photograph Collection, RU 53. Raw files, Student Services. https://repository.tcu.edu/handle/116099117/6873. Courtesy of TCU Special Collections. Mary Couts Burnett Library. Texas Christian University.

RIGHT
Chancellor James Moudy preparing to speak at the Spring 1973 Commencement. "James M. Moudy," 1973. TCU Photograph Collection, RU 53. Photo Number: 2380. https://repository.tcu.edu:443/handle/116099117/3481. Courtesy of TCU Special Collections. Mary Couts Burnett Library. Texas Christian University.

ABOVE
Flagpole and centennial marker and flame with Mary Couts Burnett Library in the background. "Centennial flag with Memorial Urn, Mary Couts Burnett Library," 1973. TCU Photograph Collection, RU 53. Photo Number: 954. https://repository.tcu.edu:443/handle/116099117/2914. Courtesy of TCU Special Collections. Mary Couts Burnett Library. Texas Christian University.

delivered an emotional convocation address.

At a luncheon following the convocation, centennial medallions and centennial flags were presented to faculty members and alumni. Attendees also received a copy of TCU Press's first centennial book, *A Hope of Wisdom*, which included two educational philosophy essays, one by Joseph Addison Clark and the other by Chancellor James Moudy.

At an April 6 Centennial Alumni Founders Day dinner, Chancellor Moudy paid special recognition to some thirty members of the Clark family. Alumni received awards and honorary degrees, while the Texas State Historical Commission honored TCU by naming it a historical site and presenting a historical plaque that today hangs in Sadler Hall. Throughout the remainder of the year, TCU hosted concerts, theatrical performances, and a series of lectures. Perhaps nothing more symbolic occurred than a September 23rd excursion to Thorp Spring, which included a centennial litany held in the front of the old Randolph Clark home. The words read that day by Granville T. Walker, minister of University Christian Church, Chancellor Moudy, and TCU students encouraged all to consider the university in relation to its past—a century had modified and changed much of what was once AddRan College and is now TCU. That progress continues even today.

RIGHT
"Centennial Marker," 1973. TCU Photograph Collection, RU 53. Photo Number: 940. https://repository.tcu.edu:443/handle/116099117/3340. Courtesy of TCU Special Collections. Mary Couts Burnett Library. Texas Christian University.

OPPOSITE
Vice Chancellor W. Earl Waldrop and SGA President Bill Stotesbery lighting the centennial flame.
"W. Earl Waldrop," 1973. TCU Photograph Collection, RU 53. Photo Number: 956. https://repository.tcu.edu:443/handle/116099117/2124. Courtesy of TCU Special Collections. Mary Couts Burnett Library. Texas Christian University.

Acknowledgments

This book is the result of almost 150 years of institutional history. As the university prepares to celebrate its sesquicentennial in 2023, a relatively recently created (2003) Center for Texas Studies celebrates all that makes Texas distinctive, including TCU, Fort Worth, and Texas history. In 2010, the Center prepared to celebrate the centennial of TCU's relocation to its current campus in Fort Worth. However, that celebration was somewhat understated, as the university did not embrace it. Nonetheless, the Center published a book with TCU Press in 2011, *A Century of Progress: Fort Worth and TCU* to celebrate the event. Now, as we approach the 150th year of TCU's existence, several university entities began discussing how to celebrate the momentous event.

Dan Williams, director of TCU Press, indicated to me that the press would publish a series of books about TCU to celebrate its sesquicentennial. One book he shared with me was a 1973 photographic version of TCU's past—Jim Corder, *More Than a Century*, with photographs by Michael Chesser and Linda Kaye. It told one version of TCU's story, but certainly not the complete version of the rising institution's complicated past. As a professional historian, I approached LeAnna Schooley, executive director of the Center for Texas Studies, and suggested that the Center should spearhead a photographic history of TCU as well as other sesquicentennial events. After discussing the prospect with Dan Williams and with Chancellor Victor Boschini, I enlisted the support of one of my doctoral students, Jackson W. Pearson, and we started the project.

This project started with us exploring the photographic holdings of TCU Special Collections, which gave us a basic understanding of the chronology of the university. We then spent weeks reviewing its scrapbook collection, which included more than forty scrapbooks from former students, faculty, and staff. These scrapbooks revealed to us a more complete story of TCU. What the students from different eras described and discussed convinced us that there were important events not apparent in more readily available accounts. These collections introduced us to influential students, prominent faculty and staff, as well as to the types of events that students engaged in during their time at the school. The images spanned the period from Fort Worth to Thorp Spring to Waco and back to Fort Worth.

Many archives and special collections helped us to complete the story, and each location added a different piece to the narrative. Ann Hodges and her staff at TCU Special Collections—who include Anne Dorf, Mary Saffell, Kerri Menchaca, Allison Kirchner, and student assistants Brandon Isensee and Valeria Aguilar Rodriguez—have done Herculean work, including moving heaven and earth to deliver us the cache of high-resolution photos we requested in a timely fashion. Since TCU was founded in Fort Worth, the project also embraced the photographic collections of the Fort Worth Public Library. Linda Barrett and her staff at the downtown branch graciously shared photos of the city during the nineteenth century, which helped us illustrate the location of the school's inception and its return home in 1910. The Texas Collection at Baylor University possesses many photographs of the years (1896–1910) that TCU was in Waco, and Geoff Hunt and his staff provided reproductions of these images. These photographs helped us understand the growth and development of the institution and introduced us to some truly interesting TCU characters.

TCU's return to Fort Worth, and the emergence of the *Fort Worth Star-Telegram* newspaper, produced many published images that reflected the school's athletic growth and other newsworthy events. Fortunately, the *Star-Telegram*'s early photos have been preserved at the Special Collections of the University of Texas at Arlington. Sara Pezzoni and her staff provided us images almost as soon as we requested them, which made our job much easier. Dawn Youngblood of the Tarrant County Archives has permitted us to use a few images that date to the era of World War I, when an airplane crashed into a TCU building. The TCU Athletic Department and Mark Cohen provided images of noteworthy athletes who brought recognition to the school and who helped advance the school's athletic reputation. The Perry Castaneda Library Maps Division at the

University of Texas in Austin provided access to the Sanborn maps, while UT's Dolph Briscoe Center (also in Austin) allowed us to access the Calvin Littlejohn Collection, thanks to the support of Ron Abram. Both collections have helped to complete the story. The Billy W. Sills Center for Archives of the FWISD and Lenna Hughes provided us an important image that highlights TCU's racial past. We also included a few images from the personal collections of Sue Monk Kidd, Bob Lilly, and Ben Procter, as well as a few images from the book by Stella Brooks, *Unbelievable: The Unmasking of Dr. Harrison Miller Moseley.*

This wealth of images does not tell the full story, so we decided to include short vignettes of 250-400 words throughout the book to advance the historical narrative. The vignettes plus the images reveal a more complete history of TCU than the 1973 published book. Providing diverse vignettes about one hundred years of TCU's past has required considerable expertise, however. Fortunately, I had been studying TCU's past since 2003, which certainly assisted me in this project. Ronald Burriss, who wrote a TCU history dissertation on the Clark Brothers, contributed vignettes about the founding of the school and its early period in Thorp Spring. Sylviane Ngandu-Kalenga Greensword, as a part of the TCU Race and Reconciliation Project, provided a couple of vignettes about the school's racial past. Mark Z. Mourer, a TCU master's graduate and friend and associate of Dan Jenkins, offered several vignettes about golf, football, and basketball, while Caroline Collier, the editor of *TCU Magazine*, contributed vignettes about the 1960s and early 1970s. Jackson Pearson and I helped fill in the gaps: I focused primarily on the early period through the 1940s, and Jackson primarily wrote pieces about TCU during the period 1950–1970. I would not have been able to complete this project in the timely way its publication demanded had Jackson not offered his writing, research, and technical services and expertise.

Having been at TCU for twenty-eight years and being a historian, I have always been interested in the history of the school. I passionately and persistently tell my undergraduate students that you need to know the history of where you are living or even where you are going to school, and I often offer extra-credit opportunities for them to learn about Fort Worth's past. LeAnna Schooley, as executive director of the Center for Texas Studies, and I have spent years trying to promote Fort Worth's and TCU's history through Community History Workshops and other events. She has also provided encouragement and financial support for this project, and without her assistance this book would not have been possible. Chancellor Victor Boschini also has a passion for TCU's past and has supported our vision of this project; he has also supplied some of the financial support that has made it possible. The sesquicentennial should be an outstanding celebration of an important event in the university's past.

Finally, this project would not have been possible without the moral support and encouragement of my wife, Darla Robinson, a 1985 graduate of TCU who played on the women's basketball team, and her son, Alex Robinson, a 2018 graduate of TCU who also played basketball here and garnered many awards. Given that much of this project was undertaken during the recent Covid pandemic, Darla's support and encouragement bolstered my spirits when I needed it most. My son, Banning A. F. Smith, also often forced me to look at things somewhat differently, and I believe that, too, helped this book come into existence. Finally, I want to acknowledge TCU for the two-plus decades of employment that have permitted me to become the scholar and person that I am today.

GENE ALLEN SMITH

Contributors

Gene Allen Smith

Chapter One:	"TCU's Origins" - Vignette No. 3
	"Leaving Fort Worth" - Vignette No. 4
Chapter Two:	"AddRan Relocates to Waco" - Vignette No. 1
	"Football Comes to Texas!" - Vignette No. 2
	"Olive Leaman McClintic, Head of Oratory" - Vignette No. 5
	"The Night that Changed TCU!" - Vignette No. 9
	"Returning to Fort Worth?" - Vignette No. 10
Chapter Three:	"Return to Fort Worth!" - Vignette No. 1
	"The Girl Graduate: Amboline Tyson, 1915" - Vignette No. 2
	"Let's Take the Streetcar" - Vignette No. 5
	"Professional Schools Come and Go" - Vignette No. 6
	"Airplanes and CRASHES!" - Vignette No. 7
	"The Epidemic—Spanish Influenza and TCU Nurses" - Vignette No. 8
	"Mary Couts Burnett: Savior of TCU!" - Vignette No. 11
Chapter Four:	"1923—The Golden Jubilee" - Vignette No. 1
	"Amon Carter, Fort Worth, and TCU" - Vignette No. 2
	"Fort Worth (TCU) School of Art" - Vignette No. 3
	"Colby Hall, a Building or a Person?" - Vignette No. 4
	"Brite College of the Bible" - Vignette No. 5
	"Memorial Arch" - Vignette No. 6
	"History Professor and Mayor of Fort Worth" - Vignette No. 8
	"From Clark Field to Amon Carter Stadium" - Vignette No. 10
	"Expanding TCU's Educational Mission" - Vignette No. 13
Chapter Five:	"McGruder Ellis Sadler and Development of TCU" - Vignette No. 1
	"TCU and World War II" - Vignette No. 2
	"Clay Tile Roofs and Foster Hall" - Vignette No. 3
	"Air-Conditioning Finally Comes to Campus" - Vignette No. 7
	"Brown-Lupton: Finally, a Student Center" - Vignette No. 10
	"TCU Airport" - Vignette No. 11
	"Robert Lewis (Bob) Lilly" - Vignette No. 14
Chapter Six:	"Ben Procter" - Vignette No. 7
	"Civil Rights and Integration- Just the Beginning" - Vignette No. 8
	"The TCU Frog Fountain" - Vignette No. 15
	"TCU Centennial—the First Hundred Years" - Vignette No. 16

Jackson W. Pearson

Chapter One:	"Student Codes at Thorp Spring" - Vignette No. 6
Chapter Two:	"The Clarks Take Leave" - Vignette No. 3
	"Name, Colors, Mascot" - Vignette No. 4
	"The *Skiff*" - Vignette No. 6
	"Summer School and Year-Round Education" - Vignette No. 7
	"Student Employment on Campus" - Vignette No. 8
Chapter Three:	"Braxton B. Wade Prohibition Library" - Vignette No. 4
	"A TCU Power Couple: The Cockrells" - Vignette No. 9
	"Expanding Opportunities for Women's Sports" - Vignette No. 10

(continues)

Chapter Four: "Literary Societies and Student Organizations" - Vignette No. 7
"TCU and Music" - Vignette No. 9
"Golden Gloves and Fencing" - Vignette No. 12

Chapter Five: "Navy V-12 Program at TCU" - Vignette No. 4
"Folk Ballads and Atomic Bombs: Newton Gaines and Harrison Miller Moseley" - Vignette No. 5
"Ranch Week" - Vignette No. 6
"Evening College, Professional Programs, and TCU Integration" - Vignette No. 8
"Dean Lucy Harris and the Harris College of Nursing" - Vignette No. 9
"Evolution of TCU's Mascot: Addy the Frog" - Vignette No. 12

Chapter Six: "KTCU Radio" - Vignette No. 3
"TCU TV" - Vignette No. 4
"Marguerite Potter and the GE Scholar's Bowl" - Vignette No. 6
"TCU/Fort Worth Week" - Vignette No. 10
"Sue Monk Kidd" - Vignette No. 13

Ronald D. Burriss

Chapter One: "The Clarks and Slavery" - Vignette No. 1
"The Clarks and the Civil War" - Vignette No. 2
"Decision to Turn over to Disciples of Christ" - Vignette No. 7
"Music Row in the Church" - Vignette No. 8

Caroline Collier

Chapter Three: "One Tree Hill" - Vignette No. 3

Chapter Six: "Phi Beta Kappa Comes to TCU" - Vignette No. 1
"Lyndon B. Johnson Comes to Town" - Vignette No. 11
"Queen Jennifer Giddings" - Vignette No. 12

Sylviane Ngandu-Kalenga Greensword

Chapter One: "Charley Thorp" - Vignette No. 5

Chapter Six: "Demands for Change and Accountability" - Vignette No. 14

Mark Z. Mourer

Chapter Four: "Football Puts TCU on the Map" - Vignette No. 11

Chapter Five: "Dan Jenkins" - Vignette No. 13

Chapter Six: "Worth Hills Campus Evolution" - Vignette No. 2
"Dr. James Cash" - Vignette No. 9

Index

ABOUT THE AUTHORS

Gene Allen Smith, professor of history at TCU, is an award-winning teacher and the author/editor of thirteen books. He is the director of TCU's Center for Texas Studies.

Jackson W. Pearson is an adjunct instructor and PhD candidate in history at TCU. He has published portions of his research in *Transactions of the American Philosophical Society*.